THE ARCHITECTURE OF DAVID LYNCH

Senalda Road, Hollywood Hills.
Credit: Photograph by Yana Stoime

THE ARCHITECTURE OF DAVID LYNCH

Richard Martin

Bloomsbury Academic
An imprint of Bloomsbury Publishing Plc

B L O O M S B U R Y
LONDON • NEW DELHI • NEW YORK • SYDNEY

Bloomsbury Academic

An imprint of Bloomsbury Publishing Plc

50 Bedford Square   1385 Broadway
London   New York
WC1B 3DP   NY 10018
UK   USA

www.bloomsbury.com

**BLOOMSBURY and the Diana logo are trademarks of
Bloomsbury Publishing Plc**

First published 2014
Reprinted by Bloomsbury Academic 2015

British Library Cataloguing-in-Publication Data
A catalogue record for this book is available from the British Library.

ISBN: HB: 978-1-4725-0548-4
PB: 978-1-4725-0881-2
ePDF: 978-1-4725-8643-8
ePub: 978-1-4725-2023-4

Library of Congress Cataloging-in-Publication Data
Martin, Richard, 1981–
The architecture of David Lynch/Richard Martin.
pages cm
Includes bibliographical references and index.
ISBN 978-1-4725-0548-4 (hardback) — ISBN 978-1-4725-0881-2 (paperback)
1. Lynch, David, 1946—Criticism and interpretation. 2. Architecture in motion
pictures. 3. Motion pictures and architecture. I. Title.
PN1998.3.L96M37 2014
791.4302'33092—dc23
2014004676

Typeset by RefineCatch Limited, Bungay, Suffolk
Printed and bound in Great Britain

To Alice Honor Gavin, and to Seba Davies

CONTENTS

Prologue: Three Journeys viii

Introduction: Mapping the Lost Highway 1

1 Town and City 15

2 Home 63

3 Road 107

4 Stage 133

5 Room 163

Acknowledgments 187
Notes 189
List of Illustrations 209
Bibliography 217
Author Biography 227
Index 229

PROLOGUE:
THREE JOURNEYS

Łódź, on a gray winter's day

In December 2009, Frank Gehry unveiled designs for a new cultural center in the city of Łódź—a multi-purpose facility including Poland's largest movie theater (Plate 1). Set alongside a rusting power station, Gehry's cluster of spectacular interlocking forms in many ways exemplifies contemporary architectural trends: a decaying industrial landscape is transformed thanks to a global "starchitect." Yet, one feature of the indicative images caught my attention: the projection onto the center's glass façade of a scene from David Lynch's film *Inland Empire* (2006). Walking around the site of Gehry's plans, I tried to imagine the connections between a Polish regeneration project and one of Hollywood's most perplexing film-makers. In what sense, I asked myself, do Gehry's designs reflect the architecture of David Lynch?

Paris, in the spring

Designed by Jean Nouvel and completed in 1994, the Fondation Cartier in Paris is a building with cinematic ambitions. It features a series of enormous screens—an elongated façade and two glass frames positioned between the building and the Boulevard Raspail—which manipulate light and perception. The intention, Nouvel claims, is to "blend the real image and the virtual image."[1] "I sometimes wonder," the architect says, "if I'm seeing the building or the image of the building, if Cartier is about transparency or about reflection."[2] Between March and May 2007, the Fondation Cartier hosted *The Air is on Fire*, an exhibition of David Lynch's paintings, photographs and sculptures. Amid the drapes and platforms, I noticed a crude sketch, in marker pen, of a domestic interior (Plate 2). Facing the sketch was a three-dimensional manifestation of the same space, the furnishings finished with a scribbled texture (Plate 3). Here, the real and the represented were again in conversation. Walking through this eerie stage set, inside a building self-consciously exploring perception, I found myself wondering: is *this* the architecture of David Lynch?

Los Angeles, in the sunshine

I can't drive, so getting around Los Angeles was a struggle. One day, in the summer of 2009, I hired a local woman named Karen to drive me to various locations in the city. Our first destination was Senalda Road, tucked beneath Mulholland Drive in the quiet curves of the Hollywood Hills. Surrounded by rich vegetation, the street contains three stark concrete structures, built in the late 1950s and early 1960s, and now owned by David Lynch. As we drove along Senalda Road, I asked Karen to slow down. The first building we met, an image of which adorns the cover of this book, was an unnerving distortion of domestic modernism, with a mottled façade broken only briefly by narrow glass slots and a larger window wrapping around one corner. It was instantly recognizable, despite slight remodeling, as the setting of Lynch's *Lost Highway* (1997), and it now contains the director's editing suite and a screening room. As we drove by, I took as many photos as possible, trying to recreate the perspective Lynch's camera held on the building. What was I doing with this familiar sight (or site)? Was I, in Nouvel's terms, seeing the building or the image of the building? Was I projecting, like Gehry, Lynch's own images onto the exterior of the house?

The next building on the street, a less distinguished structure with heavy discoloring on its once-white walls, serves as offices for Lynch's company, Asymmetrical Productions. As we approached the third building, Karen suddenly shouted, "He's there! He's on the street!" Sure enough, in front of his home, the Beverly Johnson House (Plate 4)—a hulking form with Mayan touches and a pinkish hue, designed by Lloyd Wright (son of Frank)—stood David Lynch. He was impeccably dressed in a crisp white shirt, buttoned to the collar. He looked just like David Lynch. He was talking with a group of people spread across the street. As we stared at them, they began to look at us. Given our slow pace and my conspicuous camera, our presence started to seem rather creepy. Excruciatingly, our car parted the group. I sat embarrassed in the passenger seat as Lynch stared into the vehicle. We parked around the corner and returned to the house on foot, expecting (dreading) a face-to-face conversation. But the street was now empty. A lone man surveyed us from the balcony of Asymmetrical Productions, and his look was enough to hurry us along. I took a few more photos and we left, sharply. Back in the car, I thought: was *that* the architecture of David Lynch?

INTRODUCTION: MAPPING THE LOST HIGHWAY

Architecture is the first manifestation of man creating his own universe.

LE CORBUSIER, *TOWARDS A NEW ARCHITECTURE* (1923)[1]

All my movies are about strange worlds that you can't go into unless you build them and film them.

DAVID LYNCH (1990)[2]

This book explores the relationship between architecture and David Lynch's films. In a career spanning six decades, Lynch has exhibited an acute spatial awareness. He has traveled across the United States, taking us from apartments immersed in industrial noise to hill-top mansions lit up by the Californian sun. He has charted the woods and waterfalls of the Pacific Northwest, decrepit towns in the Deep South, and green fields and grain elevators in Iowa and Wisconsin. He has plotted small-town family homes, grubby motels and empty highways. He has crossed continents to record London and Łódź. And, though neither he nor we may care to be reminded of it, he has flown us to the planet Dune.

According to Rem Koolhaas, "the most important thing about architecture is arriving in new worlds, rather than returning to old ones."[3] Whether they feature factories or freeways, the worlds built and filmed by Lynch feel utterly distinctive. They are among the most remarkable locations in contemporary culture. Not for nothing is "Lynchian" now embedded in popular parlance; the extent to which the term relies upon architecture will be demonstrated in the following chapters. In particular, the physical and mythical landscapes of the United States—the nation's cities, small towns, homes, roads and natural wonders—shape the dimensions of Lynch's universe. As a consequence, two questions form the backbone of our discussion. First, what can be learned about Lynch's films by examining the architecture we see within them? Second, what can be learned about architecture, especially the spatial developments of post-war America, by examining Lynch's films?

"Many filmmakers," Hitchcock once complained, "forget how important geography is to a story."[4] Surveying Lynch's work, its awareness of place is immediately apparent. The titles of *Dune* (1984), *Twin Peaks* (1990–91), *Mulholland Drive* (2001) and *Inland Empire* all refer to real or imagined locations, while *Lost Highway* and *The Straight Story* (1999) also indicate spatial concerns.[5] Moreover, as the philosopher Gaston Bachelard reminds us, "There are minds for which certain images retain absolute priority."[6] No Lynch film is complete without an ominous close-up of a mysterious numbered door, and other specific architectural forms, brimming with intensity, recur throughout his work: corridors, staircases, rhythmic machinery and red curtains. His camera frequently pauses on vacant spaces, encouraging us to comprehend their meaning. Elsewhere, it leads us disturbingly around corners. Occasionally, we are thrust, without warning, into dark openings. On entering a room, the layout can feel Lynchian at once: the walls faded, the furniture too perfectly arranged, the entire atmosphere askew. Our experience of the space may be radically changed by a shift in lighting or sound. The materials of this universe are vital, too. Velvet drapes, spinning vinyl, lush lawns and firing matches are instilled with cosmic implications. His architecture is tactile and sensuous, filled with textures and a striking attention to surfaces. While watching Lynch's films, spatial awareness is both demanded and undermined. His worlds combine murky geography with absolute precision. Lynch's films are littered with sign-posts, informing the audience we have entered Big Tuna, Texas or are traveling along Sunset Boulevard in Los Angeles. Characters, very deliberately, intone addresses and street names as if they hold magical significance. We are repeatedly told *exactly* where we are. Equally, we often feel without any bearings at all. This, perhaps, is what it means to map a lost highway.

Over the course of his career, Lynch has shot on location in busy cities and within deserted forests, as well as in studio environments. His films demonstrate an exceptional ability to uncover places with complex pasts, enabling our own excursions into wide-ranging territory. This book will discuss the decline of the American downtown, will question how architecture shapes social relations, and will reconsider the translation of European modernism across the Atlantic. Assessed as a whole, Lynch's career constitutes an idiosyncratic history of architecture and design.

Perhaps, then, we might consider his films as forming an imaginative and unconventional architectural project in their own right. In the words of Peter Eisenman, "All our lives are spent learning how to get it: Lynch un-learns us."[7] Yet, how does this process of "un-learning" take place? What kinds of architectural thinking does Lynch's work affirm or disavow? Or, if we are not seeking "how to get it"—which, in this case, might mean attempting to "solve" Lynch's puzzling films, a common desire they provoke—then what else might we discover in watching them?

The importance of buildings and places certainly emerges in interviews with Lynch. There is a libertarian streak in his approach to architecture: "People should be able to build what they want to build, when they want to build it, how they want to build it."[8] The architects Lynch admires—"all the students of the Bauhaus School, and Pierre Chareau, he did the House of Glass in Paris, Ludwig Mies van der Rohe, all the Wright family, Rudolph Michael Schindler and Richard Neutra"—hail from the early to mid-twentieth century, an era marked by its engagement with industrial design and innovative changes to the notion of home.[9] Lynch's formal listing of these celebrated figures, registering their full names, suggests great reverence. About contemporary architectural trends, he is more scathing: "the little mini-malls and postmodern stuff—they're *killing* your soul."[10]

Lynch's early biography also reveals clues towards a developing awareness of space and place. Born in 1946, his nomadic childhood, which included spells in Montana, Idaho, Washington State, North Carolina and Virginia, enabled him to see considerable swathes of the United States, though mainly small towns and rural areas. Being uprooted so often taught Lynch, he later said, to "get the lay of the land" in each new environment.[11] In 1965, Lynch organized a summer visit to Europe, during which he planned to study under the Austrian expressionist painter Oskar Kokoschka in Salzburg. Compared with his homeland, he found Europe to be "much stranger"—a continent where "it felt like way more of the last century was manifest at that time."[12] The trip was aborted after two weeks, with Lynch concluding: "I knew I was American and I wanted to be there."[13] However, while Lynch's work is rooted in the history, culture and landscape of the United States, a broader geographical perspective is essential to understanding it. As such, this book assesses Lynch not only in the context of spatial developments in America, but also within a wider transatlantic history of urban and architectural design. Indeed, it is to the rich and strange exchanges between these two continents that took place during the twentieth century—not least in architecture and in cinema—that Lynch's films so often return.

Back in America after his European trip, Lynch worked briefly as an architectural draftsman, drawing up blueprints, before being fired because "I only liked to work at night."[14] He subsequently moved to Philadelphia to study at the Pennsylvania Academy of the Fine Arts, where he shifted from an early focus on painting to creating short films. His explanation for the switch is telling: looking at his paintings, Lynch claims, he "wanted the edges to disappear. I wanted to get into the inside. It was spatial."[15] Another move, this time to Los Angeles in 1970, at the behest of the American Film Institute, offered Lynch greater opportunities to build and film his own worlds. He has been based in Los Angeles ever since, directing ten feature films, as well as leading a wide range of television, music and art projects. In recent years, these supra-cinematic activities have included establishing a nightclub in Paris (named after Club Silencio in *Mulholland Drive*, and with interior designs by Lynch himself), drawing sketches for a bungalow based on Vedic principles, and attempting to purchase the site of a former American spy station in West Berlin.

Despite Lynch's evident interest in architecture, the large scholarship his films have prompted has tended to neglect their spatial qualities. The most persuasive critics of Lynch, Slavoj Žižek and Todd McGowan, have instead emphasized a psychoanalytic perspective, although McGowan's schema—which sees each of Lynch's films as composed of two distinct units: a world of desire (sparse and bleak) and a world of fantasy (excessive and compensatory)—has considerable spatial implications.[16] Justus Nieland's monograph, however, broke new ground in discussing Lynch's sophisticated engagement with post-war design, especially in his filmic interiors. Nieland's approach reconfigures one of the central debates surrounding Lynch: the frequent presence of styles from the 1950s in his films. "Lynch's thing for the 1950s is a form of attentiveness to a transformed material environment," argues Nieland. By stressing the ambivalence Lynch maintains "toward the lure of the mid-century," as part of the director's broader interest in twentieth-century architecture, Nieland counters the accusations of nostalgia and postmodern pastiche habitually attached to Lynch's work.[17]

This book aims to develop further an understanding of the spaces Lynch has created by assessing his work alongside a diverse range of urban and architectural thinkers, as well as synthesizing insights from film studies, modern and contemporary art, and literature. It is structured around the prime symbolic spaces Lynch has manipulated: the small town, the city, the home, the road and the stage. It begins with an examination of Lynch's towns and cities—from his response to industrial urbanism in *Eraserhead* (1977) and *The Elephant Man* (1980), and the tales of fraught neighborhood life in *Blue Velvet* (1986) and *Twin Peaks*, to his depiction of Los Angeles in *Mulholland Drive*. The second chapter moves—to borrow Lynch's terms—"into the inside," and charts the dimensions of his cinematic homes. Corridors, staircases and closets define the territory here; surveillance, security and media are key themes. The montage of sights provided by the American highway is the context for Chapter 3's examination of Lynch's road movies, *Wild at Heart* (1990) and *The Straight Story*. Chapter 4 peels back the red curtains and steps onto the Lynchian stage to discuss his famous platforms and arenas. How might we explain the Red Room in *Twin Peaks*? Why is there a lady singing inside a radiator in *Eraserhead*? Finally, we arrive at a chapter that confronts the singular architecture of *Inland Empire*—a film that demands a different approach. Łódź, with its factories, palaces and passageways, provides a starting-point; Los Angeles, with its mansions, studio sets and boulevards, comprises another layer; but ultimately this is an old tale haunted by the sites (and sights) of cinema's past. In the alley behind the marketplace, we will have the perfect space in which to assess Lynch's career as a whole and the lessons it might hold for architecture, design and cinema today.

In prioritizing a spatial rather than a strictly chronological approach to Lynch's work, the book's structure is designed to demonstrate how each of these key symbolic locations contributes to his overall architectural project—from an engagement with vast urban layouts to the objects decorating a single room. Emerging through these chapters are the defining features of Lynch's architecture. The most immediately apparent of these is his ability to create discrete cinematic worlds—highly pressurized environments that operate with their own internal logic. These are meticulously designed, yet distinctly fallible, worlds, constantly at risk of decay or interruption. However, if Koolhaas stresses the importance of architecture "arriving in new worlds, rather than returning to old ones," then the worlds Lynch has built and filmed demonstrate the impossibility of such a clean separation. Different historical eras exist throughout his cinematic architecture, so that, for instance, his characters continue to live with traces of downtown decline or the death of modernism's domestic dreams.

Historicizing Lynch's spaces is a vital task, especially as he is often seen as the creator of ahistorical psychological dramas. Lynch's films intimately engage with the different ways in which space has been conceived and produced, from London in the 1880s to contemporary California. In particular, it is the legacies of modernist design in post-war America that haunt these films—how Loos, Schindler, Neutra and Le Corbusier entered the American home, and how decentralized cities, industrial decline, highways and roadside paraphernalia marked the nation. In Lynch's stages, moreover, we see diverse designs from throughout twentieth-century culture (including art, film and architecture) fused to form arenas for affective performance.

Above all, these cinematic worlds are obsessively attentive to symbolic places and objects, to the investments we make in certain spatial forms. We can identify these forms at once—the factory, the neighborhood, the downtown movie theater, the family home, the modernist house, the open road and the theatrical stage—but they are placed under unbearable scrutiny by Lynch's camera, so that their conventional meanings slip, distort and shatter. These symbolic forms constitute the tense social relations seen in Lynch's films. Friends, enemies, marriages and love affairs are, Lynch shows us, shaped by the urban street and the small-town fence, the framed photograph and the car radio, the staircase and the corridor. This involves the dense intertwining of psychological and material space, the real and the represented, and thus requires close critical scrutiny of both physical locations and the interpretations they have provoked. To examine Lynch's cinematic architecture, to consider how these worlds have been built and filmed, is to encounter familiar spatial forms reworked in radical new ways. Before we embark on this journey, however, we must first consider in detail the intimate relationship between film and architecture.

Cinematic Architecture: The Locus of a Secret

Vitruvius was a demanding man. An architectural education, the Roman author argued, must not be limited to drawing and geometry, but should also include history, philosophy, music, medicine, law and physics. Vitruvius was aware that these requirements were tough, so excellence in each discipline was not expected. Instead, the architect should possess "a fairly good knowledge of those parts, with their principles, which are indispensable for architecture."[18]

To Vitruvius' subjects, outlined over two thousand years ago, we should offer a modern addition, indispensable for a comprehensive architectural education: knowledge of the cinema. This is partly because of film's exceptional ability to depict three-dimensional space. Bruno Taut argued in 1920 that a student seeking "a lively notion of the true essence of architecture" must study film to "free himself of the pictorial notions fostered hitherto by perspectival renderings."[19] Since then, computer-aided design technology may have provided a more sophisticated rendering of space, yet cinema retains other advantages. Any substantive account of how we now experience space must assess how such encounters are mediated. This slots into a wider, often neglected, architectural tradition. The history of architecture includes the representation of space—on canvas, on the page and on the screen. Architectural thinking takes place across a variety of forms. As Katherine Shonfield points out, our culture contains "an untapped spatial and architectural understanding. The site of this understanding is in its fictions."[20] Wim Wenders agrees: "architects who are interested in city planning ought to know something about paintings and music and cinema. How else are they going to be able to talk about cities and the people who live in them?"[21]

Many contemporary architects not only "know something" about cinema, they also express a desire to engage with film. Peter Eisenman, for example, once planned a "virtual museum of David Cronenberg" and claims: "A lot of things I think about, I see and think about first in film. Basically, architecture is boring compared to film."[22] Rem Koolhaas studied at the Netherlands Film and Television Academy before beginning his architectural studies, while Jean Nouvel talks of turning to film at the end of his career: "I dream that one day, after I've built what I want to build, I'll have a bit of money in hand and I'll try to make a film."[23] It is now almost a cliché for an architect to identify himself, as Nigel Coates has, as a frustrated movie-maker.[24]

Yet, what of contemporary film-makers: should they, in turn, "know something" about architecture? There is certainly precedent—Sergei Eisenstein, Fritz Lang and Patrick Keiller all studied architecture, and Nicholas Ray worked under Frank Lloyd Wright at Taliesin. Architectural leanings also underpinned Michelangelo Antonioni's youth:

The other things I would have been able to do are, in order: architecture and painting. As a kid I didn't design puppets as most children of my age did; I designed doorways, capitals, plans of absurd battlements; I constructed city districts in cardboard and painted them in violent colours.[25]

The architects represented in films, however, are invariably arrogant and egotistical, epitomized by Harold Roark in *The Fountainhead* (dir. King Vidor, 1949) and Stourley Kracklite in *The Belly of an Architect* (dir. Peter Greenaway, 1987). Lang's student experiences evidently provoked some ambiguity towards the profession: the protagonist of his Freudian thriller *Secret Beyond the Door* (1948) is a sinister architect who "collects" famous rooms in which murders have taken place. Cinema may offer a unique opportunity for spatial investigation, but it has not been kind to architects.

What, though, are the theoretical consequences of the links between cinema and architecture? What techniques do both architects and film-makers employ? Such questions necessitate a definition of architecture that is extensive and imaginative, encompassing cities *and* stage sets, the built *and* the unrealized, the real *and* the represented. This entails embracing the terminology employed in geography and urban theory, as well as film studies. It also demands that we talk about studio constructions as architecture, rather than framing the debate in terms of set design or art direction. Indeed, many film sets display more attention to detail than countless environments in which we spend our lives. Lynch himself sounds a little like Harold Roark when describing his approach to cinematic architecture: "There's no compromise possible. You keep looking until you find the place that will work for the story. And that holds for the objects, too. Many places are painted or rearranged, new furniture is brought in. You can't make compromises. Compromises kill the film."[26]

At the same time, assessing the architecture of a film director requires an open-minded approach to cinema. It means understanding that cinema functions spatially; that when buildings and places appear in films, they are not passive; that there is a perceptual framework shared by film-makers and architects. As Hans Dieter Schaal confirms, cinematic architecture is never "a silent shell, standing there indifferently." Filmic spaces speak to us, they exude presence: "every façade, every building is involved and has something to say."[27] Cinema involves forms of spatial manipulation critical to the understanding of architecture. Through a variety of techniques, a film director generates space, immerses us in a sequence of scenarios, creates a narrative from rooms and corridors, focuses the traveling eye on specific features, commands our sensory experience—all of which requires an architectural imagination. Lynch, who works closely with his production designers, retains a reputation for careful supervision of sets, props and furnishings. A mere "setting" for his work is rejected; Lynch demands a holistic environment in which "the design of each and every thing is important if the whole film is to hold together."[28] There are certain worlds, he stresses—and thus certain experiences—that can only be accessed if they are built and filmed.

From the earliest days of cinema, the medium's ability to render and transform space has been noted by practitioners and critics. In 1923, Dziga Vertov outlined the magical architectural capacities of film:

> I am kino-eye. I am a builder. I have placed you, whom I've created today, in an extraordinary room which did not exist until just now when I also created it. In this room there are twelve walls shot by me in various parts of the world. In bringing together shots of walls and details, I've managed to arrange them in an order that is pleasing and to construct with intervals, correctly, a film-phrase which is the room.[29]

The film-maker, Vertov emphasizes, is involved in an architectural procedure—producing, organizing and sequencing space. Notably, Vertov highlights the role of montage in "bringing together shots of walls and details." Through montage, cinematic architecture transcends the restrictions of geography, creating an impossible singularity from disparate elements "in various parts of the world." Montage also enables architecture to subvert temporal limitations. For instance, the lengthy production process for Lynch's first feature film, *Eraserhead*, meant that, as he explains with obvious excitement, "There was one shot where Henry walks down the hall, turns the doorknob and a year and a half later he comes through the door!"[30] In Lynch's more recent film *Inland Empire*, the temporal and geographical leaps that montage makes possible are also shown to have harrowing consequences, as we will see. Yet, the assembled spaces of cinema highlight how all architecture is concerned with sequencing, with the construction of a "pleasing" order from various "walls and details." It was structural montage that led Sergei Eisenstein to label the Athenian Acropolis "one of the most ancient films," while Koolhaas has also argued: "the largest part of my work is montage [. . .] spatial montage."[31]

The ultimate invention of cinematic architecture, Vertov notes, is "a film-phrase which is the room." That a singular "room" lies at the heart of film-making's labyrinthine process seems apt, given that, at its Latin root, the camera exists as an "arched or vaulted roof or chamber" (*OED*). What the "builder" designs with his camera is another framing mechanism, the host for an amalgamation of objects and characters, and a structure for desire or anxiety. Lynch's films, as will become evident, repeatedly pivot on a single, decisive room.

Among contemporary architects, Jean Nouvel's work stands out for the cinematic analogies it has provoked. Nouvel himself has encouraged such allusions, discussing architecture using filmic terms such as "depth of field" and "sequences"—a reminder that cinema and architecture employ a shared vocabulary that also attaches shifting meanings to terms such as "plot" and "frame."[32] Nouvel describes the photoelectric cells that comprise the southern exterior of his Institute du Monde Arabe in Paris as "camera shutters" and the movements in light they create as "a series of camera angles and apertures."[33] In 2000, he decorated a boutique hotel in Lucerne with filmic images, including two bedrooms where stills from *Lost Highway* adorn the ceilings (Plate 5). Reyner Banham has argued that "architects are educated and influenced primarily by the force of visual example."[34] For Gehry's project in Łódź and Nouvel's hotel in Lucerne, Lynch's cinematic images moved beyond the realm of inspiration to become literal architectural material. Indeed, as well as citing directors such as Godard and Wenders as influences, Nouvel has also declared himself "impressed by David Lynch and his aesthetics."[35]

Nouvel's extensive comments on cinema and architecture deserve to be examined in detail, for they offer an instructive summary of the relationship between the two disciplines, as well as specific observations that suggest why Lynch's films are so architecturally significant. To begin with, consider the following statement by Nouvel, which outlines some practical similarities:

> I often compare the architect to the film director, because we have roughly the same limitations. We're in a situation where we have to produce an object within a given period of time, with a given budget, for a specific group of individuals. And we work as a team. We're in a situation where we can be censored, directly or indirectly, for reasons of safety or money, or even because of deliberate censorship. [...] We are situated in an environment that is bound, limited. Within that

environment, where can we find an unrestricted space and the means to overcome those limitations?[36]

As Nouvel suggests, notions of individual authorship are complicated by both architecture and cinema, where production relies on external endorsement and collaboration. For Fredric Jameson, the "constitutive seam" between economic conditions and aesthetic production is most visible in architecture, while film, although similarly affected, must "repress and conceal its economic determinations."[37] What is intriguing in Nouvel's account is how he describes these conditions—the fear of "censorship" and the invocation of a "bound, limited" environment. Questions of financial backing and artistic restraint have emerged throughout Lynch's career, particularly in the aftermath of *Dune*, a commercial and critical disaster. Indeed, Lynch admits to "a hair of paranoia" in his distaste for boardroom meetings.[38] Such anxieties permeate his work—not only in the explicit portrayal of directorial compromise seen in *Mulholland Drive* (enacted by the character of Adam Kesher), but also in the recurrence of delineated arenas where personal expression wrestles with spatial restriction. These stages are a response to the repression and concealment that Jameson identifies; they are perilous manifestations of the search for "an unrestricted space" that Nouvel desires. The predominance of screens in both Nouvel's architecture and Lynch's films also suggests a shared obsession with this ultimate framing device—a space that both restricts and heightens its contents.

Nouvel offers further insights into the formation of bound environments in architecture and cinema:

> Both the architect and the movie maker create or invent things that interrelate imagery and time. For the one, it's a product that plays on total illusion, because there is no physical reality other than the set of pictures; for the other, the product is experienced as a piece of space that works to a sort of scenario, a bit like a small invented world. Both of us—film director and architect—invent small worlds.[39]

Cinema's capacity to create immersive spaces is exemplified by the hermetic "small worlds" built and filmed by Lynch, such as Henry's apartment in *Eraserhead*, Jeffrey's neighborhood in *Blue Velvet* or the Red Room in *Twin Peaks*. No small world, however, can remain completely sealed, and Lynch's protagonists are continually threatened by secret passageways and unwanted intruders. For this reason, the buildings designed by Nouvel—ethereal high-tech environments, dominated by glass and steel—do not feel Lynchian, whatever their cinematic overtones. Lynch's small worlds are designed with interruption and fallibility in mind; Nouvel's work seems immaculate by comparison.

Furthermore, when Nouvel claims that film-makers have "no physical reality" to consider when inventing their "small worlds," he ignores the architecture of the cinema itself. While cinematic décor has become less ostentatious over the years—as screens have moved from urban palaces to suburban warehouses—audiences today continue to sit in a distinctive environment. This "physical reality" is especially important to remember when discussing Lynch, whose work is filled with enclosures and stages, curtains and screens, intense darkness and sharp light—the architecture of the cinema itself. How film is housed and how we inhabit this space are essential factors in any consideration of the medium.

For, regardless of a film's locale, there is already a geographical dualism at play when we enter a cinema. Tom Conley rightly talks of spectators feeling "unmoored" during an experience in which our position—are we here, in the theater, or there, on the screen?—becomes a matter of uncertainty.[40] The study of cinematic architecture reveals the wider geographical registers in which a "set of pictures" reverberates. When Lynch films Los Angeles or London, his images interact with a spectator's previous experience of those cities, as well as the myths prompted by the location. Accordingly, we should keep in mind the "physical reality" of the terrain in which Lynch's films were created—the cities that pretend to be elsewhere, the cardboard sets that stand in for historic structures, and the small towns that function as national archetypes. There is always slippage between the place in which filming occurred (whether it be a studio set or an outside location) and the place depicted on the screen, even (perhaps especially) if they profess to be one and the same. In any space, moreover, we remain hovering between the "physical reality" of our surroundings and our thoughts, memories or assumptions. As Juhani Pallasmaa, another architect who has explored cinema, explains: "We do not live separately in material and mental worlds; these experiential dimensions are fully intertwined." Consequently, Pallasmaa believes that a film-maker "often recognises the mental ground of architectural impact more subtly than an architect."[41] Lynch's work emphasizes the intertwining of physical and psychological space. More than any contemporary architect, he prioritizes the subjective nature of architectural experience.

These complications highlight the competing purposes driving architecture and cinema. Nouvel suggests: "One of the big problems with architecture is that it must both exist and be quickly forgotten; that is, lived spaces are not designed to be experienced continuously."[42] A similar case has been argued for filmic locations. For Oscar Werndorff, an art director in the 1920s and 1930s, cinematic architecture was a subservient backdrop to characters' actions: "The best 'sets' in my experience are those which you forget as soon as the film is over and the lights go up again in the theatre."[43] Many Hollywood films continue in this vein, presenting an initial urban cliché (such as an establishing shot of the Manhattan skyline) before a plot emerges that requires little geographical specificity (often filmed in Los Angeles or Toronto). Such an approach negates cinema's spatial capabilities. Contrary to Werndorff's view, a forgettable setting tends to result in a forgettable film. To this extent, cinema *is* architecture, a space we inhabit for a designated period.

In one sense, this book rests on a notion that Lynch's architecture is "designed to be experienced continuously." If, as Nouvel implies, architects should ensure that buildings fade from their inhabitants' minds, and if Werndorff feared architecture distracting from cinematic action, then Lynch guarantees that architecture *is* the story. Lynch's locations cannot "be quickly forgotten." His characters remain trapped within exceptional architectural scenarios, places that become equally lodged in his audience's consciousness. Ironically, Nouvel admits to admiring American cities because "you can go through them without thinking about the architecture."[44] Watching Lynch's films, even banal urban environments are imbued with persistent tension.

One final, rather cryptic observation by Nouvel deserves attention:

We are still dealing with invention, the unknown, risk. This unfamiliar place, if we succeed in figuring out what's going on, could be the locus of a secret. And it might, assuming that's the case, then convey certain things, things we cannot control, things that are fatal, voluntarily uncontrolled. We need to find a compromise between what we control and what we provoke.[45]

This statement might hold for any exploration into the mysteries of cinematic architecture, but it has particular resonance for Lynch's films. One defining feature of Lynch's work is the feeling that something fundamental to our very being is stored within his small worlds, if only we can discover it. The "locus of a secret" haunts Nikki Grace's passage through the corridors and rooms of *Inland Empire*; it fuels the performance in Club Silencio in *Mulholland Drive*; it propels Alvin Straight's journey across the Mid-West; it might even, perhaps, inspire someone to journey to Łódź, Paris or Los Angeles in search of an answer. This is an elusive space, yet Nouvel identifies the primary conflict it hosts: a tension between control and chaos. For Lynch, as we will see, heavily prescribed places are ripe for distortion; environments carrying excessive symbolic weight are liable to shatter; the homely environs of the cinema can become distinctly uncomfortable.

1 TOWN AND CITY

The real United States lies outside the cities.

HENRY FORD (1922)[1]

The Plot against American Cities

Contrary to popular belief, David Lynch has been as much a director of the city as of the small town or suburb. This chapter explores the Lynchian urban paradigm through his representations of London, Philadelphia and Los Angeles, and it assesses these cinematic cities alongside the famed small towns of Lumberton and Twin Peaks. The notion that Lynch's "real" interests lie outside the city, akin to Henry Ford's judgment on the United States, will be demonstrated as manifestly false: here is a director acutely conscious, if often critical, of American urbanism.

Ford's comment alerts us to the peculiar ambivalence that has characterized American attitudes towards the city. As Jonathan Raban has put it, "in America the city is widely regarded as the sack of excrement which the country has to carry on its back to atone for its sins."[2] Central figures in American intellectual life have frequently advocated the superiority of rural life, criticized the incivility of American cities, and claimed the evils of manufacturing and industry should be left to Europe.[3] Even the nation's most celebrated architect, Frank Lloyd Wright, yearned to dismantle America's existing urban structures in favor of low-density, organic and semi-rural settlements, epitomized by his Broadacre City project. Democratic life will "degenerate and die" in a centralized urban form, according to Wright, while dispersal offers salvation.[4] In response, Jane Jacobs fought the battle for an alternative perspective on American urbanism, claiming: "It is silly to deny the fact that we Americans are a city people, living in a city economy." Jacobs refused to accept Americans as intrinsically anti-urban, and pointed out that the demand for lively and diverse city districts has far outstripped their supply. What Americans truly hate, she declared, is "city failure."[5]

The post-war era in which Lynch's films have been produced and received has been marked by constant debates over American urban decline and the nation's relentless suburbanization. These discussions have included a distinct sense—slotting into older frontier myths—that America's destiny is moving inexorably to its western and southern borders. While eastern and northern icons such as Detroit, Philadelphia and Pittsburgh (part of the "Rust Belt") have suffered substantial declines in population and status since the 1950s, cities in Florida, Texas, Arizona and California (the "Sun Belt") have experienced rapid growth, predominantly based on a decentralized, car-dominated urban model. Robert Beauregard argues that, for modern Americans, cities have become "the focal point of the nation's collective anxieties, the object around which to debate injustice and inequalities, and the scapegoat for ills not of their own making."[6]

Lynch is perfectly placed to manipulate such "collective anxieties." His sensibility remains deeply marked by the politics, culture and designs of the 1950s, a time characterized by the widespread movement of white middle-class Americans to the suburbs, and a decade in which Los Angeles was the only one of America's ten largest cities to increase its population.[7] The most critical piece of legislation in the period was the 1956 Interstate Highway Act. This $26 billion program, one of the largest infrastructure projects in American history, created a vast national road network that would ensure further dispersal of the urban core, as well as a proliferation of shopping malls, motels and gas stations.

Lynch's career can be seen as emblematic of these post-war spatial developments. Not only did he personally migrate from the East Coast to the West, but his films have also moved from tiny rooms and pumping machinery in industrial cities to the expansive homes and winding roads of California. The focus, in the mid-period of his career, on small towns soaked in 1950s iconography at a time when debates concerning nostalgia and New Urbanism were emerging only adds to the sense that Lynch's films offer a unique reading of modern American urban design. In this chapter, attention initially will be given to Lynch's industrial cities, before the focus shifts towards his small towns. The chapter finishes with an analysis of Lynch's relationship with Los Angeles—a city that functions, as David Brodsly declares, as "a living polemic against both the large industrial metropolis and the provincial small town."[8]

In combining the realities of post-war urban America with Lynch's cinematic interpretations, my analysis will straddle the distinction, outlined by Raban, between the "hard" features of the city (physical buildings, cartography and statistics) and its "soft" elements (individual perceptions of space, our urban illusions and nightmares).[9] The separation of these factors is the latest round in a long conflict, famously noted by Georg Simmel, which pits the mental projections of the city against its materiality.[10] Edward Soja characterizes the division as a distorting opposition between an "illusion of opaqueness" (which sees spatial theory through the lens of a superficial materiality) and an "illusion of transparency" (which dematerializes space and sees only pure representation).[11] A strict demarcation between "hard" and "soft" urbanism offers a false dichotomy for contemporary urban studies.

The analysis of cinematic architecture, by contrast, exemplifies the expansion of perceptual range needed to understand our experience of the modern city. For film maintains an umbilical relationship with urbanism. The very first sequence of moving images projected in public by the Lumière brothers in 1895 showed workers leaving a Lyon factory, while the early city-symphonies captured the frenetic movements of the modern European metropolis. As Andrew Webber has pointed out, "the city/screen relation" has remained "a defining cultural nexus."[12] The likes of Berlin, Rome and Paris have not only been vital centers of cinematic production; but also our perception of these cities has been shaped, via the screen, by Ruttmann and Wenders, Rossellini and Fellini, Godard and Rivette. Urban dwellers, theorists and designers are not immune to the potency of these images. In fact, cinema's ability to change our impression of material space has been of on-going concern to urban thinkers. Films provide a fresh ontology to confront urban space and the social relations within it. We should pay close attention to how directors imagine the city because, as Henri Lefebvre reminds us, "An image or representation of the city can perpetuate itself, survive its conditions, inspire an ideology and urbanist projects. In other words, the 'real' sociological 'object' is an image and an ideology!"[13]

Notably, in *The Image of the City* (1960), Kevin Lynch examined in detail how residents of Boston, Jersey City and Los Angeles perceived their home cities. He found the urban image generated in the drawings of local people "was not a precise, miniaturised model of reality, reduced in scale and constantly abstracted. As a purposive simplification, it was made by reducing, eliminating, or even adding elements to reality, by fusion or distortion, by relating and structuring the parts." In their mixture of fantasy and reality, their irregularities, contortions and omissions, the images created by city dwellers mirror the representational tendencies of film-makers. Indeed, many participants in Kevin Lynch's project pictured their own city "as though seen by a motion picture camera."[14] Cinema, then, is both an index to our urban past and an influence on future forms. We might even say that cinema, produced by an assembly-line of images and beams of stark lighting, functions as both "Rust Belt" and "Sun Belt." An investigation into David Lynch's urban forms, in which physical and psychological spaces are woven together, adds new dimensions to a persistent negotiation between city and screen.

Walking the Industrial City

The modern city has consistently been explicated, especially by European theorists and film-makers, through an investigation of walking. Baudelaire and Benjamin obsessed about the *flâneur*, Le Corbusier contrasted man's rational direction with the donkey's meandering path, while Michel de Certeau took an aerial view of the "ordinary practitioners of the city [. . .] whose bodies follow the thicks and thins of an urban 'text' they write without being able to read."[15] The city-symphonies of the 1920s and 1930s similarly focused on the movement of crowds.

In Lynch's first two feature films, *Eraserhead* and *The Elephant Man*, walking is again how urban identity is established. Early sequences in these films contain journeys on foot that illustrate the death and life of modernity's defining spatial form: the industrial city. In *The Elephant Man*, Frederick Treves' exploration of Victorian London displays the noisy variations of the city. There are horse-drawn carriages and stray dogs, fruit sellers and industrial laborers, accordion players and tottering drunks. The brutal exposure of urban life is epitomized by the raw meat hanging from the market stalls (Figure 1.1). *Eraserhead* may precede *The Elephant Man* in Lynch's oeuvre, but its setting is the spatial descendant of the Victorian city. Beginning with Henry Spencer's lonely walk through the wastelands of post-war Philadelphia, *Eraserhead* demonstrates the industrial city at its lowest point. Here, there are no masses occupying the train station, the theater or the public house. Indeed, amid the blank façades and broken windows, Henry appears to be Philadelphia's last inhabitant. In the film's opening moments, Lynch uses eight lengthy shots,

FIGURE 1.1 *The Elephant Man*: Treves walks through Victorian London.
Credit: *The Elephant Man* (dir. David Lynch, 1980), © Brooksfilms.

six of which feature little or no camera movement, to create an alienating urban stage.

Lynch's fascination with industrial designs can be seen throughout his work. In *Dune*, the planet Giedi Prime is immersed in steam, fire and bubbling water; the Packard Sawmill lies at the heart of Twin Peaks; while *The Straight Story* romanticizes grain elevators and combine harvesters. In his first two films, Lynch wanders through the temporal and spatial dimensions of the modern city, essaying his own history of the bodily and psychological effects of industry. In a moment, we will examine the American context of this journey, via the malfunctioning Philadelphia depicted in *Eraserhead*. First, though, we should consider its historical antecedent— London, at the epicenter of the Industrial Revolution, as portrayed in *The Elephant Man*. It is the mesmerizing horror of this European setting that underpins the later industrial forms seen in Lynch's cinema.

The Abominable Forms of London: *The Elephant Man*

In *The Elephant Man*, London is a capital at the height of its powers—the world's largest city, an industrial powerhouse and the center of a global empire—in the midst of a "volatile decade."[16] The city's public life in the 1880s appeared increasingly grotesque, exemplified by sordid coverage of the Jack the Ripper murders. Londoners were also able to devour press reports concerning the condition of Joseph Merrick (1862–90), the "Elephant Man," whose name is distorted as "John" in Lynch's film.

However, the journalistic churning of gossip is nothing compared to the smoking chimneys, foaming pipes and roaring furnaces that engulf *The Elephant Man*. Lynch's London is a throbbing metropolis, oozing with surplus matter. Even the dreams of the city's inhabitants are infected by the hypnotic pounding of industry. In a critical sequence, Merrick's sleep is punctuated by the repetitive chug of labor. His mind fills with images of men welded to the operations of heavy machinery. The dream concludes with one worker emerging from his toil to approach the camera with a mirror, a maneuver with clear implications: Merrick's deformed features are a reflection of this worker's labor; his misshapen body, as Lynch has suggested, is "a product of the Industrial Revolution's smoke and fire."[17] Here, human flesh is subjugated to the ruthless logic of machinery and the ceaseless demands of a ravenous city. In its inexorable growth—the population is rising, the economy is booming—London is manufacturing monstrous forms.

Of course, Lynch's alliance of industrial machinery and human deformity is not a surprising one. Factories in the Victorian age were a common source of injuries, and in *The Elephant Man* Treves operates on one such victim. The surgeon's comments during this procedure, "abominable things these machines—you can't reason with them," allow for some intriguing exegesis. Lynch's cinema constantly prioritizes alternative forms of inquiry above conventional reasoning—this, we might say, is one way in which it "un-learns us." In *Twin Peaks*, for example, Dale Cooper's intuitions are more incisive than the hyper-rational observations of his FBI colleague Albert Rosenfield, a metropolitan cynic. The narrative of *Inland Empire* emphasizes association and allusion rather than a focus on linear progress. What is more, Lynch's aversion to Hollywood's commercial considerations suggests a mind-set that rejects raw efficiency. On the one hand, then, industrial methods represent a form of relentlessly consistent movement—the symbol, contrary to Treves' suggestion, of an ideology founded upon reason, law and organization—that is antithetical to Lynch's thought process. The predictable chug of machinery fits uneasily with the director's embrace of a more fluid mode of cinematic expression. As Henry Ford admitted, "Repetitive labour—the doing of one thing over and over again and always in the same way—is a terrifying prospect to a certain kind of mind."[18] Yet, Ford's own rational planning was a response to the chaotic and irrational nature of nineteenth-century industrialism, which Merrick's features brutally embody.

Conversely, though, industrial processes also evoke forms of repetitive imagery and ritualized behavior that occur throughout Lynch's work, via the regular grooves of vinyl (*Inland Empire*) or the whirling blades of a ceiling fan (*Twin Peaks*). His online film *Industrial Soundscape* (2002) distilled this obsession into a ten-minute symphony created by a looping sequence of mechanical reverberations—apparatus recalling the desert "thumper" of *Dune*. Industrial processes have a form of abstract motion, immune to rational explanation, that corresponds with Lynch's emphasis on internal, subjective logic. This coincides with his evident delight in rituals (such as Cooper's daily coffee routine) and repeated phrases (for instance, *Mulholland Drive*'s refrain: "This is the girl"). Lynch's camera, itself a form of "mechanical reproduction" in Benjamin's famous definition, remains both horrified and mesmerized by the "abominable" processes and products of industry.[19]

In the swirl of activity that Treves encounters during his walks around London, Lynch's preoccupation with urban movement extends from industry to the intricate practices of the city's inhabitants. These scenes are fertile territory for a confrontation between modernist urban critics— no doubt Le Corbusier (and perhaps Ford) would see their noise and disorder as exemplifying the "foul confusion" of the Victorian city—and those observers who resisted the allure of freeways and skyscrapers.[20] Indeed, Treves' experiences constitute a grubby version of the "daily ballet" in Greenwich Village that Jane Jacobs frequently promoted as the model for urban living, a counterpoint to Le Corbusier's plans to decontaminate the city.[21]

Although they indicate how, for Lynch, the architecture of the city constitutes its social relations, these sequences also represent a vision of urban life unmatched in his cinema, in which protagonists are usually isolated in their travels through America's towns and cities. Consider, for example, Rita's dazed walk through the Hollywood Hills in *Mulholland Drive*; the quiet streets of Lumberton that Jeffrey and Sandy stroll through in *Blue Velvet*; and the ghostly Southern towns in *Wild at Heart*. In *Inland Empire*, moreover, the only people occupying Los Angeles' streets are prostitutes and the homeless, leading Nikki Grace to wail, "I'm a freak," when she emerges onto Hollywood Boulevard. With the exception of *The Elephant Man*, neither traditional civic spaces nor large urban crowds exist in Lynch's work. To a director shaped by the post-war dispersal of America's cities, the notion of a swarming urban core is an anachronistic European phenomenon. Yet, Treves' walks can no longer be so easily replicated in London, either.

These scenes of Victorian life were shot within the tight streets around Wapping, Shad Thames and Clink Street—areas comprehensively gentrified since Lynch's crew departed in 1980. The soot-stained warehouses of *The Elephant Man*, which once served the city's shipping industry, now house scrubbed apartments and estate agents' offices, while souvenir shops and expensive cafés have replaced the market stalls (Plate 6).

Returning to Jacobs, her vision of successful urbanism centred upon dramatic street life. Streets, for Jacobs, should function as a stage for unexpected performances; "the show" that is the daily product of the city's interactions. "A lively street," she explains, "always has both its users and pure watchers."[22] Jacobs' predilection for theatrical language, her emphasis on performance in urban life, is highly relevant to *The Elephant Man*, where Lynch draws links between the carnivalesque activities of the street and the public's hunger for freakish spectacle. These two aspects of Victorian culture are explicitly combined in the climactic encounter at Liverpool Street train station—a scene that exemplifies a simplistic humanism at the heart of *The Elephant Man* (Figure 1.2). Merrick is hounded by Londoners until, huddled amid the bedlam in the public toilets, he is forced to exclaim: "I am not an animal! I am a human being!" Such uncomplicated moralizing—the one-dimensional shaming of voyeurs—is usually absent from Lynch's cinema, whereas Nikki Grace's disturbing embrace of her freakishness is more typical. The Liverpool Street scene does, however, acknowledge the violence and hypocrisy of crowds, challenging Jacobs' vision of an animated yet benign form of urban theater. Given the psychological afflictions Merrick experiences in his journeys between hospitalization and public exposure, it seems ironic that Liverpool Street station was constructed on the original site of the world's

FIGURE 1.2 *The Elephant Man*: Merrick arrives at Liverpool Street station.
Credit: *The Elephant Man* (dir. David Lynch, 1980), © Brooksfilms.

oldest psychiatric hospital, Bethlem Royal Hospital, from which the term "bedlam" derives. Today, with its profusion of chain stores and CCTV equipment, Liverpool Street epitomizes the twin forces driving contemporary notions of public space: consumerism and electronic surveillance (Plate 7).

Implicit within *The Elephant Man*'s critique of voyeuristic urban crowds is cinema itself. Set in the last decade before moving pictures were publicly demonstrated, Lynch's film hints at the social appetites that would make downtown movie theaters such popular venues. Both cinema and the freak show where Merrick performs involve another form of labor, non-productive and spectacular in nature, that compensates for the mechanical grind of industrial urbanism. We will return to the venues that stage such performances, and the desires they provoke, throughout this book.

The Elephant Man stands alone in Lynch's canon in its depiction of a busy, high-density, walkable city. Victorian London functions, therefore, in contrast to the "witlessly murdered" post-war American cities that provoked Jacobs' ire and which dominate Lynch's films.[23] In this sense, it is the symbolic urban form against which his American cities must be assessed. With this in mind, we might consider America's vast project of decentralization in the 1950s, including the systematic reduction in the authority of downtown districts, as a spatial metaphor for Lynch's cinema. After all, *The Elephant Man* not only contains the solitary example of a thriving urban core in Lynch's work; it is also his most conventional film (rivaled only by *The Straight Story* in this regard), a mainstream production with a classical narrative structure. Elsewhere, Lynch's films, their narratives diffused and twisting, rarely congregate on a clear focal-point. Although both films deal with the warped products of industrialism, a fundamental difference between *The Elephant Man* and *Eraserhead* concerns how their contrasting narrative structures reflect the design of their settings: the conventional linearity of Merrick's tale befits the classically centripetal city he inhabits; the hollowness of Philadelphia, lacking the distractions of a pub, theater or circus, leaves Henry Spencer to daydream a more imaginative urban story.

The Horrible, Horrible Decline of Philadelphia

Once the second-largest city in the British Empire, Philadelphia's history contains important transatlantic connections. When drawing up the city's famous grid, a manifestation of rational urbanism, William Penn was influenced by schemes to redesign London following the Great Fire of 1666.[24] By 1776, when the Declaration of Independence was signed in Philadelphia, the city was America's most productive settlement. It was the national capital from 1790 to 1800, and home to Benjamin Franklin, a pioneer of urban infrastructure. In 1876, Philadelphia staged the Centennial Exposition—America's first World's Fair—when its host was not only the nation's leading industrial center, but was also among the most prosperous cities on the planet. Completed in that year, the ornate Furness-Hewitt building, home to the Pennsylvania Academy of Fine Arts where Lynch would later study, was one symbol of Philadelphia's success. The bicentennial celebrations of 1976, however, took place in a city that had lost 40 percent of its manufacturing jobs in a decade, was facing a $73 million municipal deficit and had been shedding its population to the suburbs for over thirty years.[25] Few people in 1976 recognized the imminent arrival of another key event in the city's mythology: *Eraserhead*, described by Lynch as "the real *Philadelphia Story*," was in the final stages of production.[26]

These hundred-year cycles offer an emblematic tale of industrial life and death. Philadelphia's fall from grace epitomizes modern American anxieties concerning industrial urbanism. The city's problems with reproduction had made themselves apparent to Henry James at the beginning of the twentieth century. James noted that Philadelphia was the one major American city "that didn't *bristle*." He saw a place with "a fixed quality" and "its history behind it," a city where static perfection pointed towards eventual decline.[27] In the post-war era, such doubts hardened. In John Updike's *Rabbit, Run* (1960), Harry Angstrom sees Philadelphia as the "dirtiest city in the world" where inhabitants "live on poisoned water, you can taste the chemicals." By 1981's *Rabbit is Rich*, Harry sees Philadelphia as "one big swamp of miserable humanity." *Rabbit at Rest* (1990) confirms a relentless urban deterioration: "there is no such thing any more as a good Philadelphia neighborhood."[28]

Like Updike, Lynch is a product of small-town America who has mapped the decay of this industrial icon. Lynch worked and studied in Philadelphia between 1965 and 1970. During this time, he lived with his family in the Callowhill area, a district north of downtown especially affected by the city's manufacturing slump. Lynch has since called Philadelphia "a very sick, degenerate, decaying, fear-ridden place where things are totally absurd and confusing. I saw horrible things, horrible,

horrible things while I was there."[29] Intriguingly, though, he felt an attendant excitement in the city: "I saw things that were frightening, but more than that, *thrilling*."[30]

Forty years after Lynch left Philadelphia, Callowhill remains an assortment of industrial detritus and railway infrastructure, where isolated homes and abandoned warehouses sit alongside parking lots and auto-repair shops (Plate 8). Cut off from downtown by the Vine Street Expressway, it maintains a feeling of desolation and poverty, though the remnants of glorious Art Deco hotels and factories have led to the area's inclusion on the National Register of Historic Places. The transformation of several of these buildings into upscale apartment blocks has also placed Callowhill at the center of gentrification debates in the city. Callowhill is, like Łódź and downtown Los Angeles, brimming with fertile decay, the kind of ill-defined terrain that sparks Lynch's imagination. Fittingly, the area now enjoys a new nickname: the "Eraserhood."[31]

Manufacturing Malfunction: *Eraserhead*

Though the setting is never formally named in *Eraserhead*, the rotting urban realm depicted in the film symbolizes both a generation of "Rust Belt" decline and speaks to specific woes within Philadelphia's history. What emerges is a vision of reproductive failure, dysfunctional labor and manufacturing stasis.

Eraserhead's dream-like prologue forges an immediate connection between industrial apparatus and sexual reproduction. It features a disfigured man (another victim of those "abominable" machines, perhaps) cranking mechanical levers to release a sperm-like substance into the atmosphere. In this world, technology is controlling matters. Indeed, matter itself, especially human flesh, is subjugated to machinery. Beneath the gaze of this deformed foreman, Philadelphia's factories require no further supervision. In fact, human agency is now redundant in the city. Consider the curious employment status of *Eraserhead*'s protagonist, Henry Spencer. He claims to be a printer—a job Lynch held in Philadelphia, and also the occupation of Benjamin Franklin and Updike's Harry Angstrom. Consequently, when quizzed by his mother-in-law, Henry confesses to being "on vacation" and we never do see him at work. Henry's lack of occupation affects his ability to occupy space successfully: he is perennially displaced and terrified by his surroundings. His failure to be economically productive is combined with the production of a malfunctioning human form—the grotesque baby Henry fathers. Given that images of industrial architecture smother the film, this deformed creature feels like the result of a problem on the production line. Just as mounds of earth and stray piping sprout in the city's public spaces, Mary and Henry have created a misshapen child, prone to bizarre illnesses. Perhaps Harry Angstrom was right and Philadelphians have been drinking poisoned water.

The birth of Henry's child is a form of dysfunctional labor and manufacturing malfunction overshadowed by temporal confusion. When he is first told he has become a father, Henry responds, "That's impossible, it's only been..." before Mary interrupts: "They're still not sure it *is* a baby!" The child's questionable conception and birth suggest that time has become distorted amid Philadelphia's waning fortunes. In a film containing such sparse dialogue, we should take note of Mary's first words: "You're late, Henry." Producing couples and celebrating the products of marriage are two of Hollywood's most persistent themes. In Philadelphia, though, production has faltered. The temporal inconsistencies in *Eraserhead* echo the film's own difficult birth: it took Lynch five years to complete his first feature-length production.

If Merrick's condition in *The Elephant Man* warned of the chaotic products of industrialization, then *Eraserhead* confirms that manufacturing difficulties can overwhelm all city processes. Philadelphia's alienating factories are accompanied by a disintegrating public realm in which Franklin's famed achievements, which included paved streets, urban lighting and a city police force, are now long gone (Figure 1.3). Even Penn's grid, a spatialization of social order, has turned to dust. Whereas London's throbbing streets generate grotesque public spectacles, Philadelphia's hostile public spaces drive Henry towards domestic retreat, where the baby's screams engulf his tiny apartment. The body of Mary's father also betrays the legacy of industrial practices, his knees ruined by thirty years of plumbing, while his family's home contains an invasion of random pipes.

It is in this context that we should view the fantasmatic scenes late in the film in which Henry dreams of his own physical disintegration. Henry's decapitated head falls to the ground next to a homeless man, before a young boy carries it to a workshop to be turned into pencils. The incident represents a neat metaphor for the production of *Eraserhead*

FIGURE 1.3 *Eraserhead*: negotiating the rubble of the post-war American city. Credit: *Eraserhead* (dir. David Lynch, 1977), © David Lynch and the American Film Institute for Advanced Studies.

itself: the cinematic reel is the assembly-line upon which Lynch's industrial dreams were manufactured; the workshop is a dream factory to rival Paramount Studios. Within the film, though, Henry's imagined death is the culmination of industrial practices that have already erased the city's infrastructure. His daydreaming was a response to the surrounding alienation—a small act of creative resistance amid machine-driven rationality—yet, like Merrick, he merely imagines more machines and more deformity. Industrial labor demands that workers place their bodies on the assembly-line; unproductive Henry has only his day-dreams to contribute. After devouring its own physical fabric, Philadelphia is now consuming the city's inhabitants, colonizing their minds as well as their flesh. Warped manufacturing processes have produced another victim.

Critics often highlight the fears of fatherhood evident in *Eraserhead*, an idea discussed in the following chapter. What is more often ignored is Lynch's terrified reaction to the aggressive paternalism of capital and its irreversible effects on the self. The personification of this threat is the owner of the workshop in which Henry is finally erased—a businessman, dressed in pinstripes and unraveling rolls of cash, so brash as to be a clear parody. Furthermore, McGowan, in one of the best readings of the film, describes the urban landscape that surrounds Henry as a world of absence, the inevitable consequence of the sacrificed enjoyment that industrial production demands.[32] Indeed, Henry's city feels almost entirely barren. While crowded industrial cities like Victorian London exemplified violent proximity, it is emptiness that defines the Philadelphia of *Eraserhead*. The rapid circulation associated with modern urbanism is absent, a vision of "city failure" to make Jacobs shudder. Whereas conventional urban dramas emphasize the movements of the city through sharp cuts and vertiginous tracking shots, Lynch's camera is largely immobile, reflecting a stagnating city where the flows of images and capital are grinding to a halt.

Eraserhead, then, is an indictment of Philadelphia's failure to renew itself once its industrial pre-eminence faded. Lynch's films frequently present places hovering between different eras. For instance, *Blue Velvet's* blending of American iconography from multiple decades has often been remarked upon, with Eisenman noting how its "complex and intentional tissue" comprising past and future forms creates "temporal dislocation."[33] In *Eraserhead*, Lynch registers a city caught between its industrial heritage and an uncertain future. Here, Edward Dimendberg's work, which explores *film noir* in the context of the centrifugal forces that devastated post-war urban America, is of particular use. Dimendberg sees *noir* as both a celebration and mourning of centripetal space. He claims the films function as "a social memory bank that provides a means for the film spectator to remember disappearing urban forces." The end of *film noir* at the end of the 1950s, Dimendberg states, coincided with "the end of the metropolis of classical modernity, the centred city of immediately recognisable and recognised spaces."[34]

Extending these conclusions to *Eraserhead* positions Lynch's representation of Philadelphia as "a social memory bank." Lynch envisions an American industrial powerhouse in a distinct identity crisis, a period of limbo between manufacturing success and the narratives of gentrification and post-industrialism that would dominate urban theory from the late 1970s onwards. Indeed, Lynch's archive of urban decline has ensured a certain form of immortality for the Callowhill area. *Eraserhead* now operates as a central element in the cultural memory of this district. A mural of Henry adorns the Philadelphia Mausoleum of Contemporary Art, a few streets north of where Lynch once lived (Plate 9), while the gallery itself hosts exhibitions inspired by Lynch and the "Eraserhood" in general (Figure 1.4).

We might, then, view Henry as a pioneer of the warehouse lifestyles now emerging in Callowhill, but the contemporary preference for such cleansed industrial spaces sees only irony where Lynch senses uncanny remnants. Henry's travels through Philadelphia's wastelands

FIGURE 1.4 "Eraserhood" exhibition poster by Karli Cox (2013).
Credit: Copyright Eric Bresler. Poster design by Karli Cox.

more suitably confirm what Dimendberg positions as a key characteristic of the post-war American metropolis: "the psychic hazards of dwelling in an urban space whose historical mutation yields real spatial gaps and temporal voids between the modern as 'yet-to-come' and the urban past as 'yet-to-be-destroyed'."[35]

With this in mind, let us return to those early shots in *Eraserhead* where Henry walks past a concrete viaduct, piles of rubble and a large anonymous façade (Figure 1.5). He is dwarfed by his surroundings, stranded in indeterminate spaces awaiting regeneration. Solitary and confused, Henry seems a relic from an earlier era, an instinctive reminder of Charlie Chaplin or Buster Keaton. Notably, those two stars were much admired by Le Corbusier, who saw their struggles as typical of the American soul in its ability to survive "an overwhelming situation, inhuman dimensions." Chaplin, Keaton and Henry all fight against a sense of epic urban space, a disproportionality that, Le Corbusier concludes, "is the rule in the USA: an abyss opens up before sensitive persons at every step."[36] Chaplin, of course, highlighted the alienation of industry in *Modern Times* (1936), and the memorable sequence in which his body slides through machine cogs finds a successor in Henry's workshop erasure. *Eraserhead*'s connections with a cinema of anachronism and decay are further evidenced by the ruined urban environment of *Film* (1965), directed by Alan Schneider from a script by Samuel Beckett. Set in 1929, a year that combines associations of economic uncertainty with the changes sound brought to cinema, *Film* features Keaton scuttling past the

FIGURE 1.5 *Eraserhead:* Henry begins his lonely urban walk.
Credit: *Eraserhead* (dir. David Lynch, 1977), © David Lynch and the American Film Institute for Advanced Studies.

crumbling walls of an old factory before, like Henry, he settles (or, more precisely, unsettles) himself within a tiny room.

That *Eraserhead* presents us with a place somewhat out of time is an idea, perversely, with its own historical context. The film's temporal uncertainty reinforces how the 1970s are often perceived as an interim stage in American history, an uncertain void between the upheavals of the 1960s and the conservative revival of the 1980s. Fredric Jameson talks of a decade "whose specificity seemed most of the time to consist in having no specificity"; Marshall Berman describes living "in the shadow of the speed limit and the stop sign"; while Updike labelled the era "somewhat amorphous."[37] Though it is rarely read alongside celebrated examples of American urban cinema in this period—the connections between city and screen in New York dramas such as Scorsese's *Taxi Driver* (1976) and Friedkin's *The French Connection* (1971) are more commonly discussed—*Eraserhead* follows a similar trajectory in siting disparate social anxieties within an urban framework.[38] For Lynch, Philadelphia becomes a scapegoat for broader national ills and thrills. The confusion, fear and hesitancy omnipresent in *Eraserhead* indicate modern America's anxiety about a particular form of East Coast urbanism involving the proximity of industrial and human production.

Thus, Lynch's Philadelphia precedes the major elements of the postmodern American city—yuppies and gentrification, high-rise financial centres and waterfront developments—and instead offers decay, decline and a certain tense excitement. By the time we reach his vision of contemporary Los Angeles in *Mulholland Drive*, the classical industrial metropolis represented by Victorian London has been superseded by a different urban paradigm—a city of freeways and downtown skyscrapers, where production means boardrooms and film sets. Yet, Lynch's cinematic journey, like that of many post-war Americans, has swapped one set of barren streets on the East Coast (caused by faltering downtown districts and a population heading to the suburbs) for another set of empty sidewalks on the West Coast (epitomized by car-dominated Los Angeles). Walking through the city, in the sense that Benjamin, Baudelaire, Le Corbusier or even Jacobs theorized, is far from the primary form of urban experience for modern Americans.

One final irony cements this story of urban change. Echoing the move from "Rust Belt" to "Sun Belt" that Lynch and other Americans undertook, the gloom of *Eraserhead* was shot entirely in Los Angeles. Like many urban fictions, Lynch's Philadelphia was an exercise in imaginary architecture. *Eraserhead*'s interiors were built in the stables of the Greystone Mansion in Beverly Hills, a Tudor-style house completed in 1928 (and the site of a horrific murder-suicide case the following year), which was leased to the American Film Institute from 1965 to 1982. The early shot in which Henry enters a dark viaduct was filmed under the 4th Street Bridge in downtown Los Angeles (Plate 10). Moreover, in a perfect example of America's shifting urban priorities, the abandoned oil well near West Hollywood—a wasteland filled with tanks and tar pools—that was used by Lynch for further exterior shots in *Eraserhead* was replaced in 1982 by the enormous Beverly Center shopping mall (Plate 11). *Eraserhead*'s production history brings to light what has been won and lost in America's regeneration battles: the landscape that served to recreate a "frightening" but "*thrilling*" city has been supplanted by a banal space of consumerism. As Lynch himself notes, the instruments of production and manufacturing have become "a congestion of shops and parking and lights and signs."[39] Ironically, recent efforts to diversify Philadelphia's economy have included government incentives designed to encourage film-makers to use the city as a shooting location.[40] The production of images is, it seems, one form of urban manufacturing with a sunny future.

Neighborhoods or Nothing?

"The success story of America," Ronald Reagan declared in 1982, "is neighbor helping neighbor."[41] As with many of Reagan's public remarks, the statement resonates with folksy common sense, not least because it draws upon a familiar, biblical source—specifically St Paul's edict: "thou shalt love thy neighbour as thyself."[42] Indeed, the concept of neighbor-love has become, as Žižek, Santer and Reinhard remind us, "the central law or moral principle par excellence, the ethical essence of true religion."[43] On first glance, then, the spirit of Reagan's assertion, regardless of its historical accuracy, seems hard to dispute. However, its unspoken implications remain contentious. What constitutes a neighbor? Who is excluded from this category? Where are these neighbors located?

Perhaps Reagan himself might be a source of further guidance. Here was a President who claimed to understand America's social divisions. Describing his childhood, Reagan quipped, "We didn't live on the wrong side of the tracks, but we lived so close we could hear the whistle real loud."[44] An advertisement for his 1984 re-election campaign offers a perfect illustration of Reagan's approach to social relations. Gentle music accompanies a soothing voice—"It's morning again in America," we are told—while an array of cosy images slide past: white picket fences, wooden-framed homes, red roses and a shiny fire engine. Despite brief shots of an urban taxi and a rural farm-worker, there is no doubt about the commercial's message: small-town America remains the nation's most reliable site of neighborly goodwill and harmonious relations.[45]

Reagan's advertisement presents a collection of images uncannily similar to the opening sequence of Lynch's *Blue Velvet*, released two years later. Here, again, the picket fence is white, the roses are red, the houses are wooden and the fire service friendly and on hand. In contrast to the urban alienation in Lynch's vision of Philadelphia, this exemplary neighborhood seems to signal a community at peace. From the urban malaise of the 1970s, we are transported to a sunny small town in a new decade.

The evocation of an idyllic small town has been a recurring feature in the history of the United States. Since Puritan settlers sought perfect villages in New England, a craving for a utopian balance between man and nature, and between the community and the private citizen, has found its expression in a mythology of small-town life. These myths have maintained a particular presence in American film, while their political potency continues long after Reagan left office.[46] In October 2008, for instance, Republican Vice-Presidential candidate Sarah Palin offered this address to an audience in Greensboro, North Carolina:

> We believe that the best of America is in these small towns that we get to visit, and in these wonderful little pockets of what I call the real America, being here with all of you hard-working, very patriotic, very pro-America areas of this great nation.[47]

Her comments were very much in the vein of Ford's earlier anti-urban stance: not only are small towns hospitable; they are also more authentically American than the nation's cities.

Contemporary architecture has played its part in imbuing the American small town with intense symbolic weight. Consider the conception of community articulated by the promotional literature for one of the most discussed new developments in recent American history: the town of Celebration, Florida, established by the Disney Corporation in 1994. The manner in which the town was described to potential residents had more than a hint of *Blue Velvet*'s opening images, Reagan's electoral pitch and Palin's rhetoric:

> There was once a place where neighbors greeted neighbors in the quiet of their summer twilight. Where children chased fireflies. And porch swings provided easy refuge from the care of the day. The movie house showed cartoons on Saturday. The grocery store delivered. And there was one teacher who always knew you had that "special something". Remember that place? It held a magic all its own. The special magic of an American hometown. Now, the people at Disney—itself an American family tradition—are creating a place that recalls timeless traditions and boundless spirit that are the best parts of who we are.

The imagery here longs for a retreat to an earlier period in American history—an era when social conflicts did not intrude on neighborhood life. Less well publicized was the fact that this nostalgic community, surrounded by a white vinyl fence, was partly built by illegal Mexican workers.[48]

Although Celebration attracted the cream of postmodern architects— Michael Graves, Philip Johnson, Cesar Pelli, Robert Venturi and Denise Scott Brown have all designed buildings there—its basis lies in the more earnest ideas of New Urbanism, which first emerged in the 1980s. New Urbanism promotes compact, mixed-use environments as an antidote to sprawling residential suburbs. Small-town America and its imagined community values form the backbone of its philosophy. According to three of its most vocal advocates, "traditional towns" have now become "a crime in America."[49] The potential for transgression is certainly high in Celebration: residency is dependent on compliance with a 100-page book of conditions, which includes rules concerning the color of curtains and edicts on plant types.[50] Celebration is a fragile utopian vision requiring high maintenance, as if the town was carved from a wilderness always threatening to return. Alongside such heavy regulation, the broader New Urbanist approach to social relations—defined by their fundamentalist cry, "Neighborhoods or Nothing!"—remains intensely prescribed.[51] As Ada Louise Huxtable pointed out, New Urbanism reduces notions of community "to a romantic social aesthetic emphasising front porches, historic styles, and walking distance to stores and schools."[52] This, then, is the political, cultural and architectural context in which we should assess *Blue Velvet*, a film that raises significant questions concerning small-town social relations, the corrupting powers of industrial urbanism and the notion of propinquity. What follows is an attempt to map the Lynchian conception of "neighbor helping neighbor."

A Friend from the Neighborhood: *Blue Velvet*

Blue Velvet is set in the *town* of Lumberton. This is important to stress, as critics of the film often conflate the terms "small town" and "suburb" as if these locations, created by different forces and laden with contrasting cultural overtones, were interchangeable.[53] Where community values are concerned, small towns, as we have seen, are frequently praised for their harmonious qualities—the symbolism *Blue Velvet* manipulates. By contrast, suburbs, particularly in their post-war American form, are more commonly associated with alienation, isolation and consumption.[54]

Such categorical uncertainties partly stem from designers of suburban housing estates appropriating the emblematic features of small-town America, such as white picket fences, regardless of a development's context—a problem that gained momentum in the 1980s.[55] To clarify the distinction, Kenneth T. Jackson's definition, made in 1985, is instructive. For Jackson, suburban areas consist of a single function (residential), a predominance of middle- and upper-class citizens, a clear separation of homes from places of work, and low-density development.[56] Lumberton— like Twin Peaks, another small town often deemed a suburb—clearly fails to fulfill Jackson's criteria. Lynch's towns are multi-functional (they contain factories, diners, hotels and stores alongside family homes and apartments), with little sign of any commuting, and they maintain a broad social mix, including a strong working-class element. These are self-contained small towns—independent entities, not satellites of larger conurbations.

This is more than mere semantics. It highlights a key feature of Lynch's best work: *Eraserhead*, *Blue Velvet*, *Twin Peaks* and *Mulholland Drive* all derive intensity from a single, bubble-like location, whether it be a city or a small town. Lynch, in Nieland's words, is "an engineer of atmosphere," who creates concentrated environments.[57] His films are Petri dishes for experiments in mood manipulation, where conditions can be tweaked, variables changed, pressure heightened and everyday assumptions tested to the limit. In Lynch's laboratories, there is little sense of a world outside. These locations maintain their own logic without the possibility of relief elsewhere.

Lynch grew up in a Cold War era in which "containment" was a dominant political and cultural idea, a notion that found architectural expression in Buckminster Fuller's domes and Paul László's bomb shelters. Moreover, Walt Disney's original plans for a model city in Florida, prompted by his disdain for Los Angeles, featured a community encased in a giant bubble.[58] Notably, before collaborating on *Twin Peaks*, Lynch and Mark Frost worked on an unrealized comedy investigating the effects of a top-secret military program on the residents of a small town. From its title onwards, *One Saliva Bubble* alerts us to Lynch's preference for sealed, self-sufficient environments in which he can tamper with conventional expectations.[59] By contrast, the parasitic form of the suburb, with its reliance on other places for employment or leisure, is antithetical to Lynch's holistic worlds. That is not to say there are no social or spatial demarcations within these small towns. In fact, Lynch highlights the divides and connections preserved within apparently homogenous communities—issues of separation and proximity that will demand our attention in due course.

Let us first examine Lumberton in more detail and how *Blue Velvet*'s initial succession of small-town signifiers operate in a radically different fashion from those ostensibly similar examples raised earlier. For the Reagan campaign, white picket fences and red roses were a form of ideological short-hand—a way of evoking a return to the abundance of the 1950s and a time before the economic woes of the 1970s (so perceptible in *Eraserhead*). Ironically, of course, the 1950s, often lionized as a prelapsarian paradise by American conservatives, are better considered as the decade in which suburbs and highways, at the expense of small towns, began their dominance of the American landscape, underwritten by the Eisenhower administration. Such complexities rarely troubled Reagan, nor Sarah Palin. For the New Urbanists, the various social, economic and political forces leading to sprawl will be neutered by a return to the "special magic of an American hometown."

Lynch's employment of small-town iconography may at first suggest sympathy with conservative ideals. Many critics have concluded that Lynch's work displays, in Jonathan Rosenbaum's words, a reactionary predilection for "nostalgic regression."[60] However, *Blue Velvet*'s opening is as much a disruption as confirmation of small-town mythology. Our suspicions are aroused by the excessive nature of Lynch's images: the immaculate clarity of the colors, with patriotic red, white and blue to the fore, is scarcely believable; the fireman's measured wave is creepy, not friendly; the children are strangely well behaved. This sequence is altogether *too* archetypal for comfort: instinctively, such a flawless vision of small-town America evokes sinister connotations. Lynch has taken the already nostalgic and highly suspect symbols of the Reagan campaign and elevated them to the point at which the images begin to undermine themselves, parodying their subject through over-identification. National symbols are placed under such unbearable scrutiny that their usual meanings distort and shatter. In so doing, as Laura Mulvey points out, "*Blue Velvet* restores an uncanny to American culture that the uncanny President disavows."[61]

Furthermore, the gentle tone of *Blue Velvet*'s beginning is transformed when Jeffrey's father suffers a heart attack in his garden. Unsettling the local equilibrium is a common characteristic of Lynch's work: both *Twin Peaks* (when Laura Palmer's body washes up on the shore) and *The Straight Story* (when Alvin falls in his kitchen) also begin with tranquil communities destabilized by physical pain: someone must get hurt when the symbols of small-town America shatter. In *Blue Velvet*, Lynch doubly subverts his peaceful setting by switching attention from the human suffering upon the turf to the insects festering beneath it. Evidently, small towns such as Lumberton are not as perfect as they seem; these lush lawns harbor processes usually ignored. Leo Marx famously outlined how "the machine as a sudden, shocking intruder upon a fantasy of idyllic satisfaction" has been an important image ordering American literature.[62] In *Blue Velvet*, though, it is natural forces that intrude upon the garden fantasies of Lumberton. It is a reminder that even the most controlled environments contain unwelcome elements. Indeed, over-determined spaces, such as these domestic lawns, are most vulnerable to corruption.

One final element of this opening sequence deserves explication. Lynch's emphasis on Lumberton's white picket fences (they appear in five of the first six shots following the credits) alerts us to *Blue Velvet*'s preoccupation with the socio-spatial divisions within the town and the anxieties these boundaries generate. In this community, territory is less secure than it appears and transcending divisions will become the film's primary focus. The white picket fence seeks to protect a homeowner's lawn from the befouling tendencies of the neighbor; disobedience of these signifiers is a declaration of turf war.

Lynch reveals the rest of Lumberton to be a riverside settlement, with sturdy turn-of-the-century architecture. It has a prosaic downtown, filled with cars; paternal authority is present through the church and police station; while a radio show informs us that "logs, logs, logs" are the main local industry. Other unremarkable settings, such as Beaumont's hardware store, Arlene's Diner and the high school, complete the feel of an archetypal small town. These exterior shots were filmed, like almost all of *Blue Velvet*, in Wilmington, North Carolina, situated on the Cape Fear River. Wilmington is now far from being a small town: its population has more than doubled since the 1980s to over 100,000, and—as the nickname "Wilmywood" suggests—cinematic production is a major industry here. It is also just a few hours' drive from Greensboro, Palin's approved slice of "real America."

In *Blue Velvet*, the language of Lumberton's residents divulges much about the town's social conventions. When Jeffrey Beaumont discovers a severed ear on a patch of wasteland—the antithesis of the perfect lawn encountered earlier—his explanation is telling: he describes the location as "the field, behind our neighborhood, there behind Vista" (Plate 12). Dismemberment is thus in shocking proximity to the idyllic community unveiled at the beginning of the film, but only a new field of perspective has allowed Jeffrey to see it. From now on, fresh vistas will emerge around the town, avenues that were "always hidden" to Jeffrey, while additional viewing mechanisms—cameras, closets, binoculars—will continue to propel his investigations.

These adventures will necessitate breaking Lumberton's social codes. Leaving home for a stroll, Jeffrey is quizzed by his aunt: "You're not going down by Lincoln, are you?" He replies: "No, I'm just going to walk around the neighborhood. Don't worry." At this stage, there is a clear separation between the respectable area where middle-class families like the Beaumonts reside and Lincoln Street, where Dorothy Vallens lives. Lincoln Street is not considered part of the Beaumonts' neighborhood. Consequently, Dorothy is, by Jeffrey's definition, not his neighbor. Any Reaganite suggestions of assistance or Pauline demands for love are redundant.

The neighbor, then, is a category that excludes as much as it includes, depending on our vista. This was among Freud's complaints with the notion of a Christian community centred on Paul's doctrine of universal neighborly love. Such a move, ignorant of its exclusionary values, meant "the extreme intolerance of Christianity towards those left outside it was an inevitable consequence."[63] Neighbor-love creates a heightened form of outsider: it denies full status, even existence, to those excluded from the injunction. Soon, however, Jeffrey is told by Sandy that Dorothy's home, Deep River Apartments, is "real close to your house. It's also close to the field where you found the ear. [...] It's really close by, that's what's so creepy." Her comments indicate a form of social myopia: Sandy is unable to see elements of her own community and is surprised they occupy adjacent territory. Notably, Sandy is also closely aligned with religion: she pretends to be a Jehovah's Witness as part of Jeffrey's scheme; she makes a speech about the "blinding light of love" in front of a church and to the sound of organ music; and her own home has a steeple-like roof. Yet, her desire to "love thy neighbor" is questionable. Jeffrey's neighborhood, though, is expanding. There are no physical changes to the buildings around him, but his perceptions of proximity are shifting.

Despite his aunt's warnings, Jeffrey explores the Lincoln Street neighborhood and beyond, new places springing up on his mental map of the town. He is awestruck by Deep River Apartments—its imposing brick façade a foreign body amid Lumberton's single-story, wooden-framed homes—and Frank Booth's warehouse-style apartment block. The latter location reaffirms Lynch's desire to confront spatial ideologies. Jeffrey's neighborhood, with its lawns and roses, exemplifies a small-town philosophy of channeling nature to create a semi-bucolic paradise. Frank's apartment block, by contrast, is surrounded by sights reminiscent of *Eraserhead* and *The Elephant Man*—a corrugated iron hut, gas canisters and a silhouette of pumping machinery. This is a neighborhood where nature has been overwhelmed by industrial apparatus. It is, in Lynch's logic, a thoroughly urban setting. Frank is the embodiment of these processes, another warped product of industrial urbanism, along with Henry's baby and John Merrick.

Lumberton, therefore, is more than just a small town: it is a small town and a city in one; a microcosm of American fears and desires. Lynch creates an overarching environment in which competing, yet dependent, forms co-exist. Indeed, Lumberton's combination of characteristics is, in McGowan's analysis, proof that "when we fantasize about our ideal, we fantasize simultaneously about the threats that imperil that ideal."[64] Thus, the urban menace of Frank's neighborhood is, like the collapse of Jeffrey's father and the insects under the lawn, part of the fall-out generated when the vulnerable symbols of small-town innocence begin to shatter.

Initially, Jeffrey believes he can observe at a distance as Lumberton's landscape unfurls before him, as if he is one of Jacobs' "pure watchers" without the responsibilities of social engagement. He hides in Dorothy's closet, peering through the slats at her torment, and he photographs Frank's home using a secret camera. However, these secure, detached positions cannot be maintained for long. Jeffrey's relentless curiosity, a surrogate for the voyeuristic desires of film directors and spectators, means the distance between Lumberton's residents is narrowing by the scene. The social implications of this constriction are immense. As Jacques-Alain Miller explains, "it is a simple matter to love one's neighbor when he is distant, but it is a different matter in proximity."[65] What, we wonder, will happen when Jeffrey, Dorothy and Frank come together?

Dorothy's apartment hosts the inevitable encounters. Whereas neighbors have conventionally been perceived as binding a community together, to the subsequent exclusion of outsiders, Žižek positions the neighbor as "a traumatic intruder," a figure who "disturbs us, throws the balance of our way of life off the rails, when it comes too close."[66] It is this force that both Jeffrey and Frank bring to Dorothy's world. After breaking into Dorothy's flat, Jeffrey's interstitial surveillance is only a temporary position, to be superseded by a relationship combining pleas for assistance ("Help me") with a desire for pain ("Hit me"). In this regard, Frank offers Jeffrey a lesson in neighborly behavior. The famous scene in which Jeffrey observes Frank abusing Dorothy is unsettling, Michel Chion has argued, "because it resembles a ritual played out for someone else."[67] Readings of this scene tend to position the characters, via a psychoanalytic framework, in a familial hierarchy, an understandable move given the language of "mommy," "daddy" and "baby" involved. However, the scene's horizontal social relations are often overlooked. What occurs here is a form of education: Frank is demonstrating to Jeffrey what being a neighbor truly involves. Here, the American success story of "neighbor helping neighbor" is given a radical twist: the implicit violence in social relations—especially in Reagan's America, an increasingly unequal place—is made thoroughly explicit. Such traumatic neighborly intrusions are a recurring theme in Lynch's work, the consequence of overlapping spatial philosophies. *Inland Empire*, for example, introduces Hollywood to its "new neighbor" in the form of a European woman who knocks on Nikki Grace's door to discuss "brutal fucking murder."

Likewise, Dorothy is at first uncertain of Jeffrey's motives, but soon finds a suitable way to describe him: Jeffrey is "a friend [...] from the neighborhood," she tells Frank. This ambiguous expression—as we have seen, defining the neighbor or the neighborhood is far from straightforward—grips Frank's imagination. His response is mocking, a parody of small-town civility—"Oh, you're from the neighborhood?"—confirming an incongruous juxtaposition. No longer is Jeffrey the intrepid detective or the commanding lover: his boyish, middle-class demeanor is swept aside by Frank's authority.

Frank will address Jeffrey as "neighbor" for the rest of the film, imbuing the term with ferocious implications. These meetings are *Blue Velvet*'s pivotal moments, the scenes in which the logic of the Lynchian neighbor reaches a crescendo. One particular outburst contains an incoherent, yet fascinating, philosophy of social relations. Frank, in the process of warning Jeffrey away from Dorothy, smothers his "neighbor" in kisses before almost collapsing as the symbolic differences between the two men finally shatter. He explains with terrifying solemnity:

Don't be a good neighbor to her. I'll send you a love letter. Straight from my heart, fucker. You know what a love letter is? It's a bullet from a fucking gun, fucker. You receive a love letter from me, you're fucked forever.

This is closer to William Burroughs' imperative to "Love Your Enemies"—"give him the kiss of life, stick your tongue down his throat and taste what he's been eating and bless his digestion. [...] Let your love enter into him and penetrate him with a divine lubricant"—than Reagan's patronizing rhetoric.[68] Frank offers an alternative small-town sermon, embracing a desperate form of neighborly relations.

For Freud, loving thy neighbor without qualification or merit was absurd. In fact, "nothing else runs so much counter to basic human nature." Our innate hostility means a stranger is not only "altogether unlovable," but actually holds "a greater claim to my enmity, even to my hatred."[69] Accepting an unbridgeable divide between humans is, for Freud, a sign of maturity and self-awareness, while Burroughs twists this logic into a truly radical form of social relations. In Frank's confused words in *Blue Velvet*, neighbour-love and social hostility merge in a melting pot of anger and desire. Frank is capable of loving his "neighbor" Jeffrey, but love itself is inverted: it becomes a form of hatred, a deadly weapon, a profound violence. Here, neighborly assistance provokes aggression, not harmony. For Žižek, in a characteristic reading of Lynch via Lacan, Frank exemplifies the neighbor who is "a Real which is all too possible, and *that* is what is traumatic."[70] Recalling Frank's warehouse ghetto, should we regard this "Real" as the unleashed voice of urban America, those citizens whose authenticity has been doubted by the likes of Ford and Palin? Have America's cities, in Lynch's eyes, become so degraded their inhabitants cannot separate love letters from bullets? Is this backlash now threatening the nation's small towns?

Perhaps, but Lynch typically complicates things. For Frank and Jeffrey maintain an inextricable bond: both the urban and the small town harbor a predilection for social violence. "You're like me," Frank tells his rival, recognizing their shared appetite for sexual brutality. The scenes of recognition that occur at spatial borders are "the only chance for people to confront fixed, sociological pictures," Richard Sennett contends.[71] Just as Lynch found Philadelphia's grime to be "*thrilling*" as well as "frightening," Jeffrey prefers the thrilling, frightening urban attractions of Lumberton to the domestic stasis of his family. Yet, while Sennett sees this displacement as wholly positive, following Jacobs in stressing urban interaction in benign terms, Lynch demonstrates that an expanded neighborhood increases the possibility for transgression rather than harmony. Exemplary in this regard is the scene late in *Blue Velvet* in which Dorothy appears naked and beaten—as if from nowhere—on a perfect domestic lawn. As McGowan states, her intrusion into "the fantasmatic ideal world of Lumberton [...] rips apart the fantasy structure."[72] No white picket fence can stop this neighborly disturbance with all its traumatic dissonance—a sociological picture that cannot be assimilated by those who witness it, except for Jeffrey. Dorothy's journey from Lincoln Street, beyond his vista, to the heart of his community, is complete. In reciprocating Jeffrey's earlier intrusion into her world, Dorothy is now his "friend [...] from the neighborhood."

In this context, the end of *Blue Velvet*—when the death of Frank is followed by a return to images of a white picket fence, a fireman and roses—is easy to misread as the triumph of small-town values over urban evil, a Reaganite restoration of former glories. Too much has taken place for this conclusion to satisfy. As Mulvey points out in her analysis of Douglas Sirk's melodramas, the dust kicked up by such films, their ideological contradictions and willingness to tackle sensitive issues cannot be settled by five minutes of peace at the finish.[73] *Blue Velvet*'s ending, like its beginning, feels strange because the images are too perfect—they seem ready to crack at any moment. This uncertain atmosphere is heightened by the film's final shot: Dorothy, united with her son, sits anxiously on a park bench. The lyrics that drift over this scene—"And I still can see blue velvet through my tears"—signal caution: Lumberton has not suddenly become a place where neighbor greets neighbor in the quiet of the summer twilight.

Before leaving *Blue Velvet*, we should return to Jacobs, a figure co-opted by many New Urbanists, despite her doubts about the movement. In *The Death and Life of Great American Cities*, she writes:

> Neighborhood is a word that has come to sound like a Valentine. As a sentimental concept, "neighborhood" is harmful to city planning. It leads to attempts at warping city life into imitations of town or suburban life. Sentimentality plays with sweet intentions in place of good sense.[74]

First published in 1961, Jacobs' warning has gathered resonance in the intervening years. Sentiment, from Reagan to the New Urbanists and beyond, continues to cloud American conceptions of the neighborhood, in an unthinking celebration (or Celebration) of imagined community values. *Blue Velvet* is a vivid rejoinder to the idealization of the small town and to comfortable notions of community in general. By reminding us that the valentines sent from neighbor to neighbor are not always tender—sometimes a love letter is "a bullet from a fucking gun"—it emphasizes the antagonisms driving social relations, in stark contrast to other rosy images of the 1980s. Lynch is acutely aware that intense, over-determined conceptions of community are hypocritical and exclusionary when we examine their underside—the swarm of insects Disney always seeks to hide from its customers, but which Lynch revels in revealing. *Blue Velvet* asks us to consider who *really* constitutes a "neighbor," while stressing that any call for neighborly assistance must go beyond the usual parameters to be truly enacted. To embrace neighborhood life, we must embrace the bugs under the lawn. *Blue Velvet's* imagery may be in close proximity to that employed by Reagan, Palin and the New Urbanists, but, in Lynch's laboratory, the symbolic shatters.

Finally, if Jacobs distinguishes between the planning requirements of cities and those appropriate for small towns and suburbs, then Lynch reminds us that such settings are far from homogenous—there are many divisions within each spatial form. Attempting to fuse different elements, to turn them into a single, harmonious neighborhood, may not be "good sense." Žižek proposes that alienation, in the form of social distance, is sometimes "indispensable for peaceful coexistence."[75] The problem, it seems, is proximity. Indeed, we should remember how Jeffrey finally saves himself from Frank's lethal propinquity: he steps back into the closet.

The Price We Pay: *Twin Peaks*

"Five miles south of the Canadian border, twelve miles west of the state line. I have never seen so many trees in my life. As W. C. Fields would say, I'd rather be here than Philadelphia." Urban America, especially in its East Coast industrial form, is far from proximate when Dale Cooper enters Twin Peaks in the series' pilot episode. Cooper has been summoned from FBI headquarters in Philadelphia because an interstate crime has been committed. Indeed, borders and thresholds will continue to prove malleable throughout his investigation into Laura Palmer's murder. Furthermore, Cooper's first comment on the town, juxtaposing its spatial co-ordinates with the abundant scenery, emphasizes that the relationship between man and nature is of vital importance in this community. There is a meta-fictional element to Cooper's arrival, too: viewers familiar with Kyle MacLachlan's role in *Blue Velvet* might assume that in the intervening years Jeffrey Beaumont has learned to hone his detective skills for federal purposes. Yet, high up among the woods and waterfalls in the north-western corner of the nation, Twin Peaks is a long way from Lumberton.

Such territory represented a homecoming for Lynch. He was born in Missoula, on the western edge of Montana, and lived as a child in Spokane, Washington and Sandpoint, Idaho—all places within a part of the Pacific Northwest known as the Inland Empire.[76] Shooting for *Twin Peaks* and *Fire Walk With Me* took place in small towns across Washington State, including North Bend, Fall City and Snoqualmie, as well as in California's studios and suburbs. With Cooper's precise instructions, we can even pinpoint where Lynch's fictional town joins these locations on a map.

Compared to other informal American regions, such as the Deep South or New England, the Pacific Northwest remains relatively unburdened by symbolic weight. Paul Giles notes the area's continuing "ontological instability" created by its uncertain boundaries, an ill-defined history (no written records of the region pre-date 1800) and the threat of geological rupture.[77] Surprisingly, despite its natural assets, the Pacific Northwest has failed to attract significant attention from film-makers, although Oregon has recently played a prominent role in the work of Kelly Reichardt and Gus Van Sant.

If images of the Pacific Northwest are comparatively rare, they often return to a powerful set of associations, as Raban explains:

> In no other American region has solitude been so exalted as a virtue, or society—especially in its concentrated urban form—tolerated, if not quite as a necessary evil, then as the acceptable price to pay for living so conveniently and romantically close to nature.[78]

The Pacific Northwest, then, evokes some specific spatial tensions: the balance between the private citizen and wider society, between the call of the wild and the needs of the neighborhood, between the development demanded by economic growth and the delights of an environment left untouched.

What does *Twin Peaks* have to say about these matters? Considerations of community are primarily addressed by the television series rather than the film. *Fire Walk With Me* bypasses many sites and characters to concentrate on domestic drama. In *Twin Peaks*, though, the town and its inhabitants are the series' true subjects. To define the spirit of the project, Lynch employed cartography. "We had drawn a map of the city," he explains. "We knew where everything was located and that helped us to determine the prevailing atmosphere and what might happen there."[79] We should note Lynch's unexpected use of the term "city" here: Twin Peaks, with a population of 51,201—according to its welcome sign— combines urban and rural characteristics.

Comparable to indicative architectural sketches, Lynch's map suggests potential openings rather than a fixed program (Plate 13). He includes a main road running between two snow-capped mountains and dividing the town's districts. Consequently, there are few streets in *Twin Peaks*: the series' many destinations slide off this one strip. This is a town without a civic centre, reflecting the emptiness of its dead protagonist. The Canadian border is also marked on Lynch's map, encircled by several buildings, including one, the brothel One-Eyed Jack's, beyond even the FBI's jurisdiction. Additional lakes, hills and forests foreground nature's presence in the community, while a misty quality is felt across the image as a whole. Overall, the map is an expressionistic reminder of the urban cartography analyzed in *The Image of the City*, sharing the indicative simplicity of Kevin Lynch's specimens. Yet, whereas those maps were attempts to represent existing spaces, the map of Twin Peaks is a blueprint for future geography, a framework for potential storylines. Furthermore, David Lynch's adoption of a flattened, two-dimensional perspective insists on the superiority of individual perception over strict geographical plotting. A "plot" can be a sequence of events, a piece of land or a secret plan: Lynch's map of Twin Peaks encompasses all three definitions. Throughout the series, cartography, including Cooper's map of Tibet and the cave drawings leading to the Red Room, continues to play its part.

The sense of place palpable in Lynch's map is fleshed out to produce an enthralling community on-screen. Lynch's ability to imbue a single small town with abundance is demonstrated by Twin Peaks' extended pilot episode. There is a marked economy, not always a term associated with Lynch's work, in how he establishes so many settings in the space of ninety minutes, each meticulously imagined and filled with personal touches. The Double R diner instantly seduces with its retro styling. Like its nocturnal cousin, the Roadhouse bar, the diner's leather booths stage the intense discussions that made Twin Peaks feel so joyously conspiratorial. The local high school, a staple of American drama, is quickly defamiliarized by a menacing tracking shot of empty corridors echoing to the announcement of Laura's death. The Palmer household, with its fussy furnishings and stuffed ashtrays, is a pit of middle-class misery. Leo and Shelly Johnson inhabit a half-finished wooden shack where temporary plastic sheeting offers a reminder of Laura's deathly wrapping. Such evident class distinctions are never fully explored by Lynch or his collaborators—Blue Velvet is more explicit in its social conflicts—with the series happier to suggest mystical connections between characters. Property speculation, however, underpins one of Twin Peaks' lengthiest storylines: Ben Horne's real-estate plans imperil the town's natural assets in a comic enactment of the problems that accompany development in rural settings. Ben already owns another iconic location introduced in the pilot episode: the Great Northern Hotel. Perched atop Snoqualmie Falls in Washington, this is a magnet for visiting strangers—a crucial piece of architecture for any long-running drama.

Dale Cooper is one such intruder. Subverting the traditional role of the villainous outsider who descends on a small town—as, for instance, in Hitchcock's Shadow of a Doubt (1943), where the criminal Uncle Charlie escapes from Philadelphia to California—Cooper is a source of purity in the community. Indeed, by the series' conclusion, it is he who is corrupted by Twin Peaks: the last episode sees him inhabited by the satanic spirit of

Bob. If further confirmation is necessary, then Cooper's struggles remind us of the difference between social relations in Lynch's small towns and the neighborhood guarantees offered by the likes of Reagan and the New Urbanists. In Twin Peaks, "neighbor helping neighbor" might involve cherry pies or cocaine.

Twin Peaks also contains its own industrial power, harnessing the surrounding landscape. The show's credits are dominated by images of production—a wide shot of the Packard Sawmill with its smoking chimneys is followed by close-ups of sparking machinery. Lynch's camera is mesmerized by these interactions, but, unlike the industrial processes in *Eraserhead* and *The Elephant Man*, there is no malignancy in the movements of the metal. Later in the pilot, there are further close-ups of the mill's machinery, as well as a wider shot of a log-infested lake next to the factory—a scene filled with steam, electricity pylons and manufacturing detritus (Plate 14). In Lynch's first two films, human nature is deformed by the demands of industry, with vegetation either invisible or sprouting erratically. In *Twin Peaks*, nature is a partner in the cycles of the sawmill. Wood is the town's defining element: it feeds industry, it structures buildings and it cloaks nocturnal adventures. Rather than those famous red curtains, it is trees that frame the action in *Twin Peaks*: nature is a veil for conspiracy and the arena for self-discovery. Interiors pulse with stuffed animals and hunting prizes—a large stag's head lies on a desk in the Sheriff's Department, while the products of taxidermy clutter the Great Northern. Outside, we are inundated with shots of rustling leaves and gushing waters. Lumberton, despite its logging, was manifestly urban by comparison. Twin Peaks incorporates industrial processes into the mechanics of rural life.

Yet, this apparently productive partnership between nature and industry has unforeseen consequences. For Frank Lloyd Wright, along with Louis Sullivan and others in the Chicago School, nature provided the beautification and humanization of machinery, which remained potentially chaotic. Emerging throughout the Progressive era was the thought that nature's curves could harmonize industrial urbanism to create an organic order.[80] For Lynch, though, nature and industry are both beautiful and chaotic: the forest is as fallible as machinery. Just as he highlighted fences and lawns as symbols waiting to shatter in Lumberton, in *Twin Peaks* Lynch places intense pressure on the role of nature in small-town life. Raban claimed the Pacific Northwest embodies a clash between solitude and society—the latter being "the acceptable price to pay" for proximity to nature. In episode three of *Twin Peaks*, Sheriff Harry S. Truman expounds a comparable philosophy:

> Twin Peaks is different. A long way from the world. [...] And that's exactly the way we like it. But there's a back end to that that's kinda different too. Maybe that's the price we pay for all the good things. [...] There's a sort of evil out there. Something very, very strange in these old woods.

Natural splendors appear to demand sinister compensation. In Truman's doctrine, though, the dark side of paradise is not found in urban society, as Raban claims, but within the natural landscape north-western residents adore. Twin Peaks may be an isolated bubble—"a long way from the world"—but it offers no retreat from social anxiety. Indeed, fantasmatic versions of community and chaos exist alongside each other within the same world. The exact shape of the town's "sort of evil" is never clarified— *Twin Peaks'* second series veers increasingly into supernatural territory— yet it is clear that the threats facing the community are internal. Strangeness is part of Twin Peaks' nature, not the product of an outside agency.

The trauma of neighborly relations has thus been transported from Lumberton's sidewalks to Washington's woods. In *Blue Velvet*, the confrontation between the opposing forces of Frank and Jeffrey takes place in an urban environment: Dorothy's apartment. In *Twin Peaks*, it is the woods that hosts the critical encounters between Leland and Laura Palmer (in *Fire Walk With Me*, he drags her through the forest) and between Cooper and Windom Earle (in the final episode, the Red Room emerges from the trees). Industrial urbanism cannot be blamed for these social and familial conflicts. Instead, nature is implicated.

Twin Peaks, then, represents a shift in Lynch's thinking. *Eraserhead, The Elephant Man* and even *Blue Velvet* scrutinized how industrial processes and designs affect society. *Twin Peaks* engages with an older mythology than American anti-urbanism: the thrills and threats of the woods. The likes of Emerson and Thoreau personify an American Romanticism still evident in the celebration of hunting and camping, and the suspicion that city life is somehow less authentic. Americans, Jacobs claimed, are "the world's champion sentimentalizers about nature."[81] This Romanticism clashes with other national myths, not least an economic model that devours land.

Lynch's American pastoral laces the myths of solitude with peril: the price to be paid, perhaps, for an unthinking embrace of nature. His vision is perhaps best expressed by Bachelard: "We do not have to be long in the woods to experience the always rather anxious impression of 'going deeper and deeper' into a limitless world."[82] If the forest offers a sense of boundlessness, a world within a world, then Lynch extends this idea to social relations: the woods, in *Twin Peaks*, is where the most unbounded behavior can take place.

By contrast, the rest of the town exhibits humor and warmth—a community pride rarely found in Lynch's locations, especially his cities. This is clearly a place for which the director feels much affection, and the locations Lynch used continue to attract large numbers of visitors and an annual Twin Peaks Festival. The opening section of *Fire Walk With Me* emphasizes the point by contrasting Twin Peaks with its own ugly twin, Deer Meadow—a town with a grotty diner, uncooperative authorities and a low-rent trailer park. It is as if Lynch, having demonstrated, via Lumberton and Twin Peaks, how even idyllic small towns harbor social conflicts, wanted to offer a glimpse of a truly inhospitable environment. Yet, as *Fire Walk With Me* progresses, we learn of entanglements between Deer Meadow and Twin Peaks: Deputy Cliff upholds the law in the former and deals drugs in the latter, while Teresa Banks and Laura Palmer turn tricks together. We might, therefore, conclude that the two towns are best described as neighbors—and neighbors helping neighbors is the story of America.

The Exemplary Extraordinary City: Los Angeles

David Lynch and Los Angeles are an ideal pairing: twin authors of spatial frustration. Consider, for instance, one contributor to Kevin Lynch's *The Image of the City*, whose description of Los Angeles mirrors many responses to Lynch's work: "It's as if you were going somewhere for a long time, and when you go there you discovered there was nothing there, after all."[83] This is someone—to again borrow Peter Eisenman's terms—who is still "learning how to get it."

Los Angeles occupies a unique position in both urban and film studies, making it difficult to ignore in any discussion of cities and cinema. This is a location, raised by land speculation and showcased on celluloid, where city and screen are irrevocably intertwined. Moreover, in recent decades,

Los Angeles and its surrounding region have become highly productive sites within critical theory, to the extent that Jacques Derrida declared: "The state of theory, now and from now on, isn't it California? And even Southern California?"[84] Derrida's claim, made in 1987, has not aged well: urban theory, at least, has shifted its gaze from America's West Coast towards the rapidly expanding metropolises of Beijing and Dubai, Lagos and São Paulo. There remains, however, a pertinent dilemma within the debates Los Angeles has provoked: is this an exceptional city or the epitome of urban changes occurring elsewhere in America and the rest of the world?

On the one hand, Los Angeles has often been seen as extraordinary, as a bizarre combination of features that are impossible to compare with other cities and which many observers dismiss as freakishly abnormal—assumptions also occasionally placed upon Lynch's work. Even a sympathetic critic such as Reyner Banham argued that Los Angeles' "splendours and miseries" are "as unrepeatable as they are unprecedented."[85] This reputation is partly based on a perception that Los Angeles has avoided the heavy industry that scarred cities such as London and Philadelphia. Film reels and real estate are often understood as the engines of its growth, given that the city's population grew by 609 percent between 1900 and 1925, just as the American film industry took root there.[86] Mark Shiel has recently shown how the film industry's "distrust of central cities and preference for suburbs"—which mirrored Henry Ford's philosophies—helped drive the suburbanization of Los Angeles and boost the city's real estate market.[87] As Brodsly confirms: "Los Angeles' appeal lay in its being the first major city that was not quite a city, that is, not a crowded industrial metropolis."[88] In fact, Los Angeles has hardly lacked large-scale industry and manufacturing—from automobile production to aerospace technology—with Lynch utilizing the city's industrial detritus when filming *Eraserhead*. Los Angeles' continued reputation for sprawl is also questionable: it now represents the most densely populated urban area in the United States.[89]

Other observers have developed an alternative standpoint, in which Los Angeles, far from being an aberration, is actually the exemplary modern city. For Soja, Los Angeles is "the paradigmatic window through which to see the last half of the twentieth century," while Charles Jencks claims the city is the archetypal "global megalopolis of the future."[90] For these critics, Los Angeles is a vision of both past and impending urbanism, a place where typical contemporary concerns, such as job insecurity, large-scale immigration and environmental degradation, are carried to their extremities. While Soja highlights the exploitation that has marked the city's economic growth, Jencks sees Los Angeles as the model for a form of political, social and architectural thought that stresses "pluralism, variety and difference as positive ends in themselves." The latter's conviction that Los Angeles supplies a stage for "frictionless personal transformations" is certainly challenged by *Lost Highway*, *Mulholland Drive* and *Inland Empire*.[91] These debates, then, position Los Angeles in direct opposition to the small-town myths promoted by conservative commentators. As such, it is no surprise to learn that the New Urbanist guru Léon Krier views Los Angeles as proof of modernity's disastrous embrace of industrial processes. "Auschwitz-Birkenau and Los Angeles," Krier claims, "have the same parents."[92]

Los Angeles has come to play an increasingly prominent role in David Lynch's work, with three of his last four films set in the city. *Mulholland Drive* remains his most sustained engagement with the city's forms and myths, yet it is not a film without its local critics. Thom Andersen, director of *Los Angeles Plays Itself* (2003), an epic montage of the city on-screen, claims: "Lynch's vision of Los Angeles remains that of a tourist." His conclusion that *Mulholland Drive* shows Lynch to be "the naïve provincial in the big city" conforms to a wider perception that the director understands only small towns.[93] Is Lynch a cinematic tourist, or does his use of Los Angeles' famous features demonstrate a more complex appreciation of the city's layout and history?

Bend Sinister: *Mulholland Drive*

Our trip along *Mulholland Drive* begins in hypnotic fashion. Shots of a limousine winding around the dark canyon road are interspersed with an overview of the illuminated boulevards below. The camera pans across this cityscape, unable to comprehend it in a single gulp and offering no hub from which we might find our bearings. Los Angeles' streets, like those in most American cities, are largely structured around a grid system. Jean-Paul Sartre noted that, compared to "oblique and twisting European streets, the American street is a straight line that gives itself away immediately. It contains no mystery."[94] By beginning his film on a road that follows the natural landscape, Lynch hints that *Mulholland Drive*'s narrative will bend and arc accordingly. Instead of a traditional focal-point, he places us on an axis of disorientation, a trail that feels dangerous and uncertain. To make sense of the film, we should learn to trust the shape of these twists; to take pleasure in it, one must love the feeling of being lost. This is *not* a straight story.

If, as most critics agree, *Mulholland Drive*'s opening forms part of Diane Selwyn's fantasmatic revision of events, it is important to note how she immediately imagines Rita in a position of vulnerability, forced by a car crash to walk down from the canyons in this most vehicular of societies. Spurned and frantic, Diane hunts the most humiliating images in her psychic armoury: nothing is apparently more degrading than being without a car in Los Angeles. Later, we see that Mulholland Drive leads to the site of Diane's ultimate embarrassment—the excruciating party at Adam Kesher's house—and that Camilla Rhodes knows a "short cut" to this modernist palace, a way of cheating the city's layout to gain success. Elsewhere in Lynch's work, similar scenarios face those who lack a car in this city: Pete Dayton, in *Lost Highway*, is reduced to using the valley's bus system as his fantasmatic life crumbles, while Nikki Grace, struggling for direction in *Inland Empire*, meets prostitutes and homeless people (public transport, notably, is the subject of their conversations) on Hollywood Boulevard. Reality, in Lynch's Los Angeles, demands a car. Even Andersen admires how *Mulholland Drive* "captures the almost uncanny fear you can sometimes experience as a pedestrian in Los Angeles."[95]

Fresh from Deep River, Ontario—Canada, in Hollywood terms, being a provincial wilderness—Betty's first experience of the city is more glamorous: Los Angeles International Airport, bathed in sunshine. Light, a crucial constituent of both architecture and cinema, is essential to this scene. Betty emerges into an intense sunlight that sharply contrasts with the darkness of Rita's entrance and the murkiness that frames other characters (most conspicuously, Diane Selwyn). It is the spotlight craved by actors and it continues to illuminate Betty until a nocturnal visit to Club Silencio (sign-posted in neon, an artificial substitute for light). Of course, the film-making process, as David Thomson points out, converts light "from nature to product," with studios having been historically zoned, in an evocative phrase, as "light industrial" areas in Los Angeles.[96] The transformation of natural attributes into cinematic commodities is a major theme in *Mulholland Drive*, where singers mime, actors rely on photo résumés, and cityscapes are merely cardboard sets. Betty dreams of a career swimming in golden sunshine. Instead, Diane must witness

Adam's directorial instruction, made while seducing Camilla, to "kill the lights!"

Betty's rapture at the airport reflects a joy felt by many visiting directors, producers and actors—all tourists initially, by Andersen's logic—at their immersion in Los Angeles' sunshine. Émigré architects such as Neutra and Schindler also saw the Californian light as perfect for their modernist dreams. It is especially tempting to read Betty's entrance as a rendering of Lynch's own arrival in Los Angeles:

> I arrived in L.A. at night, so it wasn't until the next morning, when I stepped out of a small apartment on San Vicente Boulevard, that I saw this light. And it thrilled my soul. I feel lucky to live with that light. I love Los Angeles. I know a lot of people go there and they just see a huge sprawl of sameness. But when you're there for a while, you realise that each section has its own mood. The golden age of cinema is still alive there, in the smell of jasmine at night and the beautiful weather. And the light is inspiring and energising. Even with smog, there's something about that light that's not harsh, but bright and smooth. It fills me with the feeling that all possibilities are available.[97]

Here, Lynch appears as both naïve provincial, embracing Hollywood mythology, but also as knowledgeable urbanite, aware of Los Angeles' variations. Moreover, the light engulfing Betty is not, in Lynch's eyes, an unreal exaggeration: it is an everyday occurrence.

The iconic elements of Los Angeles continue to seduce Betty. Familiar images of palm trees and the Hollywood sign follow her departure from the airport. Her next destination is also infused with "the golden age of cinema." Aunt Ruth's apartment block, with its ornate iron gates and a Spanish arch hinting at the entrance to Paramount Studios, lies on a picturesque street. Betty, who recognizes, tellingly, that this place is "unbelievable," claims the apartment is located on Havenhurst Drive, which is adjacent to Sunset Boulevard and close to Hollywood Boulevard. In reality, the building—named Il Borghese and built in 1929—lies on North Sycamore Avenue in Hancock Park, an exclusive residential district south of Hollywood (Plate 15). The area contains all manner of architectural wonders—like a film studio, it compiles Tudor beams, medieval turrets and modernist volumes. This variety adds further significance to Lynch's choice of a building dressed in the stylized stucco of the Spanish Colonial Revival, as we will see. The movies infiltrate the apartment's interior, too, with a poster of *Gilda* (dir. Charles Vidor, 1946) hanging in the hall, another image laced with artifice: "There NEVER was a woman like Gilda!" reads the tagline. Fittingly, Aunt Ruth's home feels like an archetypal *film noir* setting, especially given that genre's preference for apartment blocks and courtyards rather than the detached, single-family homes that predominate in Los Angeles.[98]

Soon, though, Betty will enter a "real" film set, through the celebrated Spanish-style gateway at Paramount Studios. This is another dream-like image, for which Lynch had Norma Desmond's car from *Sunset Boulevard* (dir. Billy Wilder, 1950) transported from Las Vegas (Plate 16).[99] In fact, Betty's arrival is "unbelievable," too: visitors to Paramount are no longer able to pull up in their cars in front of the original Bronson Gate, which now leads only to a pedestrian plaza, and must make do with a replica on Melrose Avenue instead. Inside the studios, "the golden age of cinema" is palpable in the wooden interiors, glamorous black-and-white photographs and award statuettes.

These disparate elements—the sunshine, the palm trees, the Hollywood sign, Aunt Ruth's apartment and Paramount Studios—share an idealistic rendering of Los Angeles. Here, Andersen seems correct in sensing a tourist mentality guiding *Mulholland Drive*. Yet, Lynch's emphasis on such familiar features is entirely in keeping with Betty's status as a fresh-faced visitor longing to see the best in the city. We view Los Angeles through her awestruck eyes. If images of palm trees and Paramount Studios have become clichéd, then Lynch makes us feel their original force. These well-worn images are imbued with new potency, yet once again such pressurized symbols seem ready to shatter.

What Lynch assembles, therefore, is not a tourist's vision of Los Angeles, but a fantasmatic compilation stressing the powerful, unconscious influence of Hollywood myths. In fact, the famous district itself rarely appears in *Mulholland Drive*. Like Betty—who complains, "I'm in Hollywood and I haven't even seen any of it"—we spend most of our time in areas such as Silver Lake (Diane's apartment is said to be on Sierra Bonita Avenue, but is actually further east, on Griffith Park Boulevard), downtown or up in the hills. *Inland Empire* reveals the true state of Hollywood Boulevard: "the golden age of cinema" and the "smell of jasmine" are difficult to detect in Nikki's encounter with this shabby neighborhood. Elsewhere in *Mulholland Drive*, nostalgic nods to *Sunset Boulevard* are countered by a satirical presentation of a studio system Lynch has largely rejected. Indeed, he revels in the absurdity of an industry in which executives, rather than directors, decide: "This is the girl." Furthermore, through Diane's desperation in the film's final stages, *Mulholland Drive* warns against investing too much hope in Tinseltown. Lynch's representation of Los Angeles' landmarks is thus double-edged in a manner that undermines the notion that he is a "naïve provincial."

These idyllic locations are also paired with the city's less salubrious spaces. For, just as Lumberton has its wasteland "behind Vista," Los Angeles contains areas omitted from tourist maps. In *Mulholland Drive*, scenes detailing Betty's blissful journey around the city are interspersed with episodes involving hit-men, prostitutes and cleaners. Behind Pink's Hot Dogs, which sits on a dusty stretch of La Brea close to North Sycamore Avenue, low-rent gangsters meet with a blonde junkie. Again, as Jeffrey discovered in *Blue Velvet*, the proximity of these elements to Betty's world is as much psychological as spatial. Social propinquity and geographical proximity are very different categories.

Odder occurrences take place at Winkie's, a Googie-style diner said to be on Sunset Boulevard, though it actually lies in Gardena. A young man recounts a dream to a friend (or, perhaps, his analyst), which centers on the fear that "There's a man, in back of this place. He's the one who's doing it." Investigating this claim, they traverse the diner's car park and garbage area, discovering a shocking homeless figure behind a graffiti-ridden wall (Plate 17). Particularly intriguing is Lynch's explanation for a scene that, in strict narrative terms, has little to do with the rest of the film. The director claims inspiration from a diner on Sunset Boulevard near to where Frank Capra used to work. According to Lynch, this diner (which other sources describe as a haven for "prostitutes and hustlers") emanated "some kind of heavy feelings [. . .] and that fed into this thing in *Mulholland Drive*—this bum."[100] We might, then, read the scene at Winkie's in a straightforward fashion: for Lynch, the homeless embody feelings of dread. However, to complicate matters, Lynch points out that the diner was positioned at a junction, "and in the old days that was the corner where all the movie extras would line up in the morning for work."[101] Given that Diane, a struggling actor, later sits in the same booth as the anxious young man, we might read the earlier sequence as an indication of the terror she feels about her career. What Diane fears most is what waits outside Winkie's: the queue for minor roles in the movies, the alley behind the marketplace. What she most desires is Hollywood's spotlight.

In this respect, the Winkie's scene demonstrates how Lynch molds Hollywood's myths into strange new formations. Moreover, the fear that external forces "in back of this place" are in control recurs throughout *Mulholland Drive*, most notably in the maneuverings behind Adam's film. For Diane, the notion that backstage corruption prevented her from achieving stardom is a comfort, but this is a reassurance, like all feelings of security in Lynch's work, that cannot be sustained. Club Silencio represents a psychic showdown for Betty/Diane, the realization that "There is no band. [...] It is an illusion." Surreptitious forces are not conducting affairs or, to return to the words of the Los Angeles resident in *The Image of the City*, "when you go there you discovered there was nothing there, after all."

Club Silencio, among the most critical sites in Lynch's career, is situated in downtown Los Angeles. This is an area that merited only a note in Banham's study, "because that's all downtown Los Angeles deserves," and which historically has failed to command the same authority as central districts in other major American cities. Lynch, though, does not share Banham's belief in the "sheer irrelevance" of downtown.[102] In fact, he grants it a significant role in *Mulholland Drive*.

Our first view of downtown Los Angeles comes from the air. The skyscrapers in these images, built where the Bunker Hill tenements once stood, are products of a very different form of industry to Hollywood's studios, Twin Peaks' sawmill and Philadelphia's factories (Plate 18). They epitomize the triumph of the financial sector, with Los Angeles positioned on the frontier of capital—the recipient, since the mid-1970s, of a huge influx of foreign investment. Later, as Betty and Rita speed towards Club Silencio, there is a glimpse of the area's tallest building, the US Bank Tower (designed by Pei Cobb Freed & Partners), with its illuminated crown shot like one of Lynch's domestic lamps. Lynch is keen to emphasize the rigid grid on which these towers stand, highlighting a tension between downtown's intensely controlled spaces and the fluidity of Mulholland Drive.

For the grid represents the ultimate delineation of space, the transformation of formless land into identical blocks. It symbolizes, for Koolhaas, "the superiority of mental construction over reality," while Sennett notes how Americans used the grid "to deny that complexity and difference existed in the environment."[103] Lynch remains highly alert to such framing devices. In *Mulholland Drive*, he follows aerial shots of the downtown grid with a boardroom meeting at Ryan Entertainment. For Koolhaas, the grid's true ambition is "the subjugation, if not obliteration, of nature."[104] At Ryan Entertainment, artistic concerns, what we might deem Lynch's "natural" landscape, are subjugated to the incomprehensible logic of financiers. To Lynch, the unreal elements of the film industry are not his own imaginative leaps, but the mental constructions of executives who prioritize homogenous products. These are the people, *Mulholland Drive* implies, who dwell in formulaic grids. As Sennett reminds us, a grid divides land into real estate units, "a space for economic competition, to be played out like a chessboard."[105] The heightening process demanded by Lynch's worlds renders the usual gray businessmen as exotic mafiosi ("the Castigliane brothers"), but the implications are clear: Los Angeles may not be a crowded industrial metropolis like London, but the potential for commercial processes to erase all other desires ("to shut everything down," is the term employed) remains present. *Mulholland Drive*'s journey from abandoned television series—replaced in the ABC schedule by a New York drama aptly named *Wasteland* (1999)—to prize-winner at Cannes lends additional piquancy to these scenes.[106]

There is, however, another perspective on the grid. Our current reading of *Mulholland Drive* follows a conventional directorial complaint: studio executives ruin films. One of the most evocative cinematic renderings of tensions between creative and financial concerns is Godard's *Contempt* (1963), to which *Mulholland Drive* frequently alludes.[107] Yet, whereas Godard presents an ignorant producer as purely malignant, Lynch revels in the intricate networks sewn by corporate gangsters. Rather than Adam Kesher, who strongly resembles the young Godard in appearance, the true director of events in *Mulholland Drive*, the real creative genius in his manipulation of characters, is Mr Roque. Like the deformed figure at the start of *Eraserhead*, this misshapen criminal mastermind pulls levers from inside a strange booth. His elaborate system of control corresponds, as Tom McCarthy has shown, to Lynch's broader obsession with puppetry, choreography and inner chambers.[108] In *Mulholland Drive*, these machinations are, symbolically, plotted within the downtown grid. Thus, just as machinery in Lynch's early films is both repetitive and the producer of thrilling mutations, the grid potentializes strange deformities. In suggestive terms, Sennett points out the infinite opportunities provided by this layout: "The modern urban grid is centreless and boundaryless, a form of pure repetition very much like the workings of an industrial machine."[109] As such, Los Angeles' grid sits alongside the vinyl record, the sawmill and the factory in Lynch's spatial pantheon: forms of repetition that seduce, circulate and subvert reality.

Ryan Entertainment is housed in the Banks-Huntley Building on South Spring Street. This is not one of downtown's new glass towers, but an Art Deco office block built in 1930. Nearby stands the Beaux Arts-style Barclay Hotel, which in *Mulholland Drive* hosts a bungled killing. Again, the grid supports criminality in the film, although in this case the participants are more comic than ingenious. Adam confirms that his sleazy hotel, introduced via further aerial shots of the grid, is also "downtown." Lynch is evidently attracted to earlier examples of civic grandeur in an area increasingly defined by contemporary architecture (Frank Gehry, Arata Isozaki and Thom Mayne have all designed buildings in downtown Los Angeles in recent years). There is a logic to this decision. As *Mulholland Drive* is obsessed by "the golden age of cinema," it follows that the film's dark forces be based in buildings from a similar era. Once more, as with *Eraserhead* and *Blue Velvet*, Lynch combines historical eras, synthesizing spaces in an urban palimpsest. Downtown Los Angeles is the ideal setting for this uncanny maneuver, because here, in Soja's words, "All is present within walking distance: the past, the present, the future."[110]

South Spring Street, once "the Wall Street of the West" but now struggling for investment, deserves further interrogation.[111] The street gave its name to the first moving picture made in Los Angeles in 1896.[112] Directly opposite the Banks-Huntley Building on this street lies a car park backing on to the Palace Theatre (Plate 19). This desolate space will reappear later in *Mulholland Drive*, in front of the entrance to Club Silencio. Thus, two locations with opposed priorities—remorseless profit versus unyielding emotion—lie in close proximity. We may intuit the implications of this layout: Betty and Rita can only experience the sensations of Club Silencio by turning their backs on the corruption of Ryan Entertainment. Alternatively, one might highlight an unlikely alignment between the illusions of Club Silencio and the corporate deception practiced in the boardroom. Certainly, a conventional economic critique of Hollywood is not Lynch's intention.

Downtown Los Angeles also prompts discussion of an iconic feature of post-war urban decline in America: the abandoned movie theater. Cinema chains, already threatened by television, have followed white middle-class Americans out to the suburbs. An urban medium associated with centripetal space has been transported to warehouses and malls dependent on the freeway system. In Scorsese's *Taxi Driver*, for instance, Manhattan's cinemas have become porn palaces, while *Eraserhead* actually benefited from mainstream cinema's rejection of downtown by gaining cult status at late-night screenings in Los Angeles and other cities.[113]

Mulholland Drive's Club Silencio offers a unique interpretation of how downtown film culture has been silenced. Lynch distils the history of cinematic architecture into a single scene, interweaving urban decline and the "golden age" of Hollywood. Broadway, running perpendicular to South Spring Street, is the key location here. By 1931, this street contained the largest concentration of cinemas in the world, with over 15,000 seats available.[114] Amid its dozen venues, Broadway hosts the Palace Newsreel Theatre (1911), the back façade of which acted as the entrance to Club Silencio, as well as the Tower Theater (1927), the interior of which was used as Club Silencio's main auditorium. Lynch also utilized Broadway's Orpheum Theater (1926) for *Inland Empire*, when Nikki enters an empty cinema. These theatres, at the center of America's most cinematic city, are now shadows of their former selves. Yet, like the factories of Philadelphia, they retain traces of glamor. For Stephen Barber, Broadway forms "a geographically linear graveyard" and provokes thoughts of cinema's intimate relationship with death, decay and erasure.[115]

Returning to Dimendberg's terms, Lynch's shots of Club Silencio's baroque ceiling, red curtains and dusty downtown surroundings forge another branch of our "social memory bank," in which the destruction of an entertainment culture formed around compact central precincts and collective experience can be deposited. Broadway's theaters now host only occasional screenings, with some also functioning as film sets. The entrance to Club Silencio features a further nod to Los Angeles' architectural history: the tiles surrounding this strange portal are modeled on the exterior of Frank Lloyd Wright's magnificent Ennis House, which lies in Los Feliz.

The history of the Tower Theater is particularly pertinent to *Mulholland Drive* (Plate 20). It was the first solo cinema project by S. Charles Lee, who would become the region's leading architect of movie palaces. Upon its opening, the *Los Angeles Times* praised its "undeniable feeling of beauty, luxury and charm" and its "striking design." Its exterior has a clock tower, Moorish touches and a stained-glass window depicting a strip of celluloid. Lee's lavish interior once featured marble-faced Corinthian columns, a chandelier and a lounge for 450 people. This was truly a "golden age" for cinema-goers. The auditorium itself combined traditional theatrical features, such as balconies and a small stage, with the requirements of a cinema—thus presenting Lynch with the perfect framework for the performance that takes place there in *Mulholland Drive*. Shiel points out that this combination of stage and movie architecture actually contravened building regulations in Los Angeles at the time.[116] Moreover, the Tower made much of its innovative air-conditioning system, advertised as a form of manufactured weather, which adds further reverberations to the thunder and lightning that takes place under Lynch's direction.[117]

Most important of all, the Tower Theater was the first cinema in Los Angeles—if not quite, as is sometimes claimed, in the entire United States—to be equipped for talking pictures. The introduction of sound had significant architectural implications for both film studios, which now required sound-proof structures to silence the city outside, and for cinemas, where the need for stages and pits was eliminated. Though cinema could now be heard, there was, quite literally, "no band" present in theaters. Accordingly, events at Club Silencio are concerned with how sound and image combine, with cinema's illusionary potential and our complicity in this deception. Hollywood satirized its struggle to cope with sound technology in *Singin' in the Rain* (dir. Stanley Donen, 1952), which ends with the comic revelation of a miming singer. *Mulholland Drive* heightens this scenario further, adding existential weight to the distinction between image and sound dramatized by Rebekah del Rio's performance. The singer collapses, yet the audience remains entranced by her continuing voice. Once these conventional parameters are shattered, Betty's world crumbles. Aware of the illusion in the theater, she recognizes the fantasmatic foundations of her life. This realization occurs within a building no longer performing its original purpose, but which remains evocative, nonetheless. It is soundtracked by a song removed from its original context—Roy Orbison's "Crying" is sung in Spanish—but this defamiliarization imbues it with additional, uncanny emotion. Such relentless mediation of space demonstrates that, for Lynch, architectural meaning is as slippery as artistic authenticity.

What is experienced at Club Silencio is not limited to an exploration of sound; it concerns language, too. From the pronouncements made by the master of ceremonies to the extraordinary version of "Crying," this is a venue that speaks Spanish. Indeed, Betty and Rita's journey there is preceded by the latter's dream-like mutterings: "*No hay banda. No hay orquestra.*" When the couple return from the club, Rita greets Betty's disappearance with the question: "*¿Dónde está?*" Previously so tentative, Rita now finds her true voice, and it is a Spanish one.

Los Angeles' relationship with its Spanish heritage remains controversial, with both linguistic and architectural arguments surrounding the city's vernacular. Spanish missions were the first major buildings in Southern

California, but, when Los Angeles passed from Mexican to American control in 1848, it was still a small settlement. Unlike other North American cities that developed around a Spanish urban model encompassing a central town square, Los Angeles' growth was founded on dispersal.[118] Since then, a Spanish style has been adopted by generations of architects in Los Angeles to varying critical responses. Mike Davis attacks the Spanish Colonial style as "an ersatz history" that is part of the city's "Mission Myth" designed to attract investment.[119] For Banham, Spanish inflections "should never be brushed off as mere fancy-dress; in Los Angeles it makes both ancestral and environmental sense."[120] In *Mulholland Drive*, Aunt Ruth's apartment block exhibits a strong Spanish flavor, while Lynch also lends similar support to Diane's flat, naming a mock-Tudor development "Sierra Bonita Apartments."

During Lynch's time in Los Angeles, debates over the city's Hispanic identity have become increasingly difficult to silence. Davis claims the "Anglo conquest of California in the late 1840s has proved to be a very transient fact indeed." In 1970, when Lynch arrived in the state, its population was nearly 80 percent white and non-Hispanic. Los Angeles, in this era, had the highest percentage of native-born, white Protestants of any of America's largest cities. By 1998, though, Latinos outnumbered Anglos in Los Angeles by more than a million.[121] Political, cultural and spatial changes have accompanied these demographic shifts. When Los Angeles' downtown theaters began to suffer economic problems in the 1950s, several of them turned to Spanish entertainment, rather than face total silence. Widespread bitterness towards bilingualism, however, led to the passing in 1998 of a controversial proposal prioritizing the teaching of English in Californian schools. Further tensions have arisen from the poverty and racism historically endured by many Mexicans in the region.[122]

One might, therefore, read Rita's nocturnal outburst, followed by the Spanish supremacy of Club Silencio, as a return of the repressed—Lynch's acknowledgment of Los Angeles' linguistic and architectural roots. Crucially, Spanish is a language understood by Adam and Rita (and, later, Camilla Rhodes), but not by Betty (or Diane Selwyn). Unable to face the lyrical content of "Crying"—a song about the pain of a relationship ending—Diane codes it indecipherable. From the beginning, Betty is an outsider, a naïve provincial from the Canadian backwaters who has landed in "this dream place." Perhaps her failure to survive in the city— Diane is driven to suicide at the film's conclusion—is Lynch's admonishment of the tourists who obsess about Paramount Studios and the Hollywood sign, yet know so little of Los Angeles' larger history. Diane, in more ways than one, is late to the party: the "golden age of cinema" and the Anglo dominance of Los Angeles have long gone. The Spanish elements of *Mulholland Drive*, and Club Silencio in particular, encourage us to think about who or what has been silenced in Los Angeles—a city, as Shiel argues, whose emergence was "predicated upon the fading history of Native American, Spanish and Mexican California."[123]

Mulholland Drive's final congregation of images, with Betty and Rita's hopeful faces overlaid onto the Los Angeles skyline, reminds us that the Lynchian urban paradigm combines an assemblage of myths, anxieties and dreams. Yet, in concluding his journey around Los Angeles, Lynch returns us to a movie palace now as empty as the streets of Philadelphia. Despite, then, the centrifugal movements of post-war America, the end of *Mulholland Drive* focuses on downtown as a place of communal self-reflection. The film's last word on the area is either a call for ceasefire in the battles it has provoked, or an admission of permanent suppression: "Silencio."

2 HOME

The house shelters day-dreaming, the house protects the dreamer,
the house allows one to dream in peace.
GASTON BACHELARD, *THE POETICS OF SPACE* (1958)[1]

Mr Bachelard Builds His Dream House

Gaston Bachelard, like David Lynch, centers his thinking on the poetic image, an image that "in its simplicity, has no need of scholarship." In prioritizing association, allusion and a certain innocence, Bachelard's *The Poetics of Space* holds a clear affinity with Lynch's cinema. For both men, everyday space is transformed by our imagination. As Bachelard notes, in a very Lynchian phrase, "At times, the simpler the image, the vaster the dream."[2] This chapter will explore the vast implications of that most common cinematic image: home.

In Bachelard's conception, day-dreaming—a state he differentiates from nocturnal dreams, a distinction less obvious in Lynch's work—is closely allied with intimate space. Above all, it is tied to home: home is where day-dreaming is possible and day-dreams are where we are most at home. A single image is enough to provoke Bachelard's reverie: "A hermit's hut. What a subject for an engraving!" The Bachelardian home is one of romance, joy and security. It is "our first universe, a real cosmos in every sense of the word." It remains, without ambivalence, a "space we love."[3]

In Lynch's films, images of home hold immense power. A single shot of Henry's apartment in *Eraserhead*, the Palmer residence in *Fire Walk With Me* or the Madison house in *Lost Highway* is enough to induce rich associations. Yet, while Lynch's domestic spaces maintain Bachelard's faith in the poetic image and the psychological dimensions of home, they refuse to ignore more disquieting consequences. For Lynch, our most familiar surroundings inevitably contain unhomely elements. Home, he contends, is "a place where things can go wrong."[4] As such, he has built and filmed a series of domestic theaters; arenas in which characters are both participating actors and voyeuristic spectators; homes where intruders and surveillance are rife. Here, inhabitants endure a painful intimacy with domestic space.

Contemporary discussions on the familiarity of home invariably lead to the Freudian *unhemlich*. Indeed, Freud's 1919 essay "The Uncanny," which explores how everyday spaces produce uneasy sensations, risks becoming a rather over-familiar reference itself. What we term the uncanny, Freud explains, belongs to "that species of the frightening that goes back to what was once well known and had been familiar." In tracing the etymology of the German *unheimlich* (literally "unhomely," but more suitably translated into English as "uncanny"), Freud notes how it overlaps with its antonym *heimlich*, in the idea of something dangerous that has been concealed. Thus, our concept of the familiar, of home itself, contains an inherent foreignness—the return of repressed elements that provoke a unique form of dread. Through geographical examples, such as his own continual return to the red-light district of an Italian town, Freud encourages us to consider the vast spatial implications of the uncanny.[5]

Anthony Vidler takes up this challenge, stating that the uncanny "is not a property of the space itself nor can it be provoked by any particular spatial conformation." No single domestic typology has a monopoly on uneasy sensations: Freud's concept rests on a process, not a product. The uncanny is better perceived as a "mental state of projection" in which a strict delineation between the real and unreal is impossible. In Lynch's films, houses are persistently shaped by the psychological projections of their inhabitants. Other forms of projection also permeate these spaces: flickering pornography floods Andy's walls in *Lost Highway*, while television pictures play an important role in *Blue Velvet*, *Twin Peaks* and *Inland Empire*. Not unexpectedly, Vidler includes in his survey of recent cultural investigations into the uncanny the domestic and "suburban" settings of *Blue Velvet* and *Twin Peaks*.[6]

However, rather than reiterating Freud's theory, another component of Viennese modernism might provide fresher and more fruitful explication of Lynch's homes: the architecture of Adolf Loos. The domestic spaces created by Loos and Lynch speak to one another in suggestive ways. Loos' houses—with their interlocking rooms and intimate recesses, split-levels and surveillance platforms, plush surfaces and enveloping drapery—are arenas for performance and observation. In the bedroom he created in 1903 for his wife Lina (an actor), where the curtained backdrop and thick carpet are both sinister and sensuous, the associations with Lynch are stark (Figure 2.1). The space is vividly described by Panayotis Tournikiotis:

The white walls, the white draperies and the white angora sheepskins created a sensual and delicate fluidity; every object in the room was white. Even the closets were concealed behind pale linen drapes. This was an architecture of silence, of a sentimental and erotic approach. Its contrast with the more public living spaces attests to a method of composition that was strictly governed by the psychological status of each room.[7]

FIGURE 2.1 Lina Loos' bedroom in the Loos Apartment in Vienna (1903).
Credit: Copyright Albertina, Vienna.

Equally, in Lynch's films, the "psychological status" of domestic space governs its materials and layout. Both sentimentalism and eroticism are important features of his homes, yet Lynch does not favor "an architecture of silence." Rather, he emphasizes what he terms "room tone"—that is, "the sound that you hear when there's silence," a definition that again implies strong psychological forces.[8] The buzzing discontent that fills Lynch's houses, where rooms vibrate disturbingly, is a further manifestation of their intense symbolic meaning.

The sickly tones of Lina Loos' bedroom bring to mind Ludwig Hevesi's shrewd comment on the representation of Loos' architecture: "In photographs his rooms don't look well."[9] This is rarely the case with contemporary architecture. Today, many buildings seem expressly designed with images, rather than inhabitants, in mind. However, some of the most potent images within Lynch's homes, such as Diane's rotting body in *Mulholland Drive* or the baby's festering skin in *Eraserhead*, are overwhelmed by physical or mental degradation. Something is always askew in Lynch's houses: his rooms "don't look well" either.

However, the flattening perspective of two-dimensional photography is especially distorting for Loos' work. As Beatriz Colomina explains, Loos' interiors "are experienced as a frame for action rather than as an object in a frame."[10] Walking within a Loos house, one feels how rooms converge and delineate themselves unexpectedly, how optical connections are impossible to traverse physically. To use a cinematic term—and Loos himself was a keen film critic—the "cut" (or, sometimes, the lack of it) between domestic scenes is highly unusual in his designs. For Loos, Colomina argues, "the house is the stage for the theatre of the family."[11] The architect's *Raumplan*, in which the height of each room varies depending on its purpose and status, creates competing levels within the home. It produces dramatic internal vistas, as if theater boxes have been inserted into the house, as well as striking external façades, marked by windows that refuse to align. A similar sense of observation is a recurrent element of Lynch's homes. For John Merrick, Dorothy Vallens, Laura Palmer and Fred Madison, surveillance is an everyday domestic trauma. Accordingly, Loos referred to the inhabitant of his interiors as "the spectator."[12] Colomina tweaks this definition: the owner of a Loos house is "a stranger, an intruder in his own space."[13] Thus, in a Loosian home, we are liable to ask ourselves the spooky question Fred Madison puts to the Mystery Man in *Lost Highway*: "How did you get inside my house?"

When considering how ideas of domestic spectatorship fared in transition from *fin de siècle* Vienna to post-war Los Angeles, Richard Neutra is a telling figure. Neutra trained under Loos and was a frequent visitor to the Freud household, before earning widespread recognition in California. Lynch's admiration for Neutra's architecture is unsurprising given that it negotiates with dramatic forms of living. As Sylvia Lavin has demonstrated, Neutra probed the psychological effects of the home. Indeed, when asked whether domestic surroundings influence our mental health, Neutra gave a revealing reply: "How can they not? I mean, where do we go crazy?" Despite their clean lines, right angles and glass walls, Neutra's houses reject Le Corbusier's industrial modernism in favor of domestic theatricality. The home, Neutra declared, was "not a machine for living. Architecture is a stage for living." Like a director who builds and films cinematic worlds, Neutra believed "that he watched over the private lives of his clients through his architecture."[14]

Neutra's domestic theaters are constructed around the penetration of thresholds, where interior and exterior spaces are juxtaposed and the surrounding landscape framed by spidery out-rigging (Plate 21). He made persistent use of reflective surfaces—mirrors, pools and sliding doors—with flowing curtains offering a dramatic counterbalance. That these drapes were usually removed when Neutra's rooms were photographed, to allow clearer shots of the outside world, confirms him as an architect distinctly aware of media.[15] Loos adopted a contrary position—photographs of his houses emphasize the interior, with curtains drawn and little sense of the world outside—though he was also an adept media performer, organizing tours of his buildings and writing both prolifically and polemically. For Lynch, similar spatial conflicts abound. The director admits that the "inside/outside thing" is "sort of what life and movies are all about to me."[16] What is more, both Neutra (who blended his Viennese training with a love of Frank Lloyd Wright and the Californian landscape) and Lynch (who has combined Hollywood melodrama with nods to Franz Kafka and Francis Bacon) personify the rich transatlantic cultural exchanges that developed in Los Angeles throughout the twentieth century.

What follows are close readings grouped around the three principal domestic archetypes found in Lynch's work: the urban rooms of *Eraserhead* and *The Elephant Man*, the small-town family homes in *Blue Velvet* and *Twin Peaks*, and the Hollywood residence in *Lost Highway*. Considered alongside Bachelard's theories, Kafka's stories, Bacon's paintings, and the architecture of Loos and Neutra, Lynch's domestic theaters emerge as the stage for unsettling family drama.

A Little Place to Mull Things Over: Three Urban Rooms

Urban living was a central concern for two directors much admired by Lynch. Billy Wilder's comic take on sex in the city in *The Apartment* (1960) constructs "a world" to which Lynch repeatedly refers, while Hitchcock's *Rope* (1948) and *Rear Window* (1954) place murder, voyeurism and a critique of cinema itself within their claustrophobic environs.[17] Regarding *Rear Window*, Lynch says, "even though I know what's going to happen I love being in that room."[18] For Lynch, the interior built and filmed by Hitchcock is so powerful he feels he has literally occupied the space: the apartment and the movie theater have merged. At the same time, *Rear Window* promotes the urban apartment as another viewing mechanism, a theater box from which L. B. Jeffries can watch the city, but a world that cannot remain permanently secluded. Likewise, the boundaries between the observer and the observed are perilous in Lynch's work.

In the case of *Eraserhead*, earlier influences are at play, too. As the previous chapter noted, Henry mimics Chaplin and Keaton, whose anxious relations with architecture included the inability to establish an effective home. For instance, *The High Sign* (dir. Buster Keaton and Edward F. Cline, 1921) presents the home as a labyrinth full of pitfalls, and Keaton's most famous trick—executed in *Steamboat Bill Jr.* (dir. Charles Reisner, 1928) and later re-enacted by the artist and film-maker Steve McQueen in *Deadpan* (1997)—entails a house tumbling down around him. Keaton, described by Deleuze as the "Dadaist architect *par excellence*," continually traces the contours of his homes to expose their fragile nature.[19]

It is, however, in Kafka and not Keaton that we find the most insightful companion to Lynch's urban rooms. Kafka's work is filled with staircases and gates, waiting rooms and corridors, offices and courts—an architecture of the unsettled, the transient and the perplexed. The prevailing spatial anxiety in his fiction is an ambivalent homesickness shared by many of Lynch's protagonists. In particular, both Kafka and Lynch explore the alienation of a single urban room.

Lynch has often discussed his abandoned adaptation of Kafka's "Metamorphosis" (1915), via a script that transfers the tale to the 1950s.[20] In 1991, the director apparently designed and built a giant cockroach in preparation for the project.[21] Barry Gifford claims "Metamorphosis" was in mind when he and Lynch planned *Lost Highway*, and traces of this inspiration lurk in the transformation of Fred Madison into Pete Dayton.[22] Assessing *Eraserhead* and *The Elephant Man*, though, it becomes evident that Lynch has little need to adapt Kafka's story when his earliest films negotiate such similar terrain. In mapping the urban rooms of Gregor Samsa, Henry Spencer and John Merrick, we encounter three visions of the claustrophobia, and possible comforts, of the confined family home. These tales are grounded in an urban framework; they feature domestic architecture with both symbolic and material power; and, like Bachelard, they navigate the intimate relationship between day-dreaming and the home.

Philadelphia, where the row-house rules, is not a city famed for its apartment blocks.[23] Our first impression of Henry's apartment building in *Eraserhead*, at the end of his walk through urban wastelands, is not encouraging. The block resembles an abandoned factory with bricked-up windows and no external hints of domesticity. When Henry closes the entrance door, it sounds like a gunshot and the building is sealed as if it were a tomb. The lobby, however, maintains a faded glamor—reflecting the Art Deco styles of Callowhill, where decorative touches compensate for industrial rawness—while the distinctive floor pattern anticipates the Red Room in *Twin Peaks*. Framed in the lift, the doors of which are thickly varnished with an ominous Gothic tinge, Henry seems primed for transportation to another universe.

Koolhaas reminds us that the elevator, the invention of which changed spatial hierarchies in the city irrevocably, was first presented to the public as "a theatrical spectacle."[24] For Henry, the lift is a theater of cruelty, in which he is trapped as an unwilling performer surrounded by flickering lights and rumbling noises. The tight and windowless corridor leading towards his room further exacerbates feelings of constriction. Henry is tunneling deeper into the building, searching for sanctuary. Indeed, one imagines him reaching his room and exclaiming, like the self-proclaimed "old architect" who narrates another Kafka story: "I have completed the construction of my burrow and it seems to be successful."[25]

The Royal London Hospital, a grand Victorian structure looming proudly over the capital's factories, hosts Merrick's room in *The Elephant*

FIGURE 2.2 *The Elephant Man*: Merrick in his tiny attic room.
Credit: *The Elephant Man* (dir. David Lynch, 1980), © Brooksfilms.

Man—a small space in the attic (Figure 2.2).[26] Later, although housed in larger quarters, Merrick ignores adjoining rooms, never venturing beyond the minimum space needed for inhabitation. After a lifetime of incarceration, he remains locked into the idea of a solitary cage. Moreover, by focusing on the hospital's corridors and furnace, Lynch emphasizes the connections Merrick's new home shares with the industrial warehouse where he is first seen by Treves. At times, the hospital feels like another factory, with Lynch—ever alert to how a building breathes and sweats— highlighting the rushing winds and random thumps of its heating system.

As London society begins to visit Merrick in his new home, one astute nurse acknowledges the similarity with his previous role in the circus: "He's only being stared at all over again." It is no surprise, therefore, that Merrick's last night in London, the culmination of a life in captivity, is spent in a theater box. This is a venue that, as Colomina explains, existed for Adolf Loos "at the intersection between claustrophobia and agoraphobia." The theater box, like the interior of the Loosian or Lynchian home, provides both "protection and draws attention to itself."[27] Observation, from curious crowds, probing doctors or bourgeois hypocrites, structures Merrick's entire life.

The location of the Samsa household in Kafka's "Metamorphosis" is unknown. We never learn the city or the country in which the story takes place, beyond a pointed reference to the family apartment being on a "quiet but decidedly urban" street. What is revealed is a peculiar form of spatial disorientation. Gregor's physical state is itself depicted in architectural terms—"his dome-shaped brown body, banded with reinforcing arches"—while the site of his transformation is originally described as "a normal though rather too small human room." This, then, is another minimal dwelling. However, as Gregor's altered physical state affects his perception, these surroundings shift and enlarge. His bedroom is subsequently described as "the high-ceilinged spacious room." The environment feels entirely governed by the psychological status of its inhabitant, so that its volumes morph like a warped *Raumplan*. As his room becomes increasingly cell-like—the doors are locked, the furniture is removed and dirt is allowed to fester—Gregor is cut off from the outside world. Isolated from his family, who (like many in *The Elephant Man*) cannot cope with such deformity, Gregor's imprisonment evokes "an anguish he could not account for, since it was, after all, the room he had lived in for the past five years." The entire apartment also becomes a financial prison for the Samsa family, unable to move to a more affordable home because of Gregor's condition.[28]

The urban nature of Gregor's plight, an indication that his anguish is linked to a wider anxiety concerning modern spatial forms, is exemplified by his relationship with the street outside. Kafka's description of the city's intruding technology closely resembles Lynch's urban rooms: "The light of the electric street lamps flickered pallidly on the ceiling and the upper parts of the furniture but down where Gregor lay it was dark." Although Gregor reminisces about the "sense of freedom looking out of the window had once given him," that view was actually depicted earlier in "Metamorphosis" in less liberating terms: "clearly visible on the other side of the street was a section of the endless, grey-black building opposite—it was a hospital—with its regular windows harshly piercing its façade."[29] Any comforting thoughts Gregor has are undermined by an uncompromising urban setting: escape, even by day-dreaming, appears impossible.

Compare this with Henry's room in *Eraserhead*, graced with buzzing light bulbs, a humming radiator and a bleak view. Once again, modern urban forms have enclosed the apartment dweller in a hostile chamber. In customary fashion, Lynch places these electrical and industrial processes alongside natural forms. Henry's apartment is a strangely lush environment where mounds of soil and stacks of hay are found, where windows are covered in steam and liquids bubble furiously. These elements induce a confusion between the natural and the man-made, suggesting a bizarre form of urban nest. Indeed, Bachelard's characterization of the nest as "a precarious thing," but an environment that provokes "*daydreaming of security*" is apt here. For, faced with hazardous surroundings, Henry day-dreams that his radiator houses a sanctuary. Yet, Bachelard's claim that apartments are less affected "by the storms of the outside universe" is contradicted by the howling weather and brutal violence Henry sees outside his room.[30] In this respect, his home represents the type of intimate refuge Bachelard, who preferred multi-story houses, deems impossible of the modern apartment. As Lynch himself admits, "to me, even though there was plenty of ambiguous torment in Henry, his apartment—actually, his room—was, you know, fairly cosy. It was just this one little place he had to mull things over"[31] (Figure 2.3). Equally, this applies to Gregor, who is only in physical danger when he ventures into the rest of the family home. These cells are highly restrictive, but they protect their residents from external threats.

Merrick's room is more vulnerable to outside forces, both creative and terrifying in nature. His window, at the frontier between public and private realms, allows for nocturnal torment, as groups of drunken Londoners stare at his distorted features. In these scenes, Merrick's room becomes a dramatic stage, with the window ledge as a makeshift theater box. The usual rules of urban voyeurism are reversed and the city looks inwards at Merrick's performance. As L. B. Jeffries discovered in *Rear Window*, when his room was breached by a murderer, there is no such thing as a secure spectator. Merrick's ostensibly safe accommodation remains, like all Lynch's homes, porous.

Yet, the window generates imaginative activity, too. Inspired by his partial view of St Philip's Church in Whitechapel, Merrick constructs a

FIGURE 2.3 *Eraserhead*: Henry mulls things over.

Credit: *Eraserhead* (dir. David Lynch, 1977), © David Lynch and the American Film Institute for Advanced Studies.

wooden model of the building, using his imagination to complete features that remain out of sight. Indeed, the real-life Joseph Merrick built a number of such models using Victorian kits, one of which survives today in the Royal London Hospital's archives (Plate 22). In Lynch's film, the model church takes on mounting significance, as Merrick fashions an idyllic piece of architecture to compensate for the harsh realities of Victorian London. On this issue, Bachelard's thinking is again instructive:

> Miniature is an exercise that has metaphysical freshness; it allows us to be world conscious at slight risk. And how restful this exercise on a dominated world can be! For miniature rests us without ever putting us to sleep. Here the imagination is both vigilant and content.[32]

Merrick longs to sleep "like normal people." His model-making is a small victory against a world that continually denies him nocturnal comfort. Constructing the church allows Merrick to be "world conscious at slight risk" and "both vigilant and content." He has total control over at least one environment in his life. In the closing moments of *The Elephant Man*, as Merrick dies in his bed, the camera moves solemnly through this wooden sculpture, savoring its forms. It is this architectural artifact, a product of intimate day-dreaming, that is Merrick's ideal home.

The model church is also evidence of Lynch's close attention to domestic objects, a subject we will return to throughout this chapter. The tiny dimensions of Merrick's apartment expand with a growing number of gifts. His room is soon decorated with ornately framed paintings and photographs, hardback books and flowing curtains—the furnishings of a conventional bourgeois dwelling. Indeed, Merrick appears to be mimicking the elaborate décor of Treves' home after his "tour" of the doctor's house. As a further illustration of how Lynch's architecture conditions social relations, the apparent "civilization" of Merrick's domestic space goes hand-in-hand with the rising acceptance of his physical appearance, first by the hospital staff and then by the wider community. Previously, the nurses considered interaction with Merrick to be "like talking to a brick wall," but, surrounded by gilded knick-knacks, he holds greater social potential. The rather pathetic nature of Merrick's design gestures is Lynch's way of ridiculing Victorian class-based hypocrisy through the very objects it prizes. The most conspicuous of these is the luxurious dressing case presented to Merrick. Such grooming apparatus demonstrates the social importance of taming physical irregularities. In this context, Geoff

Andrew promotes an autobiographical reading of *The Elephant Man*, which sees Merrick's social progress as reflecting Lynch's (temporary) switch from freakish experimentation in *Eraserhead* to mainstream film-making.[33] Since then, Lynch's work has continually articulated a tension between the artistic grooming demanded by studio bosses and an inclination towards abstraction and poetic imagery. A tidy room, it seems, is required for a mass audience. Yet, just as Merrick's respectable home leads to his acquiescence with death, then Lynch is wary that a well-mannered film ultimately indicates creative demise.

That Merrick's domestic troubles erupt most fiercely at night—a space and time designed for recuperation and reverie—invites further comparisons between Lynch's approach and those of Kafka and Bachelard. In Kafka's "The Burrow" (1931), the "little round cells" the protagonist constructs are described in a sentence that could figure in *The Poetics of Space*: "There I sleep the sweet sleep of tranquillity, of satisfied desire, of achieved ambition; for I possess a house." Here, "the house protects the dreamer" impeccably, during the day and at night. Simultaneously, this bunker, a rural labyrinth rather than an urban room, produces a heightened awareness in its inhabitant, which rejects the slumbers of the outside world: "it is as though at the moment I set foot in the burrow I had wakened from a long and profound sleep."[34] It is, lest we forget, "uneasy dreams" that prefigure physical transformation in "Metamorphosis," an unrest that becomes permanent: "Gregor spent the nights and days almost entirely without sleep."[35] Written by a notorious insomniac, Kafka's "Metamorphosis" can be read as a manifestation of fevered reverie and nocturnal despair. If, then, Bachelard's ideal house shelters day-dreaming, and Henry's room is "one little place he had to mull things over," perhaps Gregor's room also offers an exemplary domestic space: an intimate arena where fantasmatic day-dreams have taken hold. Crucially, though, Kafka—like Lynch, but unlike Bachelard—remains highly aware that fantasies can just as easily be traumatic as transcendent.

Shot chiefly at night, *Eraserhead* offers additional nocturnal insights. The institutional iron-framed bed that dominates Henry's room is, alternately, too large and too small for him and Mary. One shot, from Henry's perspective, shows a vast landscape between the couple as they lie amid the sheets, a harrowing vision of marital estrangement. Later, they are shown fighting for space and blankets. The confines of the family home are most apparent on these dark nights, with Henry's sweet sleep murdered by the baby's horrific cries. Alongside such constraints, Lynch also presents the bed as a platform for pleasure. When Henry sleeps with his neighbor, it becomes an immersive ring of steam and water, as if such fertility is only possible with the family unit disrupted. In fact, throughout Lynch's career, the bed has remained a prime location. The psychological states it has induced include adolescent anxiety in *The Grandmother* (a film Lynch made as a student in 1970), incestuous recognition in *Fire Walk With Me*, frantic suicide in *Mulholland Drive*, erotic union in *Wild at Heart*, and sexual humiliation in *Lost Highway*.

Henry's dysfunctional marriage is the first of many irregular family units in Lynch's cinema. Families, for Lynch, are the home of incest, sibling rivalry and murder. Young children are a rare commodity in his work and are often actively absent: Dorothy's son has been kidnapped in *Blue Velvet*, for example, while, in *The Straight Story*, Rose's children have been removed by local authorities. This makes Henry's room, haunted by the realities of fatherhood, all the more intriguing. The screams of his baby, an alien-like creature as indefinable as Gregor Samsa, reverberate within the tiny dimensions of the apartment, turning a sanctuary "to mull things over" into a place of persecution. Indeed, when one of Henry's dreams ends with him behind a courtroom bar, accused of an unknown crime, we are again reminded of Kafka. Like Josef K, torn between sexual desire and the responsibilities of his case in *The Trial* (1925), the demands of fatherhood inhibit Henry's ability to satisfy other appetites. Each time he tries to leave his room, the baby's cries grow louder and Henry worries this will ruin his relationship with his neighbor. Just as Gregor's father becomes stronger with his son incapacitated, the family home in *Eraserhead* is incapable of satisfying both parent and child. Notably, Lynch himself slept on the set of *Eraserhead* when his own first marriage began to fall apart.[36] In fact, Lynch claims the "world reveals itself more" when one literally lives inside the spaces of a film set.[37] Here, the boundary between domestic space and the screen is again removed, with Henry's room metamorphosing into Lynch's home.

In *The Elephant Man*, Merrick's most intimate cravings remain a permanent home and family. The traveling circus condemned him not only to degraded accommodation, but also to a warped family model. His "owner" Bytes claims the two are "business partners"—a relationship that encompasses sporadic affection, recurrent violence and financial dependence. By contrast, the hospital's governing committee is praised for providing Merrick "with a safe and tranquil harbour, a home." When Merrick is eventually granted a permanent place there, one nurse exclaims, "Welcome home, lad." There is a sense of destiny here, a suggestion that Merrick is returning to an original setting that was always waiting for him. Yet, this "home" had to be earned, through Shakespearean recitals, personal grooming and the correct furnishings. It is a space as socially conditioned and psychologically charged as the "neighborhood" in *Blue Velvet*. Merrick's death, at the end of an evening when he has received a standing ovation from a theater audience, comes when he feels most at home—within his room, within a makeshift family at the hospital and within London as a whole. Given these circumstances, his suicidal gesture—a doomed attempt to sleep "like normal people"—suggests he rejects the most monstrous idea of all: living in a secure, homely, bourgeois environment.

Staying at home also leads to Gregor's demise. As a traveling salesman, his daily excursions released the burdens of domestic life. His transformation, however, prohibits any relationship with the outside world and he is faced only with the horrors of his family. Persecuted by his parents and their new lodgers, the communal areas of the small apartment now feel a "great distance" from Gregor's room, in another subjective rendering of space.[38] Given the distorted depiction of family life that appears in their work, Lynch's claim to fraternal affinity with Kafka—"the one artist I feel could be my brother," he famously declared—takes on a curious undertone.[39] Perhaps, though, it is fitting that their shared concerns are so apparent in *Eraserhead*—a film inspired by Philadelphia, "The City of Brotherly Love."

There is one final domestic location in *Eraserhead* that deserves attention. Henry's visit to Mary's house, a wooden bungalow covered in industrial smoke, is a darkly comic display of male fears concerning parenthood. During an excruciating dinner, Henry is confronted by Mary's mother, who interrogates him about the couple's sex life. Crucially, at the moment Henry realizes he has become a father, an exposed pipe divides the frame. It is Mary who is completely enclosed by domestic architecture, framed so that the flowers, furniture and wallpaper of the living room loom behind her. Having given birth, she is now permanently trapped. Henry is left in the corridor, a transient space, with a blank wall behind him. The insertion of the pipe offers him a bleak choice: bachelor alienation or the confines of home and family. It is little wonder he gets a nosebleed.

This scene, in the tradition of a thousand stand-up comedians, suggests there is no place more unhomely than the in-laws' house—a foreign location with an inherent familiarity. The last images of Mary's house appear via an unnerving tracking shot, the camera shakily circling the interior before it disappears into the window blinds. In the darkness that follows, we sense there is no escape for Henry. The next shot is Mary, in Henry's room, feeding the baby: his urban safe haven has become a familial cell. As Bachelard exclaims, "To live alone; there's a great dream!"[40] The image of an atomic mushroom cloud hanging next to Henry's bed is a fitting visual aid, an allusion to the murdered dreams caused by the nuclear family.

The Objects of Melodrama

Directors and critics have long been aware of cinema's distinctive relationship with domestic objects. In a 1918 essay, Louis Aragon celebrated film's ability to transform "really common objects" into "the superior life of poetry." Film, Aragon insisted, has a magical effect on our belongings: "on the screen, objects that were a few moments ago sticks of furniture or books of cloakroom tickets are transformed to the point where they take on menacing or enigmatic meanings."[41] As Godard tells us in *Histoire(s) du Cinema* (1988–98), we may forget the plot of Hitchcock's films, but we remember forever "a row of bottles, a pair of glasses, a musical score, a bunch of keys." Cinematic objects have no practical use: they exist to mean something. The medium maintains an unrivaled capacity to imbue material items with tangible life, just as it instils architecture with an animation drawings and blueprints can never match.

Lynch is highly conscious of the psychological impact possessed by on-screen objects. He repeatedly manipulates an audience's desire to attach metaphorical value to banal domestic items, so that every object he shoots—a lampshade, an ashtray, a child's hat—radiates meaning. The impact of these objects is heightened by intense close-ups and distinctive tracking shots, employed at unsettling heights, which lend Lynch's interiors a palpable strangeness. It becomes impossible in such circumstances *not* to read objects metaphorically, as actors in a domestic drama.

In particular, Lynch's interest in the objects, surfaces and structures of the American home owes a vital debt to melodrama. The tone, composition and themes of Lynch's films, with their amplified emotions, often concerning disrupted families, played out in vivid colors, make plain the wider connections his work holds with American cinematic melodrama. Here, we should follow Thomas Elsaesser in positioning melodrama as a radical form. In Elsaesser's reading, melodramas provide ambiguous and incisive social commentary through a radical excess of emotion. Moreover, Elsaesser claims the family melodrama is "almost by definition" set in the middle-class home, where the presence of suffocating objects— what Le Corbusier once called "the stifling accumulation of age-long detritus"—signals the repression of past events.[42] Elsaesser's analysis is especially intriguing when considered alongside Lavin's argument that the post-war American home became increasingly open to an array of psychological projections. The emergence of psychoanalytic discourse into American culture—like Neutra's architecture, a development that married Central Europe with Southern California—created a sense that houses were "receptacles into which unconscious psychic material about primary domestic relationships was consciously displaced," in Lavin's words.[43] Thus, Hollywood's melodramas of the 1940s and 1950s were produced within a climate of growing intensity concerning the American home. Directors such as Vincente Minnelli, Nicholas Ray and Douglas Sirk exploited cinema's charged relationship with objects, as well as the on-going absorption of psychoanalytic ideas into popular culture. Their dramas expressed serious doubts over America's domestic assumptions at a time when many of the nation's families were dispersing into isolated suburban bunkers. In *Blue Velvet*, *Twin Peaks* and *Fire Walk With Me*, we see how Lynch has followed their lead in turning familiar domestic forms—television sets, closets, staircases, ceiling fans and framed photographs—into traumatic symbols.

Television and the American Home

Darkness. The sound of a muted brass instrument. A door opens. A shadowy figure emerges, descends a staircase and announces: "I'm going out for a while." This classic *noir* scenario is our first glimpse of Jeffrey inside the Beaumont household, as his journey into Lumberton's underworld starts from the upper reaches of the family home. Following the disturbance of the domestic lawn in *Blue Velvet's* opening moments, this scene scrutinizes another ambiguous surface: the television screen. The camera pans down from Jeffrey's exit to the *noir* drama watched by his mother and aunt, in which a man slowly ascends a flight of stairs. The movement is partly a neat visual joke—little do his relatives know, Jeffrey will soon be climbing the back staircase to Dorothy's apartment. It is also evidence of the interest Lynch shares with the likes of Hitchcock and Ray in the stairs as a spatial metaphor, which we will come to shortly. However, the scene's greater significance lies in its association of the television screen with small-town life.

Lynch has already hinted at television's role within Lumberton during *Blue Velvet*'s opening sequence, where images of fences and firemen are accompanied by a shot of Jeffrey's mother watching another *noir* thriller. Lynch's focus on the television set is part of his broader obsession with the designs of the 1950s. As Lynn Spigel points out, television's ability to merge public and private spaces made it the ideal medium for the detached homes emerging across America in the post-war decades.[44] In developments such as Levittown, New York, television sets were built into the walls of standardized homes, becoming as integral to domestic architecture as staircases and closets. Neutra was especially interested in how these devices could be incorporated into the home, as part of his wider fascination with mechanisms of spectatorship.[45]

The effect of the television set on the America home was profound. A different kind of theatrical box now organized family life. As Spigel explains, television was seen as an effective way "to keep youngsters out of sinful public spaces, away from the countless contaminations of public life."[46] William L. O'Neill confirms that the post-war era was dominated by the idea that "families stayed together by staring together."[47] While his mother and aunt remain at home gripped by television, Jeffrey is outside exploring the "sinful public spaces" of Lumberton. As Mulvey emphasizes, television appeals to "staying in," to the notion of being safely "at home." Cinema, by contrast, is associated with "going out," with the excitement and danger that entails.[48] By *Blue Velvet*'s release in 1986, downtown America, the traditional home of the movie theater, was in long-term decline. Jeffrey's rejection of the domestic television set in favor of adventures in Lumberton's urban districts is, therefore, a subversion of the era's spatial trends.

The television set in the Beaumont household also depicts the tensions between two definitions of the screen itself: it both represents and conceals the nature of the world outside. The *noir* drama watched by Jeffrey's mother and aunt is far more familiar than they recognize, but their ability to understand Lumberton's realities is hindered by their absorption in television. Likewise, in *Twin Peaks*, the lives of the characters in *Invitation to Love*—scenes for which were filmed within Wright's Ennis House in Los Angeles—constantly threaten to overlap and merge with those of the soap opera's audience. In *Inland Empire*, Lynch takes this friction a step further. When Nikki enters the domestic set of the "Rabbits" sitcom—a parody of American shows, with actors in rabbit costumes performing to ill-timed laughter—her tentative movements render the screen "a permeable membrane, not a locked door," to borrow Steven Connor's phrase.[49] The television screen, like the white picket fence, offers a boundary ripe for distortion.

It is evident, then, that Lynch has a distinctly ambivalent attitude towards television, an outlook again shaped by 1950s culture. Amid the escalation of the Cold War, when Americans were encouraged to retreat into domestic havens, television became the perfect nightly companion. Between 1950 and 1960, the number of American homes with a television set rose from 9 percent to almost 90 percent.[50] Given that Hollywood relied on people "going out" to the cinema, this situation understandably troubled the film industry. As Mulvey explains, Hollywood reacted to the growth of television with a series of melodramas where the tensions of domestic life were graphically depicted.[51] In the case of *All That Heaven Allows* (dir. Douglas Sirk, 1955), the implications of "staying in" with television were explicitly rendered: to distract her from a passionate relationship with her gardener, a middle-aged widow is presented with a new television set by her children. Furthermore, in Rainer Werner Fassbinder's homage to Sirk, *Fear Eats the Soul* (1974), a television set is smashed by a son angry at his mother's new Moroccan husband. There is no doubting the associations Sirk and Fassbinder emphasize here: television belongs to a world of bigotry, hypocrisy and sexual repression. This is an especially ambivalent position for Fassbinder, given that television productions constituted a major part of his work, with series like *Berlin Alexanderplatz* (1980) among his most enduring creations.

The ambiguities provoked by communal experience are a recurring theme in Lynch's work, as Chapter 4 explores in detail. Television, therefore, with its ability to bind people together in their homes, is of obvious interest to him. It is worthwhile recalling the extraordinary viewing figures *Twin Peaks* commanded: the first installment was watched by 35 million people and the audience share for the final episode of series one was an astonishing 36 percent of the American viewing public.[52] Lynch must have relished the thought of so many suburban households engrossed in a series underpinned by domestic abuse—an updating of Hitchcock's famous quip: "One of television's greatest contributions is that it brought back murder into the home where it belongs."[53]

However, partly because of the medium's inferior technical qualities, but also frustrated by its narrow artistic parameters, Lynch has never felt quite at home in television. One ABC executive told him he found the pilot episode of *Mulholland Drive* so boring "he almost fell asleep *standing up* looking at it"—an image of tottering reverie that is decidedly Lynchian itself.[54] The core of Lynch's ambivalence lies in television's domestic setting. When watching at home, Lynch explains, "with just a flick of the eye or turn of the head, you see the TV stand, you see the rug, you see some little piece of paper with writing on it, or a strange toaster or something. You're out of the picture in a second."[55] This account again highlights Lynch's sensitivity to domestic objects. Here, though, the potency of these items is a distraction. A screen's setting is absolutely fundamental to how we perceive its images. While subscribing to Loos' notion of the home as a theater, the movie theater retains a privileged position for Lynch. His is a romantic conception of cinematic spectatorship:

> It's so magical—I don't know why—to go into a theater and the lights go down. It's very quiet, and then the curtains start to open. Maybe they're red. And you go into a world.
> It's beautiful when it's a shared experience. It's still beautiful when you're at home, and your theater is in front of you, though it's not quite as good. It's best on a big screen. That's the way to go into a world.[56]

Lynch not only prefers to work in cinema; he also imbues his filmic homes with a theatrical spatial arrangement. The worlds he creates must be all-encompassing, with no distractions. Television is, by comparison, a much less immersive medium. Indeed, his comments above cast doubt on the ability of television to create a "world" at all. Consequently, it comes as no surprise that a smashed television forms part of *Blue Velvet*'s climactic tableau in Dorothy's apartment, as if Lumberton's own urban *noir* has rendered any televisual imitation redundant (Plate 23). Even more symbolically, *Fire Walk With Me* begins with an axe ploughing into a television set. Here, Lynch follows in the footsteps of Sirk and Fassbinder in reminding his audience that cinema is the superior medium. At this point in the *Twin Peaks* project, the series had been axed, so the extreme elements of the story could emerge without constraint. *Fire Walk With Me* is, accordingly, much more explicit, in terms of sex and violence, than its televisual partner. *This*, Lynch tells us, is what family life is really about. *This* is my true home. *This* is cinema.

The Domestic Catastrophes of Bacon and Lynch

Beyond white picket fences and television sets, there are, of course, alternative post-war cultures to which Lynch is indebted. In looking at Lynch's homes, their sense of theatricality and *Blue Velvet* in particular, it is essential to consider the work of Francis Bacon. *The Alphabet* (1968), a partly animated short film in which a distorted figure is contained within a demarcated interior, demonstrates that Bacon's influence on Lynch's sense of space was present from the earliest days of his film-making career. John Russell has written, "the most persistent of Bacon's preoccupations is the problem of what a man is to do when he is alone in a room," while Bacon himself stated: "The only really interesting thing is what happens between two people in a room."[57] Similar ideas pervade Lynch's films: *Wild at Heart*'s motel confrontation between Lula and Bobby Peru, and the conversation between blurred figures at the start of *Inland Empire* are just two examples of how his cinema is structured, like Bacon's work, around erotically charged encounters within a single room. In *Blue Velvet*, additional scenarios are enacted, with the influence of Bacon again palpable: what happens between two people in a room when one thinks she is alone and the other is watching her; and what happens in a room when one person is watching two others.

Few painters hold such an affinity with cinema, as well as architecture, as Bacon. Indeed, the final image of Godard's *Histoire(s) du Cinema* is Bacon's *Study for a Portrait of Van Gogh II* (1957), rather than a film still. Bacon's adoption of the triptych format, with its cinematic style of sequencing, suggests a desire to represent the progression of an image. Similarly, in his own art school days, Lynch remembers imagining "a world in which painting would be in perpetual motion."[58] For Bacon, cinema was "a most marvellous medium," with Eisenstein and Buñuel singled out for particular praise, while cameras occasionally appear in his paintings (in, for instance, the right-hand panel of *Triptych—March 1974* [1974]). Ensconced behind glass, Bacon's images exhibit a strong awareness of screens and mediation. They also display a distinctive conception of space, with architectonic frames generating parallel worlds. "I am very influenced by places—by the atmosphere of a room," Bacon once claimed, and his mottled interiors might be read as attempts to capture the "room tone" that intrigues Lynch. Bacon's studio was itself an architectural montage, crammed with images from magazines and books, while other furtive spaces, such as photo booths and Soho clubs, also inspired his work. Most intriguingly, Bacon, who stressed that he saw images "in series" and "in shifting sequences," desired to make a film "of all the images which have crowded into my brain."[59] Lynch himself has been impelled to ask: "If Bacon had made a movie, what would it have been and where would it have gone? And how would the cinema translate those textures and those spaces?"[60] *Blue Velvet* is his most explicit attempt at answering these questions.

Before examining the Bacon-esque qualities of Lynch's imagery, it is instructive to consider Bacon's own treatment of the photographs of Eadweard Muybridge. Muybridge's work has been described as Bacon's "most fecund resource" and has been often associated with cinema.[61] In a perceptive comparison, Kenneth Silver outlines how Bacon's "schematic, perspectival box" is a reworking of Muybridge's photographic grid sequences. Silver suggests that Bacon "domesticates" Muybridge's work— turning, for instance, an outdoor wrestling scene by the photographer (created around 1887) into the private spaces of *Two Figures* (1953) (Plate 24). The relocation of the men from Muybridge's image, allied with additional sexual menace, transforms the photograph's clinical neutrality into a visceral painting. In Bacon's version, spectatorship has become voyeurism and, in Silver's words, "the protagonists have been given a home." Bacon's homes, though, are more like cells than safe havens. In *Two Figures*, as Silver points out, the participants are housed in a "private jungle" or "a zoo" where animal desire is both unleashed and contained.[62] Bacon once stated, "I hate a homely atmosphere. [. . .] I want to isolate the image and take it away from the interior and the home."[63] As such, his work strives to break loose from domestic shackles, while simultaneously housing his characters within tightly controlled limits.

This tension between inhibition and expressive release is extremely pertinent to Lynch's films, as demonstrated by Dorothy's home in *Blue Velvet*. Deep River Apartments is a stern brick building, with Gothic overtones in its ceremonial entrance. The lobby displays a series of generic horror motifs—buzzing lights, a broken elevator and dripping water—that suggest a disruption in the channeling of amenities. Like Henry's room in *Eraserhead*, it is a hybrid of nocturnal lushness and malfunctioning technology. It seems appropriate that Jeffrey's first trip inside the building is (ostensibly) to spray insect repellent.

Dorothy's apartment is a degraded space, with a faded lilac carpet and a strange green plant creeping up a wall. In contrast to the brightness of the film's early scenes, the atmosphere here is as grubby as any of Bacon's settings: these rooms *really* "don't look well." Lynch, like Bacon, has experience of interior and furniture design, as well as painting, and the two men share a sense of domestic composition. Notably, Martin Harrison describes Bacon's early interior designs as "enclosures" and "claustrophobic spaces in spite of their sleek lines," which distinguished them from "the airy sun-traps of his modernist peers."[64] The cloistered theatricality of Loos' homes again comes to mind here. Similarly, the layout of Dorothy's flat may be open-plan, with one large kitchen and living space, but this is far removed from the modernist dream of light-filled domestic harmony. Rather, this venue oozes secrecy.

Dysfunctional family relations feel inevitable in such surroundings. Dorothy is exiled from her kidnapped husband and son, and subject to the confused appetite of Frank Booth—a man who shares his initials and a predilection for sado-masochism with Francis Bacon. In Lynch's framing of flesh within Dorothy's apartment, Bacon's influence becomes even clearer. Bacon's figures, like Dorothy, John Merrick or Gregor Samsa, often seem imprisoned, struggling to assert themselves inside cage-like structures. Bacon, Kafka and Lynch's characters are uncomfortable within that most familiar, yet unhomely, location: their own body. Consider, for example, the position of Dorothy on the carpet of her living room (Plate 25). The room is overwhelmed by traumatic sex and violence— Lynch shares Bacon's obsession with the close relationship between the erotic and the terrifying. Human flesh, so vital for Bacon, is also center-stage for Lynch. Dorothy is framed by the furniture around her, trapped by her possessions. Inside this claustrophobic zone, where we can almost feel the walls closing in, the glimpse of the bathroom visible in the top left-hand corner of the frame is like one of Bacon's portals—a passage to another world. As Deleuze points out, observers of Bacon's work feel as though "a *catastrophe* overcame the canvas."[65] A similar sense of all-pervasive horror is evident in Dorothy's home.

Furthermore, Bacon and Lynch share a fascination with voyeurism. The shot of Dorothy lying on the carpet is seen from the perspective of

Jeffrey standing, as yet undetected, inside her closet. The closet is a profoundly unsettling location. A hollow interstitial space, positioned within the walls of the apartment like a hidden theater box, it is the perfect venue for concealed observation. Bacon's paintings are imbued with similar forms of spectatorship. In his triptych *Crucifixion* (1965), the third panel features two judges, sat at a curved bench, surveying the manipulations of flesh before them. Once more, *Rear Window* acts as a companion to these scenarios. Steven Jacobs explains how Hitchcock's entire set consisted of "a magisterial viewing device. The architecture becomes an instrument of the gaze, a kind of *camera obscura* on an urban scale."[66] Lynch further domesticates this situation, but uses the closet in an almost identical fashion to L. B. Jeffries' flat. This is an architecture of surveillance and intrusion, guilt and exhilaration, with relentless mediation of space.

Such theatrical feelings are enhanced by Lynch's partial adoption of Bacon's framing devices. The recurring cubes and stages around Bacon's figures are often accompanied by drapes, creating arenas for performance. Moreover, as Deleuze points out, these rings and frames are all *places*, establishing "an operative field" within the painting. Inside this field, the frame exerts a force on the central figure, isolating a suspended body. Deleuze describes this force as a "double motion," with the background fields of color pushing towards the figure and the figure pushing back. The subsequent tension accounts for the drama and oppression so characteristic of Bacon's work. The framing also separates the iconic central shape from the continuity of the outside world, suggesting a profound, even universal, scenario.[67]

Lynch utilizes domestic architecture in a comparable manner. Towards the end of *Blue Velvet*, for example, Sandy stands pressed against the wall of Dorothy's apartment, tucked into a curve that accentuates her anguish, while, in *Fire Walk With Me*, a crouching Bob emerges from a tight recess in Laura's bedroom. The idea of entrapment remains fundamental to Lynch's homes, as Henry, Merrick and Dorothy can testify. Lynch and Bacon embody a peculiar spatial formation combining confinement and theatricality, a notion of humanity as a caged animal within a boundless environment. Take, for instance, the prison-cell barking of Bobby and Mike in the pilot episode of *Twin Peaks*, which culminates in a Bacon-esque close-up of Bobby's snarling mouth, and which is then followed by a shot of the town's abundant landscape. Bacon's figures are highly restricted, but his paintings also encapsulate feelings of infinite space.

Kafka seems to have shared this sensation of a "double motion" working between interior and exterior forces: "To have the feeling of being bound and at the same time the other, that if one were unbound it would be even worse," he recorded in his diary.[68]

These spatial tensions call to mind the notion of "deliberate speed" outlined by W. T. Lhamon in his reading of 1950s culture. Lhamon explains how in this decade contradictory forces, spasms of inconsistent energy, were maintained within a controlling framework, culminating in artworks that "always seem on the verge of vibrating apart."[69] For Lhamon, works by Nabokov, Kerouac and Pollock exemplify "deliberate speed," to which we might add the taut reverberations of Bacon and Lynch's interiors—spaces that are also, in their different ways, products of the 1950s. The "containment" of the Cold War, Lhamon suggests, housed greater cultural conflicts than is often acknowledged.

Blue Velvet contains one final image that evokes Bacon's work. When Jeffrey enters Dorothy's flat for the last time, he is greeted by a grotesque tableau, a nightmarish version of the American domestic dream. The television set is smashed; the fitted kitchen is splattered with blood; beautifully composed torture stands center-stage. The camera lingers on this arrangement, a hellish parody of American lifestyle catalogs—an apartment overcome by catastrophe.

Stairway to Hell: *Twin Peaks* and *Fire Walk With Me*

From 1961 until his death in 1992, Bacon worked at 7 Reece Mews in South Kensington. His studio was situated on the first floor, accessible via a wooden staircase. Bacon's sketch of the premises reveals another theatrical venue, with his work-space depicted as a floating stage. Harrison describes this chamber and its tiny skylight as "a type of camera," and an obsession with media and reproduction was certainly housed there. Among the images found in Bacon's studio were paint-splattered copies of Muybridge's "Man Walking Upstairs" and "Woman Walking Downstairs" sequences.[70] For Muybridge, stairs were ideal for examining the movements of the human body. For Bacon, who remained fascinated by the Odessa steps scene in *Battleship Potemkin* (dir. Sergei Eisenstein, 1925), staircases held great potential for unsettling behavior.[71] The central

PLATE 1 Camerimage Łódź Center, designed by Frank Gehry (2009).
Credit: Image provided by Gehry Partners, LLP.

PLATE 2 David Lynch, *Untitled* (drawing for an interior), undated, 6 × 12.7 cm.
Credit: Collection Fondation Cartier pour l'art contemporain, Paris.

PLATE 3 David Lynch, *Untitled*, installation designed for the exhibition *David Lynch, The Air is on Fire* (2007), adapted from *Untitled* (drawing for an interior).

Credit: Collection Fondation Cartier pour l'art contemporain, Paris. Photograph by Fabrizio Marchesi.

PLATE 4 Beverly Johnson House, designed by Lloyd Wright in 1963.

Credit: Photograph by Yana Stoimenova.

PLATE 5 Olga Neuwirth, who composed an operatic version of *Lost Highway*, inside a room inspired by the film in the Hotel Luzern, designed by Jean Nouvel.

Credit: Copyright Priska Ketterer. Photograph by Priska Ketterer, with thanks to Betty Freeman and Olga Neuwirth.

PLATE 6 Shad Thames, London.

Credit: Photograph by Craig Ritchie.

PLATE 7 Liverpool Street station.
Credit: Photograph by Craig Ritchie.

PLATE 8 Callowhill, Philadelphia—part of the "Eraserhood."
Credit: Photograph by Richard Martin.

PLATE 9 *Eraserhead* mural by Evan Cairo on the exterior of the Philadelphia Mausoleum of Contemporary Art.

Credit: Copyright Eric Bresler. Mural by Evan Cairo. Photograph by Laura Jane Brubaker.

PLATE 10 4th Street Bridge, downtown Los Angeles.

Credit: Photograph by Yana Stoimenova.

PLATE 11 Beverly Center, West Hollywood.

Credit: Photograph by Yana Stoimenova.

PLATE 12 *Blue Velvet*: the field behind "Vista."

Credit: *Blue Velvet* (dir. David Lynch, 1986), © De Laurentiis Entertainment Group.

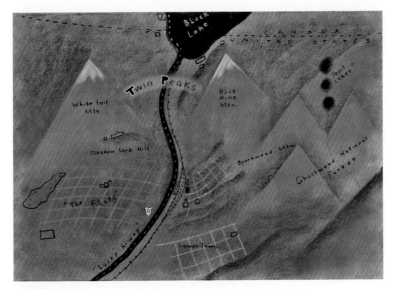

PLATE 13 David Lynch, *Twin Peaks #1* (map).

Credit: Copyright David Lynch.

PLATE 14 *Twin Peaks*, pilot episode: the Packard Sawmill.

Credit: *Twin Peaks*, pilot episode (dir. David Lynch, 1990), © Lynch/Frost Productions, Propaganda Films, Worldvision Enterprises, Inc.

PLATE 15 Il Borghese apartment building, Hancock Park.

Credit: Photograph by Yana Stoimenova.

PLATE 16 *Mulholland Drive*: the Paramount Studios gate.

Credit: *Mulholland Drive* (dir. David Lynch, 2001), © Studio Canal, Les Films Alain Sarde, Asymmetrical Productions.

PLATE 17 *Mulholland Drive*: the space behind Winkie's diner.

Credit: *Mulholland Drive* (dir. David Lynch, 2001), © Studio Canal, Les Films Alain Sarde, Asymmetrical Productions.

PLATE 18 *Mulholland Drive*: skyscrapers in downtown Los Angeles.

Credit: *Mulholland Drive* (dir. David Lynch, 2001), © Studio Canal, Les Films Alain Sarde, Asymmetrical Productions.

PLATE 19 The back of the Palace Theatre, used by Lynch as the entrance to Club Silencio.

Credit: Photograph by Yana Stoimenova.

PLATE 20 The Tower Theater on Broadway.

Credit: Photograph by Yana Stoimenova.

PLATE 21 Richard Neutra, Kaufmann House, Palm Springs, California (1946). Credit: Photograph by Richard Neutra. Kindly provided by Raymond Richard Neutra.

PLATE 22 Joseph Merrick's model of Mainz Cathedral (c. 1886). Credit: Courtesy of The Royal London Hospital Archives.

PLATE 23 *Blue Velvet*: the final tableau in Dorothy's apartment.

Credit: *Blue Velvet* (dir. David Lynch, 1986), © De Laurentiis Entertainment Group.

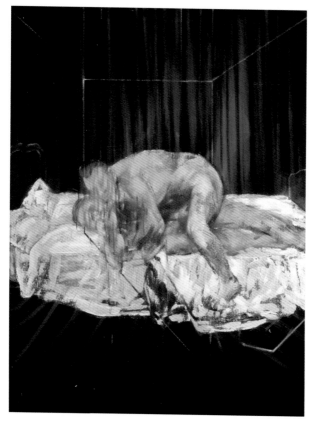

PLATE 24 Francis Bacon, *Two Figures* (1953). Oil on canvas. 152.5 × 116.5 cm.

PLATE 25 *Blue Velvet*: Dorothy framed by her furniture.

Credit: *Blue Velvet* (dir. David Lynch, 1986), © De Laurentiis Entertainment Group.

PLATE 26 Francis Bacon, *Triptych—In Memory of George Dyer* (1971) (center panel). Oil on canvas. 198 × 147.5 cm.

PLATE 27 *Twin Peaks: Fire Walk With Me*: Leland prepares to cross the landing.
Credit: *Twin Peaks: Fire Walk With Me* (dir. David Lynch, 1992), © Twin Peaks Productions, Inc.

PLATE 28 *Twin Peaks*, episode two: Leland's blood coats the famous image of his daughter.
Credit: *Twin Peaks*, episode two (dir. David Lynch, 1990), © Lynch/Frost Productions, Propaganda Films, Spelling Entertainment Inc.

PLATE 29 *Lost Highway*: the Madison house.
Credit: *Lost Highway* (dir. David Lynch, 1997), © Ciby 2000, Asymmetrical Productions.

PLATE 30 The Schindler House in West Hollywood, designed by Rudolph M. Schindler in 1922.

Credit: Photograph by Yana Stoimenova.

PLATE 31 *Lost Highway*: the Madisons' living room.

Credit: *Lost Highway* (dir. David Lynch, 1997), © Ciby 2000, Asymmetrical Productions.

PLATE 32 Diller + Scofidio, Slow House model (1989).

Credit: Photograph by Diller + Scofidio. Reproduced by permission of Diller Scofidio + Renfro.

PLATE 33 *Lost Highway*: The Mystery Man inside a desert shack.

Credit: *Lost Highway* (dir. David Lynch, 1997), © Ciby 2000, Asymmetrical Productions.

PLATE 34 The Park Plaza Hotel in Los Angeles.

Credit: Photograph by Yana Stoimenova.

PLATE 35 *Wild at Heart*: Sailor, Lula and their Ford Thunderbird.

Credit: *Wild at Heart* (dir. David Lynch, 1990), © Polygram Filmproduktion GmbH, Propaganda Films.

PLATE 36 *Wild at Heart*: a classic couple on the run.

Credit: *Wild at Heart* (dir. David Lynch, 1990), © Polygram Filmproduktion GmbH, Propaganda Films.

PLATE 37 *Wild at Heart*: the epic traffic jam in El Paso.

Credit: *Wild at Heart* (dir. David Lynch, 1990), © Polygram Filmproduktion GmbH, Propaganda Films.

PLATE 38 *The Straight Story*: man and nature perfectly balanced.

Credit: *The Straight Story* (dir. David Lynch, 1999), © Walt Disney Pictures, Picture Factory, Studio Canal, FilmFour.

PLATE 39 *The Straight Story*: Lynch tracks a combine harvester.

Credit: *The Straight Story* (dir. David Lynch, 1999), © Walt Disney Pictures, Picture Factory, Studio Canal, FilmFour.

PLATE 40 *The Straight Story*: Alvin passes the Grotto of the Redemption.

Credit: *The Straight Story* (dir. David Lynch, 1999), © Walt Disney Pictures, Picture Factory, Studio Canal, FilmFour.

PLATE 41 Detail from Christian Tomaszewski, *On Chapels, Caves and Erotic Misery* (2006). Mixed media installation.

Credit: Copyright Christian Tomaszewski. Photograph by Jason Mandella, Georg Tassev, Laszlo Toth.

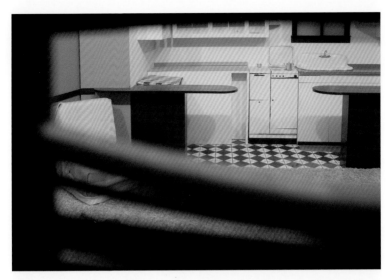

PLATE 42 Detail from Christian Tomaszewski, *On Chapels, Caves and Erotic Misery* (2006). Mixed media installation.

Credit: Copyright Christian Tomaszewski. Photograph by Jason Mandella, Georg Tassev, Laszlo Toth.

PLATE 43 *Blue Velvet*: Dorothy on stage at the Slow Club.

Credit: *Blue Velvet* (dir. David Lynch, 1986), © De Laurentiis Entertainment Group.

PLATE 44 *Twin Peaks*, episode fourteen: the giant on stage at the Roadhouse.

Credit: *Twin Peaks*, episode 14 (dir. David Lynch, 1991), © Lynch/Frost Productions, Propaganda Films, Spelling Entertainment Inc.

PLATE 45 *Mulholland Drive*: Rebekah del Rio collapses at Club Silencio.

Credit: *Mulholland Drive* (dir. David Lynch, 2001), © Studio Canal, Les Films Alain Sarde, Asymmetrical Productions.

PLATE 46 *Mulholland Drive*: auditions at Paramount Studios.

Credit: *Mulholland Drive* (dir. David Lynch, 2001), © Studio Canal, Les Films Alain Sarde, Asymmetrical Productions.

PLATE 47 *Twin Peaks*, episode two: the first appearance of the Red Room.

Credit: *Twin Peaks*, episode two (dir. David Lynch, 1990), © Lynch/Frost Productions, Propaganda Films, Spelling Entertainment Inc.

PLATE 48 *Twin Peaks*, episode twenty-nine: the corridor of the Red Room.

Credit: *Twin Peaks*, episode twenty-nine (dir. David Lynch, 1991), © Lynch/Frost Productions, Propaganda Films, Spelling Entertainment Inc.

PLATE 49 Workers' housing in the Księży Młyn district of Łódź.

Credit: Photograph by Richard Martin.

PLATE 50 *Inland Empire*: Nikki's Hollywood mansion.
Credit: *Inland Empire* (dir. David Lynch, 2006), © Bobkind Inc—Studio Canal, Camerimage, Fundacja Kultury, Asymmetrical Productions.

PLATE 51 *Inland Empire*: two men inside the Pałac Herbsta.
Credit: *Inland Empire* (dir. David Lynch, 2006), © Bobkind Inc—Studio Canal, Camerimage, Fundacja Kultury, Asymmetrical Productions.

PLATE 52 The Pałac Herbsta in Łódź (right), with the refurbished Scheibler cotton mill behind it.

Credit: Photograph by Richard Martin.

PLATE 53 *Inland Empire*: a prostitute on Hollywood Boulevard.

Credit: *Inland Empire* (dir. David Lynch, 2006), © Bobkind Inc—Studio Canal, Camerimage, Fundacja Kultury, Asymmetrical Productions.

PLATE 54 *Inland Empire*: prostitutes by Plac Zwycięstwa.

Credit: *Inland Empire* (dir. David Lynch, 2006), © Bobkind Inc—Studio Canal, Camerimage, Fundacja Kultury, Asymmetrical Productions.

PLATE 55 Plac Zwycięstwa in Łódź, with the Museum of Cinematography and former home of Karl Scheibler on the right.
Credit: Photograph by Richard Martin.

PLATE 56 Roman Polański's star on Ulica Piotrkowska.
Credit: Photograph by Richard Martin.

PLATE 57 The Hollywood and Vine intersection in Los Angeles.
Credit: Photograph by Yana Stoimenova.

PLATE 58 *Inland Empire*: Nikki enters the Orpheum Theater.
Credit: *Inland Empire* (dir. David Lynch, 2006), © Bobkind Inc—Studio Canal, Camerimage, Fundacja Kultury, Asymmetrical Productions.

PLATE 59 The auditorium of the Orpheum Theater on Broadway.

Credit: Photograph by Yana Stoimenova.

PLATE 60 Hotel Grand on Ulica Piotrkowska.

Credit: Photograph by Richard Martin.

PLATE 61 *Inland Empire*: the alley behind the marketplace.

Credit: *Inland Empire* (dir. David Lynch, 2006), © Bobkind Inc—Studio Canal, Camerimage, Fundacja Kultury, Asymmetrical Productions.

PLATE 62 The site of Lynch's proposed film studio in Łódź.

Credit: Photograph by Richard Martin.

panel of his *Triptych—In Memory of George Dyer* (1971), for instance, depicts a stairwell within a crooked environment heavily indebted to German Expressionism (Plate 26). A shadowy figure emerges onto the landing, while a single light bulb hangs from the ceiling. Observers of *Fire Walk With Me* may recall a parallel image, simple in concept, but vast in its implications: Leland Palmer crossing the landing to enter his daughter's bedroom (Plate 27).

When the body of Laura Palmer is discovered, the town of Twin Peaks discharges a collective outburst of mourning, beginning a series with more emotional deviations than any Hollywood melodrama. Upon hearing of Laura's death, Josie Packard announces the temporary closure of the sawmill, sending home her employees with the suggestion: "perhaps you can spend the day with your families." Ironically, of course, it is domestic troubles that generated this tragedy, and Twin Peaks is a town that confirms Loos' prejudice: "There are no dangers of the streets. [...] *There is only the danger of the family.*"[72]

Houses in Twin Peaks are porous, unstable and full of furtive operations. Unbeknown to Josie, her own home features a moveable wall and a hidden safe, a succession of rooms within rooms, and boxes within boxes, that anticipate the architecture of *Inland Empire*. The town's houses are rife with dysfunctional families, too: adultery, violence, drugs and madness are omnipresent, while several characters, such as Leo Johnson, Nadine Hurley and Leland Palmer, exhibit a disturbing obsession with household cleanliness.

The core of *Twin Peaks*' domestic disorders is the Palmer household. Lynch uses two different exteriors for this location—one for the television series and the other for *Fire Walk With Me*. The Palmer house in the series is an austere dwelling built in the 1920s, with substantial wooden paneling and a flat lawn. It is much more isolated from neighboring homes than its cinematic counterpart, exacerbating the Palmers' growing separation from the rest of the community. In *Fire Walk With Me*, the Palmer house sits atop a steep set of steps, producing a dramatic stage to rival Bacon's studio, and allowing Leland to watch over his daughter. The slope is also used by Lynch to emphasize Laura's arduous journey from her public persona into a private zone, with the grueling ascension continuing until she reaches her bedroom upstairs.

It is, however, the interior of the Palmer house, which retains the same décor in the series and the film, that interests us here. In particular, the central staircase and the ceiling fan above it demand our attention. While

Vidler warned that no "particular spatial conformation" guarantees uncanny sensations, certain architectural features do remain peculiarly vulnerable. As Nicholas Royle explains, "Uncanniness entails a sense of uncertainty and suspense, however momentary and unstable. As such it is often to be associated with an experience of the threshold, liminality, margins, borders, frontiers."[73] Loos incorporated similar thinking into his designs, deliberating instilling domestic architecture with pressure and doubt. Colomina confirms, "in every Loos house there is a point of maximum tension, and it always coincides with a threshold or boundary."[74] Traversing thresholds—within a home, a community or a psyche—is a Lynchian trait, too. In locations like Dorothy's closet, the corridor in *Lost Highway* and the staircase in the Palmer household, Lynch follows Loos in imbuing his domestic spaces with "a point of maximum tension." By choosing the staircase as an uncanny frontier in *Twin Peaks*, Lynch also echoes Neutra's feelings on the psychological associations prompted by this location: "What happens to one, *in* one, and around one while ascending a stair and what of it sticks with us as a strangely lasting memory—is to me a master specimen of what architectural experience means."[75] Furthermore, Lynch has outlined his particular admiration for Pierre Chareau's Maison de Verre in Paris (completed in 1932). Among the most intriguing features in this glass house is a retractable staircase—pivoting on a mechanical device so that it can be lowered or raised at will—that links a sitting room to the master bedroom. Access between the public and private spaces of the home can, therefore, be cut off whenever necessary. The interplay between the house's levels proved a compelling aspect for residents. Dominique Vellay, who lived in the house, claims it felt like "a huge theatre, with the great room as the stage and the second floor as the boxes."[76] It is unsurprising, then, that Lynch should single out this home, given that he has so often manipulated the tensions between domestic levels in his own work.

The staircase has become a crucial piece of cinematic architecture. It is a prime venue for the symbolization of unequal power or altered perspective. Indeed, its innate hierarchy creates an unusual problem of representation, in which symbolic association is difficult to avoid. These are distinctly vulnerable locations, too, with potential for uneasy encounters at their highest and lowest points. They offer dramatic platforms from which clandestine observation can occur, a tactic adopted by Donna Hayward in *Twin Peaks* and by Nikki's Polish husband in *Inland Empire*. In *The Grandmother*, Lynch's student film about an anxious young boy, a dilapidated wooden staircase acts as the intermediary between his aggressive parents and his fantasmatic relative in the attic. Other film-makers have exploited the staircase in similar fashion. Jacobs notes how Hitchcock utilized staircases for "conveying ordeal and moral change." In *The Lodger* (1926), for example, the uncertain movements of the Bunting family around the different levels of their home are exacerbated by the "oppressive and haunting" stairwell.[77] One shot of the eponymous character's footsteps on the floor above the family, as if seen through a glass ceiling, emphasizes the sinister feelings generated when outsiders enter the home. The final scene of Hitchcock's *Notorious* (1946) contains a tense and satirical manipulation of cinematic hierarchies. Cary Grant carries a drugged Ingrid Bergman down a grand domestic staircase scrutinized by Nazi agents, in a parody of the ostentatious, media-drenched entrances usually favored by such stars.

Again, though, it is Hollywood melodramas that proffer the most instructive precursor to Lynch's domestic preoccupations. As Elsaesser points out, "the vertical axis of a staircase" is used in melodramas as the backdrop to "a vertiginous drop in the emotional landscape."[78] In Sirk's *Written on the Wind* (1956), the father of the household, whose authority is rapidly deteriorating, suffers a fatal heart attack upon the staircase. In Minnelli's *Home from the Hill* (1960), it is the mother's traumatic collapse that takes place on the stairs, in limbo between the feminine territory she has staked out above and the masculine realm her husband has designed below. In Ray's *Bigger Than Life* (1956), the staircase again acts as the "point of maximum tension" between public and private activity. The film's climactic scene, in which the father threatens to murder his wife and son before clattering into the staircase, represents the disintegration of a small-town domestic model founded upon repression and hypocrisy. The continual use of the staircase as an anxious channel reveals that American culture has detected many different levels within the apparently monotonous surface of domestic life. Intriguingly, Ray claimed it was Frank Lloyd Wright's architecture, with its emphasis on horizontal forms, that helped him to understand the demands of CinemaScope.[79] *Bigger Than Life*, though, pivots on a vertical hierarchy that Wright, in shunning the stresses of the staircase, often avoided.

The significance of the staircase in *Twin Peaks* is established within the opening ten minutes of the pilot episode. Lynch positions his camera at the foot of the staircase for a lengthy shot looking upwards towards the landing that separates Laura's bedroom from her parents' room. A close-up of the ceiling fan, beating away ominously, then follows. Such repetitive machinery is a metaphor for the relentless routines of small-town life. Like the industrial practices of Lynch's cities, generic social processes in Twin Peaks produce grotesque exceptions. Later in the pilot, Sarah Palmer is asked when she last saw her daughter. Her tearful reply— "She was going up the stairs. Those stairs, right there"—is accompanied by the same shot of the staircase. To adapt Neutra's stance, this architectural gesture maintains "a strangely lasting memory" throughout the series.

In *Fire Walk With Me*, the importance of the ceiling fan is revealed: it is a symbol of recurring domestic abuse, the sign that Leland is breaking the boundaries of normal familial relations. Leland's journey across the landing reflects his move from the vertical axis of a father–daughter relationship to the horizontal line of lovers. The electric fan becomes the "point of maximum tension" in this home—the place where two competing planes collide. This incestuous relationship is a cycle of abuse that subverts the standard family model. Yet, for Lynch, habitual cruelty forms the very structure of the family home, an unmentionable activity that remains strangely familiar to Leland and Laura. In her reading of *Twin Peaks*, Diane Stevenson sees all the convoluted machinations of the series as acting "somehow as an echo, a doubling, a recurrence, of the father–daughter incest at the centre." Stevenson wonders, "It's as if every person in town were but part of a multiple personality generated by that abuse—as if not just an individual but a society had been formed in that incestuous circle."[80] To her perceptive analysis, we might add that the ceiling fan is both the symbol of this abuse and a distributor of its aftershocks, wafting domestic corruption into each home in the town.

A Homecoming Queen: The Image of Laura Palmer

Laura Palmer may be Twin Peaks' homecoming queen, but her return to the town is made "wrapped in plastic." Coming home, in fact, is where Laura's problems begin. One of the most haunting scenes in *Fire Walk With Me* develops when she returns home from school one afternoon. How a room is revealed to us is a critical architectural question. In a brilliantly maneuvered sequence, Lynch slowly walks us around the interior of the Palmer household from Laura's perspective. We share her fear as each mundane object appears charged with potential harm, while doors creak and corners are nervously approached. An unsteady camera eventually leads us upstairs, accompanied by the portentous sound of the beating fan, before plunging us into Laura's bedroom, where Bob emerges from behind a chest of drawers. Horrified, she sprints from the house, only to see her father leave shortly afterwards.

Laura's bedroom is a particularly important element in this sequence. After exploring male domestic space in *Eraserhead* and *The Elephant Man*, both *Blue Velvet* and *Fire Walk With Me* pivot on its female counterpart. Men and women, of course, have enjoyed (and endured) very different historical relationships with domesticity, while representations of the home have been filled with highly gendered implications. Through Laura Palmer's bedroom, Lynch replicates a recurrent cinematic image, epitomized by Hitchcock's *Rebecca* (1940), wherein female space is depicted as secret, enclosed and containing forbidden desires. Laura's room is a gateway, poised between innocence and experience, in which the floral bedspread and chintzy furnishings clash with the transgressive activities that occur there. Walter Benjamin famously claimed, "To live means to leave traces."[81] After Laura's death, her bedroom becomes evidence, the objects within it pored over for clues. Her surname is never more appropriate than when her belongings, her body and her reputation are in the process of relentless handling.

In fact, throughout a series in which she can never appear alive, Laura herself is presented as a deceptive topography. As Cooper is told in the Red Room, "She's full of secrets." Every positive aspect of Laura's character is presented alongside a darker double: she delivers meals to elderly residents, but has a serious cocaine habit; she works hard at the department store, but sells sex in local bars. The investigation into Laura's death is a struggle to define exactly who she really was—a longing, inevitably unfulfilled, to find a true self amid the layers of competing stories. Laura Palmer, it seems, is a space waiting to be filled with interpretation.

Here, it is useful to involve Mulvey's analysis of how cinema has depicted the female body, and femininity as a whole, as a sign and a space to be explored. Mulvey illustrates her argument with a discussion of the classical figure of Pandora—an "artefact" and "a living trick" who unleashed evil upon the world. Pandora provides Mulvey with the prototype for a patriarchal mythology that views woman as a deceptive surface masking danger. What is more, Mulvey claims, the shimmer of the cinematic screen has become indistinguishable from this vision of women.[82]

With Mulvey in mind, Laura Palmer's bedroom can be read as a contemporary illustration of Pandora's box, a space from which all the woes of Twin Peaks emanate. Its ability to contain elements larger than its volume suggests is emphasized by a dream sequence in *Fire Walk With Me*, when Laura enters a mysterious painting on her wall to find a series of dank domestic spaces that lead to the Red Room (a maneuver anticipating the drawing and installation that would later appear in Lynch's exhibition at the Fondation Cartier). As powerful as this painting is, it is Laura's own image that operates as "a living trick" throughout the series. The introduction of a still image into the continuous flow of moving pictures often creates a jolt—the uncanny sense of one media haunting its successor. In *Twin Peaks*, Lynch fully exploits this tendency by utilizing a familiar American composition: a photograph of Laura as homecoming queen. This image is seen inside the high school display cabinet (Laura is another trophy to be competed for, we might surmise), in the Palmers' living room, and in Benjamin Horne's desk, among other locations. In the second episode of the series, Leland dances wildly with the photograph, but—just like Laura herself—this symbol cannot survive such intense pressure, and the glass shatters in his hands (Plate 28). The framed photographic portrait is usually designed to make an environment more homely, as Merrick's tireless attempts at interior decoration demonstrate. Yet, in *Twin Peaks*, Laura's photo is a haunting object. Not only a relentless sign of absence, the image is also a persistent reminder of how her wholesome public face clashed with the private reality of prostitution and drug abuse.

In thinking of Laura as a contemporary Pandora, as an "artefact" or "living trick," it is notable that within *Twin Peaks* she is a character almost entirely composed of domestic media. Her identity is pieced together from the homecoming photograph, the diary hidden in her bedroom, the eerie home-video she made with Donna and James, and the home-made audio tapes she sent to her psychiatrist. That the voice, image and writings of this dead blonde woman are posthumously examined in minute detail should remind us that it was Marilyn Monroe who provided the initial inspiration for *Twin Peaks*.[83] Delving further into cinematic history, it is evident that portraits of dead women have consistently been exploited for their haunting presence. The ultimate example of this remains *Vertigo* (1958), an obvious influence on Lynch's career, though Hitchcock was manipulating similar ideas thirty years earlier in *The Lodger*, where paintings of blonde women are linked with the actions of a serial killer. Furthermore, Otto Preminger's *Laura* (1944), a film frequently alluded to in *Twin Peaks*, is dominated by a large portrait of Laura Hunt, whose surname also reflects how she is pursued. The painting contains such potency that the detective hired to investigate her "death" falls in love with the image, in much the same way that Cooper maintains a strange affinity with Laura Palmer. In *Mulholland Drive*, Lynch again repeats the idea that feminine artifice inevitably leads to murderous conclusions. In Hollywood, he implies, an actor's photographic portrait—the term "head-shot" is particularly apt—is both a reminder of celluloid performance and a portent of her future death.

While the homecoming portrait of Laura Palmer clearly raises different connotations to Lynch's other domestic symbols, such as the closet, the television set and the staircase, it functions within the same framework. For Lynch, the image of a dead woman has something familiar about it. It is, consequently, merely another part of the American domestic order that he can heighten and manipulate, an image the viewing public will comprehend in its simplicity, without the need for scholarship. In Aragon's terms, Lynch positions Laura's photograph as a "really common" object that he can raise into "the superior life of poetry." Perhaps, future generations might remember her features alongside Hitchcock's bottles and keys. Accordingly, many who found pleasure in *Twin Peaks*, such as Diana Hume George, also regarded its "sexual ethic" as "reptilian."[84]

What marks Lynch's later films is the extent to which they make us aware of our own complicity in imbuing domestic objects with excessive meaning. In *Inland Empire*, Nikki approaches a variety of items in an attempt to make sense of her surroundings, yet the watches, cigarettes and underwear she collects only confuse matters further. When, near the end of *Mulholland Drive*, a hit-man tells Diane Selwyn that a blue key will appear once he has carried out the murder, she feels compelled to ask: "What's it open?" The man's lengthy laughter in response reveals the hollowness of all on-screen objects: the key is a symbol—nothing more, nothing less—yet we are desperate, like Diane, to decipher its meaning.

In Camera: Modern Home Media

For Richard Neutra, Europe in the aftermath of World War I was mired in "extreme squalidness," whereas the United States, personified by men like Ford and Wright, represented a bright future.[85] One area, in particular, symbolized Neutra's hopes. After seeing a travel poster in Zurich, he became obsessed by its mantra: "California Calls You."[86] The Golden State subsequently became Neutra's home from 1925 until his death in 1970. In the process, Neutra helped popularize modern architecture in the region, while contributing to an image of domestic bliss that, via countless media reproductions, has resonated throughout America and the rest of the world. As the vision of a Californian lifestyle combining outdoor pleasures with modern conveniences became a powerful global symbol, Los Angeles developed its own notions of home. By 1930, an extraordinary 94 percent of dwellings in the city were single-family homes.[87] Tenements, row-houses or apartment blocks could be left to the likes of Philadelphia. What is more, the domestic designs of Wright, Neutra, Schindler, Lautner and the Eameses assured Los Angeles of a place in architectural histories of modernism.

However, Los Angeles' array of single-family homes has also found its detractors. In Nathanael West's *The Day of the Locust* (1939), Tod Hackett surveys the city's "truly monstrous" patchwork of housing and concludes that "only dynamite would be of any use." Hackett, a set designer and frustrated artist, sees the cheap façades, shameless pastiche and historical montage as indicative of the city's superficiality. In response, he plans a painting entitled "The Burning of Los Angeles" featuring "a great bonfire of architectural styles."[88] In a similar fashion, Frank Lloyd Wright dismissed Los Angeles as "that desert of shallow effects," while other observers blamed the film industry for creating confusion over architectural tastes.[89]

Housing remains the cause of intense social conflicts in Los Angeles. Mike Davis claims three characteristics define the city's suburbs. First, Los Angeles' homeowners "love their children, but they love their property values more." Second, "community" here means "homogeneity of race, class and, especially, home values." Lastly, "affluent homeowners," concerned with the defense of "home values and neighborhood exclusivity," constitute the most powerful social movement in Southern California.[90] Perhaps more than in any other American city, home has become a pressurized and highly contested notion in Los Angeles, the subject around which multiple issues have coalesced.

Davis' dissection of economic inequalities in Los Angeles may not, on the surface, appear to hold much in common with Lynch's films, which are often criticized for their lack of class consciousness. Yet, one crew member on the *Lost Highway* set told David Foster Wallace: "Read *City of Quartz*. That's what this film's about right there in a nutshell."[91] Indeed, parts of Davis' book, first published in 1990, do provide an instructive context for *Lost Highway*:

Welcome to post-liberal Los Angeles, where the defense of luxury lifestyles is translated into a proliferation of new repressions in space and movement, undergirded by the ubiquitous "armed response." This obsession with physical security systems, and, collaterally, with the architectural policing of social boundaries, has become a zeitgeist of urban restructuring, a master narrative in the emerging built environment of the 1990s.[92]

The preoccupation with domestic security, epitomized by electronic surveillance and fortress-like architecture, reaches its apotheosis in Los Angeles, but it represents a national trend, too. By 1998, 16 million Americans were estimated to live in gated communities.[93]

Lost Highway, released in 1997, takes an askew perspective on Davis' "master narrative." It is less interested in the maintenance of luxury lifestyles and property values, and more concerned with how feelings of domestic security relate to psychological well-being. Lynch uses the increasingly prevalent physical apparatus of security systems, such as intercom buzzers and burglar alarms, as a way of exploring memory, desire and guilt. Surveillance is a particularly evocative term here, bringing together associations of home security, psychological scrutiny and film-making. Reflecting on his research into the notion of home, Witold Rybczynski concluded: "domesticity proved to be an idea that had almost nothing to do with technology."[94] On the contrary, *Lost Highway* demonstrates the extent to which domesticity is now a question of media—of screens and projectors, telephones and tapes, radios and video cameras. We often think of cameras as exposing matters, of bringing issues to light. Yet, to be *in camera*, in a legal sense, is to conduct proceedings in private, behind closed doors. Highly aware of a Californian form of modern architecture that promised transparency and light, *Lost Highway* interrogates an attendant desire to conduct domestic living *in camera*.

How Did You Get Inside My House?
Lost Highway

According to Joseph Rosa, "Bad guys may no longer wear black, but they do live in white-walled modern homes." Clad in the *noir* garments of a jazz saxophonist and the inhabitant of a white modernist residence, *Lost*

Highway's Fred Madison fulfills two criteria of the archetypal cinematic villain. Rosa pinpoints a trend in which Hollywood executives, who have been living in modernist homes since the 1930s, continue to sustain an industry in which "modern domestic architecture has become identified almost exclusively with characters who are evil, unstable, selfish, obsessive, and driven by pleasures of the flesh." *Lost Highway* offers a particularly intriguing angle on this matter: Fred's house, where modern forms play host to obsessive and evil deeds, is owned by Lynch himself. Rosa concludes that cinema's equation of modern architecture with unwholesome behavior demonstrates "something in Hollywood's collective psyche that demands to be understood as transgressive, dangerous, wild, even criminal."[95] Lynch's use of his own home to explore murder, madness and media is, we might conclude, another example of how he links forms of domestic space with forms of artistic creativity and transgression.

The Madison house dominates the first forty minutes of *Lost Highway*. Its location is part of what Banham defined as Los Angeles' "foothill ecology"—a network of "narrow, tortuous residential roads" set in the wilderness and characterized by "an air of deeply buried privacy."[96] Here, the desire for seclusion ensures houses feel more susceptible to spooky encounters. Neighborly observation is obsolete when each home is carefully separated from its counterparts. The Madison house is said by Renee to be "near the observatory"—a reference to the Griffith Observatory on Mount Hollywood—though its real position is on Senalda Road, several miles to the west. Renee's reference not only emphasizes the relationship between her house and instruments of surveillance; it also brings to mind another example of Californian domestic discord and a leading Hollywood melodrama: *Rebel Without a Cause* (dir. Nicholas Ray, 1955) famously made use of the Griffith Observatory.

The Madison house is an odd concrete structure, built in 1957. Its exterior is discolored and maintains three vertical slits as rather sinister windows (Plate 29). Adam Kesher's home in *Mulholland Drive*—another modernist palace in the Hollywood Hills—is in a similar vein, with its dirty concrete and glass panels. The archetypal example of this typology is the single-story Schindler House in West Hollywood, completed in 1922, in which the eponymous architect combined tilted concrete walls with narrow slits of light (Plate 30). This home, where Neutra lived for the first five years of his time in California, combats its initial introspection with a sequence of more open spaces at the rear, aided by sliding doors and expansive glazing. In *Lost Highway*, though, the Madison house contains no such balance and remains gloomy throughout. One broader window wraps around the upper corner of the building, but this only serves to enclose residents in a glass cubicle. Fred is provided with a theatrical box to observe his neighborhood, but there is little external drama in such a cloistered society. In fact, anticipating Fred's later incarceration, this window resembles a transparent prison cell. With its garage also permanently shuttered, the Madison house turns in on itself, wary of external threats. Even the skylight above the living room is made up of fractured panels, as if the reality of the outside world should be viewed with deep suspicion.

For Loos, "The house does not have to tell anything to the exterior; instead, all its richness must be manifest in the interior."[97] The introspective façade of the Madison home hints at the repressed rage of its male inhabitant, but remains tight-lipped. The interior retains a similarly minimalist approach, yet provides more suggestions of dysfunctional behavior. Like Bacon's studio, the Madisons' living spaces are all on the first floor of the house, accessed via a twisting staircase, with only a limited intervention of light. In keeping with *Lost Highway*'s interest in psychological security, all the drama in this household takes place "upstairs." Some of the unsettling furniture in the living room was designed by Lynch—such as the VCR cabinet and the small table affixed to the wall—while the artwork was produced by his ex-wife, Peggy Reavey. As Nieland notes, the room also includes two icons of mid-century design: the Diamond Chair designed by Harry Bertoia (1952) and the Elliptical Table (1951) by Charles and Ray Eames.[98] The latter piece adds to the crooked atmosphere of the living room, which also contains two asymmetrical boxes supporting the television set and a sofa with an unexpected kink (Plate 31). The bedroom, meanwhile, is bordered by thick curtains, and contains black silk bedding and a stark red headboard in an attempt at Loosian sensuality that drifts into sterility instead. There is more than one way to be modern, of course, and the clean lines and smooth forms of Lynch's interior designs are accompanied by deliberate abnormalities. "I like a very sparse room," Lynch admits. "And I like a room that has some irregularities in it."[99]

Within such a queasy environment, Fred and Renee's relationship is suitably awkward: conversations are stilted, sex is excruciating and suspicion imbues every interaction. The deathly pace of *Lost Highway*'s opening section is an invitation for the audience to immerse itself in the on-screen architecture. When detectives are called to the house, the space is mapped as thoroughly as Laura Palmer's bedroom, with its peculiar geometries assessed for clues. Despite these lingering perspectives, though, comfort remains out of reach. Indeed, the more time we spend here, the more uneasy the space becomes. The Madison house is not a pure modernist space—its hybridity continues Los Angeles' eclecticism—yet Lynch's use of minimalist design as the site for marital disharmony emphasizes that difficult relationships cannot be tidied away in a slick storage system. Architecture, Lynch has claimed, is "a recording instrument."[100] Throughout his work, domestic spaces register the actions of their inhabitants. In *Lost Highway*, just as Fred mistrusts the ability of a video camera to document events satisfactorily, his home emits a distinct suspicion of household objects. Unlike Merrick and his growing collection of Victorian memorabilia, the Madison house tries to avoid remembering anything at all. The drama in this house lies in an ostentatious denial of the decoration Merrick embraces. However, as Nieland explains, Lynch understands "avant-garde minimalism and kitschy maximalism as always dialectically bound." Thus, the objects in the Madison house are "theatrical by virtue of their very minimalism."[101]

For modernist architects, eliminating the clutter of the bourgeois interior was designed to cleanse the house of unruly elements, thus benefiting personal relationships. "Teach your children that a house is only habitable when it is full of light and air, and when the floors and walls are clear," Le Corbusier insisted.[102] Moreover, the United States, and California in particular, seemed the ideal site for this new approach to domesticity. Not only were there the generous space and natural light necessary for new forms of living, but, Le Corbusier claimed, "Cleanliness is a national virtue in America. No filth, no dust."[103] However, disenchantment soon followed these high aspirations. Neutra, after surveying Wright's domestic buildings, was most disappointed by their inhabitants: "the people who live in these houses were rather awful. I had always hoped that this new architecture would produce a different human being. I am sorry to be proved wrong." Moreover, the first owner of Neutra's Branch House (1942), a small residence located in the Hollywood Hills, described it as "a glass cage" and claimed his family preferred to live in a thirty-year-old farmhouse "with the general proportions of a Pennsylvania barn."[104]

The gap between the progressive ideals of modern architecture and the reality of human relations occurring within it has been of particular interest to film-makers. Because of its ability to "accompany the eye as it moves," Sigfried Giedion famously declared that "only film can make the new architecture intelligible!"[105] Cinema, however, has revelled in tracking the limitations of modern housing. In *Contempt*, for example, Godard captures the disintegration of a marriage amid the pristine white walls of a modern apartment. The film's lengthy central scene sees a couple performing a destructive dance around their home, continually divided in the course of their arguments by domestic apparatus. In *Lost Highway*, Fred and Renee's occupation of their modern home is even more tortuous: they creep tentatively around this minimalist stage, uncertain of the spaces around them and barely touching one another. The defining image of the film's domestic discord, captured on video tape, is Fred dismembering his wife. In a scenario that extends Bacon's brutal treatment of flesh, Renee is transformed into a series of catastrophic objects scattered across the bedroom.

It is, though, an innovation of the late sixteenth century, the domestic corridor, that provides the "point of maximum tension" in the Madison house. It was Freud's intuition, Vidler explains, that "from the homely house to the haunted house there is a single passage, where what is contained and safe is therefore secret, obscure, and inaccessible, dangerous and full of terrors."[106] The corridor removed uncertain movements from delineated rooms into a space specifically designed to contain transition. In a zone intended for circulation, occupation thus becomes fraught with danger. The dark corridor in the Madison house was added to the building by Lynch as part of its remodeling for *Lost Highway*.[107] Here, the corridor is a kind of portal, a transformative space into which Fred repeatedly disappears. This is a secret and obscure threshold, which seems strangely unknown to Fred, yet the desires it harbors cannot remain private, inaccessible and *in camera* forever.

During one of Fred's explorations into the murky spaces of the Madison house, we see two shadows, without attendant bodies, cross the living room. There is a strong sense that Fred and Renee are not alone in this house, that the carefully ordered spaces of their home contain a dangerous intruder. Buried within the Hollywood Hills, domestic security and personal privacy remain elusive for the couple, with the appearance of unexplained video footage of their bedroom and talk of an alarm system that "kept going off." Who, or what, is inside the Madison house? Here, Kafka again offers illumination. In "The Burrow," his protagonist is anxious to maintain the security of an elaborate underground dwelling:

I seek out a good hiding-place and keep watch on the entrance of my house—this time from outside—for whole days and nights. Call it foolish if you like, it gives me infinite pleasure and reassures me. At such times it is as if I were not so much looking at my house as at myself sleeping, and had the joy of being in a profound slumber and simultaneously of keeping vigilant guard over myself.[108]

Kafka's characters continually observe their own lives as if from an external position, their surveillance both intimate and strangely detached. In *Lost Highway*, Fred's concerns over domestic security—the desire to enjoy "a profound slumber," in Kafka's words, or to "dream in peace," as Bachelard put it—are also linked to his evident need to keep "vigilant guard over myself." For it is the intrusion of Fred's own fears into the marital home that generates anxiety; jealous thoughts that feel strange to him precisely because of their proximity. "How did you get inside my house?" he asks the Mystery Man. "You invited me," is the chilling reply. "It is not my custom to go where I'm not wanted." The shadowy forces at play in the Madison house are not, therefore, the product of an outside agency: they are an internal matter. Just as Colomina deemed the inhabitant of a Loos house to be an "intruder in his own space," Fred's chaotic fears materialize as literal trespassers in his well-ordered home.

This, then, explains the video tapes that land on the Madisons' doorstep. The first package appears the morning after an evening when Fred is convinced Renee has been unfaithful, his phone calls from the jazz club having gone unanswered. It is impossible for Fred to survey the marital home like Kafka's nightwatchman, so his jealous mind generates a technological substitute to perform the task. In effect, he produces a miniature reproduction of his home in the spirit of Merrick's model-making, an exercise, as Bachelard noted, that keeps the imagination "both vigilant and content." Renee, as alert as Mike Davis to the importance of property values in Los Angeles, assumes the tape is from a "real estate agent." In fact, its source goes against reality. As Žižek notes, the Mystery Man's camera, which Fred has "invited" into the Madison home, "doesn't register ordinary reality." Rather, it directly records "the subject's fantasies."[109] We might say, therefore, that the camera records thoughts that usually remain *in camera*. In fact, Fred's interactions with his own psyche are always mediated: it is via telephone calls, video tapes and a pocket television, all controlled by the Mystery Man, that he accesses his own desires. Yet, the video's footage of the house's interior moves at a strange, impossible height that resembles a shaky architectural fly-through, as if there is a struggle between objective and subjective points of view taking place.

Indeed, Fred's mediated thoughts shake the foundations of the film itself, in disorientating switches between subjective registers. In the Madison house, the dark spaces of the corridor host Fred's encounters with Lynch's camera, moments of self-awareness that are inevitably traumatic. We know from his earlier comments to the police officers—"I like to remember things my own way [...] not necessarily the way they happened"—that Fred has a troubled relationship with cameras. For him, these devices are as threatening as an armed intruder. Alone in the corridor, he is subject to a violent tracking shot that pulls down towards him, causing him to flinch instinctively—an episode that recalls the terrified victims of a murderous camera in *Peeping Tom* (dir. Michael Powell, 1960). It is as if Fred's own fears, manifested through media, are returning to attack him. Later, we see him stride towards the camera, staring in bewilderment at the audience, before appearing to walk right through us. Just as the thresholds between Fred's psychological state and the physical spaces of the house become confused, these sequences threaten to demolish the barrier between screen and spectator.

Media, therefore, is a critical component of domestic life in *Lost Highway*. From telephones and radios to projectors and screens, an extensive list of competing technologies and electronic textures inhabit the film. Even the house's windows have electric shutters—another form of perception operated by remote control. What effect, the film asks, does such equipment have on our domestic lives, especially in terms of memory? Paul Virilio argued that VCR machines "effectively permit the distribution of time itself."[110] In *Lost Highway*, the video tapes create temporal confusion not only for Fred and Renee, but for the audience, too: how can their grainy footage be slotted into a conventional narrative structure, given that we see a replay of Renee's murder before it seems to have occurred? This is a film in which the spatial implications of media, the storage capacity and memory functions of supplementary technologies, are constantly in play. Indeed, *Lost Highway* demonstrates how architecture functions as media, via the reproduction of video images, while media takes on an architectonic status in ordering domestic space.

Exemplified by the film-strip aesthetic of the windows looping around Le Corbusier's Villa Savoye (1929), the operations of the camera have become inextricably linked with the development of modern domestic architecture. Such connections have continued to drive contemporary designers. Inspired by the famous Casa Malaparte designed by Adalberto Libera, which featured in Godard's *Contempt*, the Slow House (1989) is an unrealized project developed by Elizabeth Diller and Ricardo Scofidio for a site in Long Island, New York (Plate 32). The house takes the form of a curving chamber conceived as "a passage from physical entry to optical departure." Diller and Scofidio's plans feature video equipment that constantly records and replays the views facing the house. In "collapsing the opposition between the authentic and mediated," they claim residents will be able to control the surrounding landscape so that "day [can be] played back at night, fair weather played back in foul."[111] This is domestic architecture structured around the logic of the camera, rather than the capabilities of human memory. What role does remembering "things my own way" have here?

Colomina concludes that "modern architecture only becomes modern with its engagement with the media." At the center of her argument is a comparison between Le Corbusier and Loos. The former, Colomina contends, offered a domestic realm that looked towards the external world, with windows framing the landscape for an inhabitant's viewing pleasure. In other words, the house functions as a camera gazing outwards. The latter, by contrast, designed homes that were inherently introspective, where windows were not intended for observing the outside world, but for letting in light to the interior. Here, the home is a self-contained theater for the staging of domestic drama.[112]

In *Lost Highway*, the Madison house combines elements of both these philosophies: it functions as a camera, but one that faces inwards. A *camera obscura*, perhaps, is a more fitting architectonic model. Once again, an affinity with Bacon's studio, with its media scraps and images of distorted torsos, springs to mind. What is more, the small intrusions of light that find their way into the darkness of the Madison house ultimately produce, in the second half of the film, a series of inverted images: a cold brunette becomes a predatory blonde, and a murderous husband becomes a hapless victim. In the image-saturated environment of Los Angeles, the architecture of the media, and especially of the camera, is impossible to escape, even at home. In *Lost Highway*, subjectivity is created through modern electronic structures. Such discussions return the camera to its roots as a room, as well as reminding us of how rooms may function as cameras. As Colomina states: "Architecture is not simply a platform that accommodates the viewing subject. It is a viewing mechanism that produces the subject. It precedes and frames its occupant."[113] After its use in *Lost Highway*, the Madison house has continued to produce and project images: it now contains Lynch's editing suite and private screening room—spaces that remain defiantly *in camera*, deeply buried in the Hollywood Hills, despite the voyeuristic desires of some visitors to this street.

Notably, *Lost Highway* was released two years after *Premonitions Following an Evil Deed* (1995), Lynch's contribution to *Lumière et Compagnie*, a centennial celebration of cinema's first screening. Dozens of directors were asked to use the original *Cinématographe* camera invented by the Lumière brothers to create a film no longer than 52 seconds (the length of a single reel). The logic of the *Cinématographe*, a device that could record, develop and project images, anticipates *Lost Highway*'s extensive investigation into media and architecture. Perhaps, we might view the Mystery Man, who seems able to store and screen images at will, as the personification of such apparatus, a *Man with a Movie Camera* to follow Vertov's pioneering example.

After the film's initial section, the remainder of *Lost Highway* can be read as a series of domestic spaces that distort or challenge the major features of the Madison house. Indeed, it is as if the house itself, prompted by Fred's psychological struggles, is emitting a flood of inverted images. Paradoxically, as Nieland points out, the film's narrative becomes modernist in nature "as its interior design becomes less modernist—more irrational, secretive, and inhuman. Lynch becomes more like Bergman by defiling the visionary aspirations of a Le Corbuiser."[114] In jail for the murder of Renee, Fred finds himself inside the most secure home in California, with Lynch emphasizing the locks, gates and guards surrounding his cell. The fragmented skylight of Fred's home is replaced by a single light bulb, while his intercom system is superseded by an iron shutter. Insomnia is again a domestic torment here, with Fred unable to enjoy peaceful sleep despite the extensive fortifications and vigilant guards protecting his new home. In fact, this nocturnal unrest, caused by a stubborn determination "to remember things my own way," precipitates a physical metamorphosis to match anything depicted by Kafka or Bacon. In a fantasmatic re-imagining of his life, Fred Madison becomes Pete Dayton.

Pete and his family live in Van Nuys, part of the San Fernando Valley's sprawling suburbs, and a landscape in binary opposition to the curves and greenery of the Hollywood Hills. Strangely, though, the Daytons' house is a warped version of small-town domesticity, with a pitched roof, lush lawn and old documentaries on the television, as if Fred is fusing adolescent memories of the 1950s with contemporary Los Angeles. The garden even contains a miniature white picket fence, a purely symbolic touch, given that a formidable brick wall behind it defends the actual boundaries of the property. Pete's bedroom is an oppressive cell in line with Merrick and Henry's urban abodes, and a space with unstable foundations. As Fred's fantasmatic world begins to break down, Pete's room spins and blurs as a result.

The mansion of the pornographer Andy, located on Deep Dell Place, one of Hollywood's most affluent addresses, is also a venue in direct contrast to the Madison house. This "white stucco job" exhibits a crude taste for the vernacular and contains excessive sexual energy to compensate for the modernist sterility of the Madisons' home. Whereas the introspective Madison house rejects the world outside and is equipped with electronic alarms, Andy's home opens out onto a swimming pool so that semi-naked visitors can move freely between interior and exterior spaces in imitation of the clichéd Californian lifestyle. Simultaneously, this home is a chamber of images. Yet, whereas Fred and Renee watch video tapes highlighting their domestic problems on a small television set, Andy makes use of an impressive film projector and a giant screen to immerse his living room in pornography. Upstairs in Andy's home, the corridor again acts as a domestic portal, bleeding into the passages of the Lost Highway Hotel, another location where the sexual pleasures that elude Fred are freely enjoyed. It is noticeable that, throughout Lynch's films, sex is much more prevalent in hotels than in the marital home— from Sailor and Lula's frantic exploits in *Wild at Heart* to the scenes of Polish prostitution that begin *Inland Empire*. For Lynch, being at home seems to entail a level of sexual inhibition.

The most intriguing opposition to the Madison house comes at the end of *Lost Highway*, when Pete (who then transforms back into Fred) drives into the desert surrounding Los Angeles. With its simple wooden form and tired furnishings, the isolated shelter he encounters is the antithesis of the Madisons' sophisticated abode (Plate 33). It is one of several sordid rooms in Lynch's films—joining the room above the convenience store in *Fire Walk With Me*, where Mike and Bob host weird meetings, or the disgusting motel room in Big Tuna, which Sailor and Lula occupy in *Wild at Heart*. In *Lost Highway*, Lynch contrasts the oppressive permanence of Fred's domestic life with a desert cabin belonging to a "fence"—that is, a criminal middle-man who operates in society's marginal spaces. Indeed, there is a suggestion this "fence" is the Mystery Man, which would certainly be an apt description for his operations between material and psychological realms.

The desert itself provides an appropriately unhomely setting for the conclusion of Lynch's narrative. This is an unforgiving landscape devoid of all comforts, the very wilderness modernity sought to erase, but a terrain that has also played host to many of modernism's most interesting domestic experiments, such as Wright's Taliesin West in Arizona or Neutra's Kaufmann House in Palm Springs. Furthermore, while deserts are conventionally considered empty spaces, the story of the American desert is, as Michael Kubo points out, "fundamentally one of technology."[115] To the military maneuvers and engineering projects Kubo associates with the desert, we can add the mechanical operations of the camera. For, as Baudrillard noted, the "unfolding of the desert is infinitely close to the timelessness of film."[116] It is this sense of endless repetition that characterizes the end of *Lost Highway*. Fred's homecoming remarks— "Dick Laurent is dead"—signify continuation rather than closure, a message filtered through domestic media, once again. *Lost Highway*, then, for all its interest in domestic design, begins and ends with the image of a speeding yellow line. The road, as we will see in the next chapter, symbolizes very different spatial desires.

3 ROAD

*By travelling in America, I'm not distanced from it. No dream of
rootedness challenges the giddy exhilaration of the car and the wind.*
SIMONE DE BEAUVOIR, *AMERICA DAY BY DAY* (1948)[1]

Geography in Motion

Film moves. A medium enjoyed by stationary observers in a static venue
is predicated on the relentless progression of reels, each frame enjoying
its momentary illumination. Film moves and it moves us, too. Like the
interplanetary explorers of *Dune* who "fold space" to undergo "traveling
without moving," the film spectator is transported to distant continents
and celluloid cities from a stable seat. That cinematic motion is also
emotional, that filmic images produce movements of feeling, is the
catalyst for Giuliana Bruno's work. The affecting world of cinema, Bruno
emphasizes, emerged alongside new forms of mass tourism, with a
terminology of "panning" and "tracking" that "speaks literally of travel
space."[2] Subsequently, the road has become the foremost "travel space" in
cinema, a channel for motion and emotion to be closely aligned with the
filmic strip. A montage of material places unravels along a celluloid route,
as the landscape is framed for a spectator's attention. Aberrant tracks,
sudden detours or lost highways offer additional intrigue, while a traffic
jam, like a malfunctioning projector, signals dangerous delay. Indeed, as
Godard intimates at the end of *Week End* (1967), immobility on the
modern road represents "Fin de Cinema."

This chapter traverses David Lynch's roads, focusing on two of his
least-celebrated films: *Wild at Heart* and *The Straight Story*. John Orr
argues that, in Hitchcock's work, "love and Eros fuse *only* through the

auto-motion of the modern machine," whereas the director's houses and rooms generate sterility.[3] A similar theme has emerged in Lynch's cinema. His road movies represent his most romantic work, replete with (ostensibly) happy endings and healed families, as if motion fashions successful relationships. Yet, *Wild at Heart* and *The Straight Story* offer contrasting visions of the American road, pitting youthful adventure against elderly redemption. Having explored Lynch's interpretation of East Coast darkness and West Coast sunshine, our attention now turns to the worlds he has built and filmed in the Deep South and the Mid-West.

Before that, though, we should consider the specific relationship between motion and identity in the United States, the national symbolism with which Lynch's road movies negotiate. Why did the Pilgrim Fathers travel from Europe to America? asked D. H. Lawrence:

> They came largely to get *away*—that most simple of motives. To get away. Away from what? In the long run, away from themselves. Away from everything. That's why most people have come to America, and still do come. To get away from everything they are and have been.[4]

The previous chapter explored the symbolic weight attached to images of the American home. This chapter considers different desires—mobility, migration, the urge "to get *away*"—that imply other notions of space. To be *on the road*, as opposed to being *at home*, presupposes momentum and diffusion, not permanence or enclosure. Thus, the home and the road form a crucial cultural pairing. Tensions between the imagined confines of home and the potential for liberation on the road might be thought of as a conflict between structured space (the grid, the lawn, the neighborhood) and fantasmatic boundlessness (the highway, the woods, the desert). In Lynch's America, such binary oppositions are both overplayed and undermined. His films, shaped by an era in which isolationism and engagement were hotly debated, have been highly attentive to the spatial and psychological contradictions of American motion. In contrast to Simone de Beauvoir, Lynch is distinctly aware that—despite our desire to "to get *away*"—dreams of "rootedness" perpetually challenge the "giddy exhilaration of the car and the wind." It is no surprise that *The Wizard of Oz* (dir. Victor Fleming, 1939), one of Hollywood's most explicit renderings of the struggle between home and the road, is referenced so overtly in *Wild at Heart.*

In fact, an American traveler seeking boundless motion is often confronted by a monotonous, highly structured space. An assembly-line product of Henry Ford's decentralizing dreams, the American highway system has become, in Dimendberg's words, "the pre-eminent centrifugal space of the twentieth century."[5] During Lynch's youth, the image of endless roads filled with mass-produced vehicles emerged as a powerful symbol of American energy and freedom. Charles and Ray Eames' film *Glimpses of the USA*, projected across seven giant screens at the American National Exhibition in Moscow in 1959, depicted as a daily routine freeway trips within a baroque series of concrete interchanges. The film positioned relentless automotive motion as a key part of the American domestic order. Three years earlier, Congress had authorized the creation of a 42,500-mile highway system, promoted for defense purposes. Accordingly, the road should be considered alongside the suburban home, the television set, the fitted kitchen and the geodesic dome (the Eameses' film was screened within one of Buckminster Fuller's iconic structures) as a potent architectural manifestation of the Cold War's politics of dispersal and containment.

The highway system, then, is another piece of mid-century design to catch Lynch's attention, as the growing dominance of the car in the post-war era has spawned its own architectural forms. Highways themselves necessitate intricate interchanges and immense tunnels, but America's roadside architecture also includes garages and junkyards, billboards and parking lots, strip malls and big-box stores. Conventionally, this landscape has garnered few admirers. In response to the 1956 Interstate Highway Act, Lewis Mumford declared: "the American has sacrificed his life as a whole to the motorcar."[6] A generation later, Jane Holtz Kay concluded that America had become an "Asphalt Nation," in which "our lives and landscapes [are] strangled by the umbilical cord of the car."[7] For Mumford and Kay, car travel did not create a liberating extension of human life, that "giddy exhilaration" sensed by de Beauvoir and the Eameses. Instead, they saw collective paralysis, "motorized stasis" and the surrender of individual agency as the consequences.[8] Peter Blake pursued a different line of attack, stating that the American highway system and its accompaniments symbolized a nation "scattering debris in all directions of the compass."[9]

By contrast, Robert Venturi, Denise Scott Brown and Steven Izenour argued to great effect in the 1970s that America's much-derided "roadside eclecticism" is of considerable value to architects, revealing "a new landscape of big spaces, high speeds, and complex programs." In their view, neon signage and plastic message-boards, "an architecture of bold communication rather than one of subtle expression," embody fresh representational techniques free from the strangulations of modernism.[10] Pop Art acquired similar inspiration from this unpromising territory to form a new aesthetic order utilizing commercial iconography and highway infrastructure. Other observers at this time were also stimulated by the road and its surroundings. Philip Roth, for example, has explained how his friendship with the artist Philip Guston, which began in 1969, developed from

> a shared delight in what Guston called "crapola", starting with billboards, garages, diners, burger joints, junk shops, auto body shops—all the roadside stuff that we occasionally set out to Kingston [New York] to enjoy. [...] Independently, impelled by very different dilemmas, each of us had begun to consider crapola not only as a curious subject with strong suggestive powers to which we had a native affinity but as potentially a tool in itself: a blunt aesthetic instrument providing access to a style of representation free of the complexity we were accustomed to valuing.[11]

The crude, impure forms of Guston's late paintings and the vigorous and absurdist satires that Roth published in the early 1970s—works of bold communication rather than subtle expression—bear witness to a style of representation stimulated by the road and the roadside. This is the "giddy exhilaration" of discovering neglected Americana.

For the road has proved to be a compelling instrument for indexing America. If strolling through the city was the modernist's method of mapping the world, then in post-war America the highway system has enabled novelists, artists and film-makers to gather data, compile inventories and locate patterns in the national landscape. An especially pertinent shift in spatial perspective occurs in Nabokov's *Lolita* (1955). After the focus, in the first half of the novel, on small-town lawns and wooden-framed homes, *Lolita* becomes an ode to American travel, a dizzying directory of names and sites, "putting the geography of the United States into motion." Humbert Humbert, the archetypal cynical European, is soon enraptured by the "glossy black dance floors" of the highways and "the honest brightness of the gasoline paraphernalia against the splendid green of oaks."[12] Likewise, in *Wild at Heart* and *The Straight Story*, Lynch moved from the fences, lawns and family homes of *Blue*

Velvet and *Twin Peaks* towards a preoccupation with the texture of America's roads, the infrastructure that supports the nation's travelers, and the diverse flavors of its epic landscape.

In particular, it has been the exceptionally cinematic qualities of the car journey that have propelled the road movie. This is a genre that, as Conley explains, emerged in the 1930s "as a complement to the mapping designs of the automotive industry."[13] Americans, to clarify Mumford's complaint, were sacrificing their lives to the car *and* the camera. Such material and perceptual associations have continued to flourish. "I always connect these two media: the automobile and the audiovisual," Virilio states. "What goes on in the windshield is cinema in the strictest sense."[14] For drivers and film spectators alike, legibility is dependent upon managing motion with coherent framing. Thus, so many films, including *Lost Highway*, begin from the perspective of a speeding car, as if to stress cinema's intimate association with automotive motion.

Furthermore, as Virilio implies, the road and its surrounding landscape are heightened images produced by a structuring border, just as the cinematic screen intensifies its contents. The connections film's visual qualities have with car travel prompt Iain Borden to conclude that "cinema, more than any other representational form, provides the most direct sense of what it actually feels like to drive."[15] It is, then, intriguing to learn that the urban theorists Donald Appleyard, Kevin Lynch and John R. Myer encouraged highway engineers to utilize films when designing the visual sequences facing drivers. Roads, they wrote, are vast viewing platforms founded on the same "continuity and insistent temporal flow" as cinema.[16] The movements of the camera literalize the perceptual issues that confront us on the road, such as proximity and focus, attention and distraction. In their episodic movements, road movies and car journeys foreground questions of montage—the splicing together of disparate environments and the creation of a smooth flow from fleeting "crapola." As such, the road movie is a far from pure genre. As Jack Sargeant and Stephanie Watson confirm, it instinctively tends towards intertextuality.[17] Lynch has merged different genres throughout his career, adopting and subverting tropes from melodrama, *film noir* and even science fiction. *Wild at Heart* represents the epitome of this approach, brashly wearing its hybridity like a prime piece of "roadside eclecticism."

For this discussion, though, the most crucial element in the alignment of road and reel is intensity. Lynch's architecture is dependent on highly pressurized worlds, in which the director heightens symbolic tensions, manipulates variables and organizes traumatic intrusions. Underpinning the following analysis is a notion of the car and of America's roads as worlds in themselves, arenas that intensify experience and abhor external disturbance. Lynch is a car-orientated director: there are no subway tales, Greyhound bus trips, rail commutes or plane journeys in his films. Motion, for Lynch, means automobiles, while walking (as we have seen) is often a perilous and lonely activity for his characters. A familiar Lynchian logic lies behind this inclination. As Borden writes, "No other space is as intensively conceived, designed and experienced as that of being the driver of a car."[18] Archigram's David Greene elucidates the point, describing the car as "a self-powered mobile room" and a traffic jam as "a collection of rooms."[19] It is the intensity of driving, the sense that both vehicle and road constitute distinct spatial units, that attracts Lynch. The principal "rooms" of *Wild at Heart* and *The Straight Story*, a 1965 Ford Thunderbird and a 1966 John Deere lawn-mower, may not be housed within apartment blocks or throbbing cities, but they remain architectonic phenomena, places of total design. It is these self-powered mobile worlds, the asphalt strips upon which they travel and the landscape that surrounds them that now require closer inspection.

Crossing State Lines: *Wild at Heart*

Wild at Heart is a transitional film. Released in 1990 at the height of *Twin Peaks'* success, it finds Lynch on the road between small-town America, the territory that brought him such fame, and Los Angeles, the city that has dominated his more recent films. Indeed, *Wild at Heart's* heroes, Sailor and Lula, embark on a journey with an especially Lynchian resonance: they begin in North Carolina, the state where *Blue Velvet* was shot, before traveling west in search of "sunny California," the region that has held Lynch's attention in recent years. With four films behind him and five films to come, *Wild at Heart* occupies the middle lane of Lynch's career path.

This is no meek intermediary, though. From its first image—a firing match that builds into a ball of flames—*Wild at Heart* is Lynch's loudest, most sensational work, a lurid landscape filled with outrageous characters. While *Blue Velvet* and *Twin Peaks* were worlds Lynch wallowed in for a long time, noting each detail of the small towns, *Wild at Heart* feels like an excitingly brief excursion, something Lynch sped through saluting only the brashest sights. The road is often the site for emotional eruptions in Lynch's films—think of Mr Eddy's rage along Mulholland Drive in *Lost Highway* (though, in a twist, this is a rage urging a fellow driver to "obey the goddamn rules"), the "joy ride" in *Blue Velvet* that yields Frank Booth's confused passions, or the traumatic trip in *Fire Walk With Me* that brings Leland and Laura Palmer to the brink of break-down. In these three cases, driving experiences serve as horrendous interruptions into the flow of everyday life; car journeys generate the appalling spillage of latent tensions; motion generates wild emotion.

Yet, *Wild at Heart* is all interruption. In McGowan's words, "excess pervades each and every scene." Lynch adopts an episodic structure typical of road movies, with flash-back sequences supporting the unraveling story, but presses the conventions of the genre to their outer limits. Each segment of *Wild at Heart* is instilled with such color and passion that the filmic strip seems poised to ignite at any moment. As McGowan notes, "the narrative seems to exist in order to bring us to the next extreme image."[20] We have already observed the connections Lynch's architecture holds with his films' narrative structures—the centripetal urbanism of Victorian London supporting classical narrative progression in *The Elephant Man*, while the emptiness of Philadelphia leaves *Eraserhead* without such a focused trail—but the road makes possible particularly strong associations between space and narrative. For instance, *Mulholland Drive*'s twists and turns start, quite literally, on a curving path, the looping *Lost Highway* begins and ends on a desert road, and we might see the shots of swaying traffic lights in *Twin Peaks* as a way of marking narrative shifts and pauses in the series.[21] The shape of *Wild at Heart*, however, is disrupted and disjointed, as if each individual sequence is a small world in itself, crammed with tension, violence or humor. The road movie genre becomes in *Wild at Heart* another symbolic spatial form, like a white picket fence or the Hollywood sign, that Lynch can pressurize until it shatters. This amplification of Barry Gifford's source novel, *Wild at Heart: The Story of Sailor and Lula* (1990), is explained by Lynch in typically disarming fashion: "I just made the brighter things a little brighter and darker things a little darker."[22] Catastrophic car accidents, voodoo villainy and spectacular sex all spark within these overheating worlds.

Wild at Heart's initial setting also places us in a transitional zone. As a caption informs us, the action begins at a party in Cape Fear "somewhere near the border between North and South Carolina." Lynch loves evocative place names that imbue geographical guidance with additional connotations, as the titles *Inland Empire* and *Twin Peaks* confirm. *Wild at Heart*'s opening location indicates that terror (Cape Fear) and territorial limits ("somewhere near the border") will be thematic partners. Soon enough, Lula is "crossing state lines with a real murderer," and the film's most deadly character is named Bobby Peru, "just like the country." For Lynch, there is no exhilarating motion without attendant constraints. American travel, in his eyes, returns relentlessly to issues of borders and jurisdiction, both physical and psychological.

Held within an expansive interior featuring dark wooden paneling, an ornate ceiling mural and extravagant chandeliers, this initial party sequence situates *Wild at Heart* within a distinct regional identity: the old-fashioned grandeur of the American South. In fact, the scene was shot in "sunny California"—specifically, at the neo-gothic Park Plaza Hotel, designed by Claud Beelman in 1925, near MacArthur Park in Los Angeles (Plate 34). The Park Plaza is another Los Angeles structure that now exists for film-shoots and special events rather than its original function, with directors such as Christopher Nolan (*The Prestige*, 2006), Nicolas Winding Refn (*Drive*, 2011), Oliver Stone (*Nixon*, 1995) and the Coen brothers (*Barton Fink*, 1991) also having made use of the hotel in recent times. Of course, the Cape Fear region, in the form of Wilmington, North Carolina, was previously utilized by Lynch as the shooting location for *Blue Velvet*, but Lumberton's small-town, middle-America mood is far from *Wild at Heart*'s sweaty swing. Cinema puts into motion a geography laden with such contradictions and unexpected coincidences—the terrifying territorial conflicts Lynch would later map in *Inland Empire*.

Road movies frequently entail idealized destinations, often located on America's West Coast. Yet, Sailor and Lula never do reach California: their own staccato reel finishes in a traffic jam halfway to their target. Their interstate journey across the Deep South takes them from Cape Fear, North Carolina, to the Pee Dee Correctional Institution, South Carolina, through New Orleans in Louisiana to the Texas towns of Big Tuna, Lobo and finally El Paso. These environs, a mixture of real and imagined locations, constitute prime Southern "crapola"—a scattering of telegraph poles, low-rise shacks and gas stations amid an unforgiving desert. Outside of its metropolitan centers, the American landscape induces accusations of thoughtless clutter (from critics like Peter Blake) and provides an inspirational model of aesthetic bluntness (for Guston and

Roth), as well as a sense of vast emptiness in which architectural endeavor feels irrelevant. In *Wild at Heart*, Lynch oscillates between all three of these characterizations. There is no disguising the grim buildings of a town like Big Tuna, where visitors (greeted with a fish-shaped sign exclaiming: "Fuck you") face an ominous and sickly motel. By contrast, an earlier fuel-stop soundtracked by gentle jazz, where Sailor and Lula are pictured in front of a deep-blue sky, rustling green trees and the outline of mountain-tops—a scene that recalls Humbert's admiration for how America's "gasoline paraphernalia" complements the natural landscape—provides a moment of simple grace within their turbulent travels (Plate 35). Lynch says he was touched by *The Wizard of Oz's* presentation of "America's nowhere places," and *Wild at Heart* often extends a similar sympathy towards the nation's everyday architecture.[23]

Indeed, the auto-architecture and barren badlands of the South are the setting for the most passionate relationship Lynch has depicted. Chion goes further, describing *Wild at Heart* as "the most beautiful love ballad which the cinema has ever whispered into the night."[24] Frequently framed in iconic fashion by the windshield, Sailor and Lula are a classic couple on the run: he has broken parole and she is escaping a mother who "cares for me just a little too much" (Plate 36). Fittingly, their unified motion produces a son called Pace. The traveling couple remains the dominant configuration of the road-movie genre. It provides, as Steven Cohan and Ina Rae Hark point out, both practical advantages for framing and dialogue, and the attractive intimacy of shared experience.[25] A criminal element adds further frisson to the arrangement, as *Badlands* (dir. Terrence Malick, 1973), *Bonnie and Clyde* (dir. Arthur Penn, 1967) and *Thelma and Louise* (dir. Ridley Scott, 1991) demonstrate. If the "giddy exhilaration" of the American road is often challenged by thoughts of home, then the public manifestation of domestic order—the police force—equally binds those who try "to get *away*." Sailor and Lula's bond, stronger than any other in Lynch's canon, places the family, the home and the law in binary opposition to fierce sex and tender solidarity on the road. As we will see, this opposition is placed in doubt by the film's finale.

There remains a palpable fear to Sailor and Lula's travels, with their relationship in perpetual threat from the world outside the car. "Well, we're really out in the middle of it now, ain't we?" says Lula, as the couple cruise through the epic darkness of a Southern highway. What this "middle" is, or where exactly "it" is located, remains unclear, but the comment follows shortly after Sailor's notable quip: "We all got a secret side, baby." That the secret side of America is hidden in "the middle of it" propels the road movie—a genre where truth is mythically concealed within the country's expansive internal spaces. Defining America seems to demand driving through the nation's heartlands in search of an essential experience. Perhaps such explorers believe, to combine Ford and Lynch's terms, that they are encountering the "real United States" via its "nowhere places." Lula's comment, though, as she peers into the surrounding void, is uttered with the resignation of a traveler who understands that "the middle of it" contains no secret salvation. The only option is to keep on moving.

A Less-Than-Perfect Radio

"A good radio," according to Le Corbusier, is an American "national virtue."[26] For Lula, however, the radio is an unwelcome intrusion into the sealed world of the road trip. Driving through sterile flatlands, she scans several stations, only to encounter increasingly disturbing tales of illness, murder, necrophilia and pollution. Lynch cuts between the rotating dial and Lula's growing anguish, before she hits the brakes and leaps from the car complaining: "I've never heard so much shit in all my life!" The car radio might be considered an essential fixture of the American road trip, offering companionship, regional quirks and important news updates as a driver traverses the continent. In Jean Cocteau's *Orphée* (1949), moreover, the car radio emits coded messages from another world that take on the quality of abstract poetry. In a sense, Sailor and Lula's radio performs the same service. The elliptical reports it broadcasts merge into a grotesque communication from an alternate universe, a language that Lula, in particular, refuses to comprehend:

"Come on in there, San Antonio, Texas. What's on your almost-perfect mind this evening?" "I just had triple bypass, open-heart surgery and I want you to know it's people like you that make me wanna get out of that hospital"..."the severed"..."for her recent divorce, shot and killed her three children, aged seven"..."shot right between"..."a heinous"... "A local judge praised defendant John Roy, but was dismayed to learn that Roy had had sex with the corpse. Roy's lawyer was quoted as saying"... "murder"... "State authorities last October released five hundred turtles into the Ganges, to try and reduce human pollution, and now plan to put in the crocodiles to devour floating corpses dumped by Hindus too poor to pay for cremation"..."victim of a sexual assault"..."mutilated"..."raped"...

Once again, the road provides an opportunity for indexing America, for cataloging the nation's preoccupations. Here, Lula herself creates a "severed" and "mutilated" narrative out of the bizarre incidents she hears, stitching together an aural montage of "roadside eclecticism." Furthermore, both the form and content of this radio compilation reflect the disfigured nature of the landscape surrounding the couple, the misshapen route they are taking, and the fragmented, excessive nature of the film itself.

The horrendous directory of pain and perversion leaves Lula disgusted. Just as Marianne in Godard's *Pierrot Le Fou* (1965) turns off car radio reports of the Vietnam War—"It's all so impersonal," she laments—Lula seeks to exclude political or social interventions from the motions of travel. This radio is all interference, though the material it broadcasts—murder, rape and mutilation—is also in close proximity to Sailor and Lula's lives. The radio, then, acts as another form of screen—projecting the world outside into the mobile world Sailor and Lula have created. Yet, the car seems to demand a certain purity, screened from exterior threats. Sailor and Lula's Thunderbird may be a convertible, but they prefer psychological structures that shield them from the outside world. In fact, for this couple, a car is enough of a world in itself. With this in mind, it is notable that Lynch shot and then discarded scenes for *Wild at Heart* in which Sailor and Lula pick up a filthy hitchhiker.[27] In the final version of the film, their vehicle remains untainted.

We should follow the scene featuring the radio reports to its conclusion, not least because it is one of the most powerful Lynch has ever produced, but also as it exemplifies how *Wild at Heart* juxtaposes the traumatic and transcendent possibilities of the American landscape. Upset by the encyclopaedia of violence on the radio, Lula leaps from the vehicle demanding music. As she leaves the car, the sunlight changes dramatically, with the glaring heat mellowing to a golden hue. Once Sailor locates on the dial the aggressive chords of the heavy metal band Powermad, the couple begin to move frantically in the desert. To borrow Nabokov's description, "glossy black dance floors" have materialized and the roadside has become a theatrical stage. A moment of distress quickly morphs into cathartic passion, as Sailor and Lula sublimate external energies into their own expressive physicality. Violent news from the outside world may not be welcome on this trip, but violent music—an abstract force, not a social reminder—fully supports the pure motion required by lovers on the road. Lynch adds one further emotion to this already potent mix. As the camera rises above their gleaming car, and with the sun now setting behind them as if time were moving at record speed, the couple's angry movements become a tender embrace. The thrashing guitars give way to the soaring strings of Strauss and the surrounding terrain, which seemed unbearably hot and harsh when accompanied by those radio reports, now has a distinctly romantic flavor. This oscillation between the atrocious and the idyllic suggests that Lula's own subjectivity is shaping the landscape, that material and psychological space have merged. The rapidly shifting emotions in this visceral scene confirm that for Lynch the American pastoral does not exist independently of our own perceptions, social intrusions or electronic interventions. This is a highly mediated landscape, another desert story guided by technology.

The Crazy World of New Orleans

Alternate eras and unexpected spaces continue to intrude into *Wild at Heart*, where Americana competes with an amalgamation of European influences. There are traces of French and British culture, while the film's soundtrack features Chris Isaak's "Blue Spanish Sky" and an instrumental piece, composed by Angelo Badalamenti and Kinny Landrum, entitled "Dark Spanish Symphony."

New Orleans is *Wild at Heart*'s most intriguing site of transatlantic exchange. The city is presented as an island of eerie European urbanism and vicious voodoo practices floating within Louisiana's dusty sprawl. It emits a sinister atmosphere, which Lynch characteristically connects to the city's intense interaction with European culture. Our protagonists' visit to what Sailor deems the "crazy world of New Orleans" begins with a spooky image of the famous balconies in the French Quarter. These intricate, wrought-iron structures are shot in haunting slow-motion, akin to Lynch's treatment of the Palmers' staircase in *Twin Peaks*. Fittingly, a fan beats away on one of the balconies, alerting us to another cycle of corruption.

Having veered away from the broad exposure of the American road, Sailor and Lula find themselves within the tight streets of a city loaded with suspicious Old World trappings. Their pursuers in New Orleans,

Marietta and Johnnie, dine at a plush French restaurant and stay at a hotel staffed by pompous Englishmen. An English, distinctly colonialist, attitude also characterizes Mr Reindeer, the puppet-master of Lynch's New Orleans, who does not feature in Gifford's original novel. Controlling *Wild at Heart*'s bizarre criminal network from a luxurious mansion, Mr Reindeer sips tea from china cups, wears a dressing gown or formal evening wear, enjoys candlelit dinners with classical music, and is waited on by servants. Sailor and Lula, in the binary fashion Lynch favors, are Ford drivers, who smoke Marlboros and impersonate Elvis. The couple are at home in New Orleans' jazz bars, with their sultry musicians and croaking clients, just as they revel in the Deep South's roadside paraphernalia. Like Guston, Roth and Venturi et al, Sailor and Lula display a predilection for blunt, bold communication. Their independent highway adventure is threatened by a conspiracy rooted in an urban center and controlled by an aristocratic European.

Mr Reindeer and his cohorts represent another exotic Lynchian network, foreshadowing *Mulholland Drive*'s sinister Hollywood conspiracy. As with many similarly complex structures that appear in Lynch's work, the network in *Wild at Heart* is established through a series of phone calls and elliptical messages, sequences in which telephones and lamps in various scattered locations are highlighted. Such complicated arrangements exist for Lynch to revel in their elaborate motions and interchanges. For an audience, the movements are both mesmerizing and confusing, evoking paranoia and the sense of a world harboring unseen connections. Associations between roads and narrative forms are again apposite here, but in the case of Lynch an entire internal highway system might be a more precise comparison. His films feel like three-dimensional, multi-lane structures full of pathways, parallel streams of traffic and tense junctions. At either end of these conspiracies, there commonly stands a blunt architectural contrast: a grand home (where a main character lives) and an isolated shack (where the trail ends). Examples of this dichotomy can be seen throughout Lynch's work: the Palmer household and the lodge in the woods in *Fire Walk With Me*; the Madison house and the desert hut in *Lost Highway*; and Nikki's Hollywood mansion and the corrugated iron shed hidden in the Polish woods in *Inland Empire*. In *Wild at Heart*, the criminal network leads from the (aptly named) Fortune household to a wooden shack in Big Tuna where Perdita Durango lives. Faced with such densely intertwined enemies, Sailor and Lula have no choice but to return to the simple lines of the American highway system.

The Build-Up in Traffic

It is a home-grown phenomenon that provides a stiffer challenge to the centrifugal movements of *Wild at Heart*: American traffic and its discontents. In the early stages of the film, Lula asks Sailor: "Have you been noticing the build-up in traffic?" A sense of impending automotive catastrophe remains palpable throughout their journey, with apocalyptic fears manifested in three major traffic incidents to be discussed in detail shortly. For Lynch, the American road network represents another mechanism where repetitive movement, like the industrial machinery of *The Elephant Man*, both hypnotizes in its motions and devastates in its malfunctioning. These faults take the form of horrendous car accidents and maddening gridlock, everyday occurrences that again spark extraordinary cinematic renditions. According to Kay, 43,000 Americans die in car crashes each year, while eight billion hours are spent stuck in traffic.[28] In *Lost Highway*, Mr Eddy has his own figures to hand when confronting an impatient driver: "Fifty fucking thousand people were killed on the highways last year because of fucking assholes like you!" Accordingly, there is a strange paradox that overshadows *Wild at Heart*'s scenes of vehicular damage and delay: these are outrageous tableaux of pain, crumpled machinery and arrested motion—moments of supreme spatial tension—but equally they represent a thoroughly banal source of injury and frustration. Thus, Lynch follows a logic laid out by J. G. Ballard, who pointed out that his novel *Crash* (1973), for all its extremities, is not actually "concerned with an imaginary disaster, however imminent, but with a pandemic cataclysm that kills hundreds of thousands of people each year and injures millions."[29] On the road, there is nothing more ordinary than a car crash. It is, Ballard's narrator notes, "almost the only way in which one can now legally take another person's life."[30]

Some observers, then, have definitely been noticing the build-up in traffic. For the car crash has proved itself to be a remarkably productive cultural trope throughout the twentieth century, serving the disparate needs of Marinetti, Musil, Warhol and Ballard.[31] As Vaughan notes, in David Cronenberg's film version of *Crash* (1996), "the car crash is a fertilising rather than destructive event." Such cataclysmic wreckage is generative in nature, spawning new associations and aesthetic forms from its mangled parts. Assemblage art, especially the sculptures of John Chamberlain, has made great use of the surplus matter and warped remains of consumer societies. Bacon's constant depiction of catastrophic bodily motion also evokes the twisted tissue of automotive disaster, with the spurting paint he incorporates being described by Deleuze as "whiplash."[32] The morphing flesh of Bacon's figures registers the impact of speed on the body, the exhilaration and annihilation that cars facilitate, prefiguring the contortions of Fred Madison at the end of *Lost Highway*. This is the physiology of the car crash.

Furthermore, one need only glance at the stark voids and jagged planes that characterize Daniel Libeskind's work or the discordant forms created by Rem Koolhaas to recognize the architectural significance of the car crash. Owen Hatherley has argued that the contemporary preference for jarring structures owes less to Derrida, whose work has conventionally underpinned architectural Deconstructivism, and more to "the roadside architecture of the 1950s." According to Hatherley, it is the production of "an instantly memorable image" to be "appreciated in movement, as from a passing car" that defines both the Googie architecture of post-war California and the recent designs of Libeskind, Koolhaas and Gehry.[33] Today's iconic structures provoke additional automotive associations: created with motion and inattention in mind, as if vision has been sacrificed to the demands of the motorcar, the forms favored by contemporary architects also resemble the deformed roadside debris of a traffic accident. Other influences are, of course, at work—for Libeskind, warfare and the Holocaust are conspicuously emphasized—but more everyday catastrophes remain unmentioned. Through Venturi, Scott Brown and Izenour, architectural theory paid its dues to roadside diners and gas stations. There has yet to be similar recognition of the inspiration provided by roadside pile-ups.

In cinema, and specifically road movies, there is a genealogy of automotive woe that travels from Godard to Lynch: the rise and fall of American cars, as well as American cinema, holds symbolic importance for both directors. *Pierrot Le Fou* presents the memorable image of a burning car dangling from a single piece of elevated highway in the French countryside—the kind of violent and absurd scenario that Lynch has often repeated (consider, for instance, how Andy is impaled on a glass table in *Lost Highway*). It is *Week End*, though, that pushed the traffic jam to extremity, in a manner that demands comparison with *Wild at Heart*. Lynch's film contains two major car accidents and one epic piece of congestion in which Godard's influence can be detected. Sailor and Lula come across the first accident as they drive through the desert at night. Initially, they are confused by a scattering of clothes across the highway.

Pulling over to the roadside, they realize it is the spillage from "one bad car accident." An over-turned vehicle is surrounded by bloody corpses with a distressed victim still wandering the scene. This young woman with some "damn sticky stuff in my hair" fusses over her lost hairbrush and wallet before finally collapsing. The episode immediately calls to mind the famous scene in *Week End*, in which a car accident provokes a bourgeois woman to wail: "My Hermès handbag!" Lynch maintains Godard's aesthetic—for both men, car crashes constitute beautifully arranged fantasies—as well as a similar line in dialogue, but removes the overt social satire. Instead, Lynch offers stranger sensations: his scene is equal parts comedy and melodrama. Sailor and Lula are visibly shaken by the misery they encounter, yet the drama is so excessive the sequence is difficult to assimilate. Godard's class commentary is caustic, but more predictable.

In *Wild at Heart*'s second accident, Lula shields her son from a nasty collision they pass in El Paso. The camera rolls past the debris of a crashed motorcycle before offering a gruesome close-up of its fallen rider. Another passer-by, himself in a wheelchair, yells: "Hey, man, same fucking thing happened to me last year." Callipers, walking sticks and skin defects appear throughout *Wild at Heart*, implying a world of widespread injury and mutilation—Ballard's "pandemic cataclysm" reaching a crescendo. The film is filled with people supported by their own architectonic props—metallic supports, crutches and false limbs. In El Paso, the everyday and the extraordinary are perfectly suspended. The motorcycle scene is disturbing (and perhaps darkly amusing) in its explicit suffering, yet it feels utterly familiar to the film's participants (Lula keeps a cigarette poised between her fingers throughout). The arrangement here is in keeping with *Week End*'s numerous crashes, but Lynch's identification with excessive emotion refutes Godard's clinical satire. McGowan puts it well, in succinct and spatial terms, when he describes the key difference between these two directors: "If Godard is a filmmaker of distance, Lynch is a filmmaker of proximity."[34] Lynch's crashes draw a spectator in; Godard's emphasize a spectator's alienation.

Week End's central sequence is a remarkable eight-minute depiction of a rural road filled with honking vehicles, where the dominance of red, white and blue machines indicates a matter of national importance for both France and the United States. This is cinema's ultimate traffic jam, the cause of which is finally revealed to be, as Sailor might put it, "one bad car accident." As with *Wild at Heart*'s crashes, though, we see only the aftermath of the catastrophe, rather than the event itself. To be precise, auto-wreckage, as well as mundane congestion, is composed into a cinematic event by both Godard and Lynch. At the conclusion of this sequence in *Week End*, the camera pauses briefly to consider the blood-splattered tarmac and the sprawling roadside victims before sweeping round to follow the film's protagonists as they continue on their journey. Cinema has to keep moving and the end of this scene allows us to indulge, in Karen Beckman's words, "in a fantasy of film as a medium without end or repetition."[35] Previously, Godard's films had depicted the joys of automotive motion, beginning with the exuberant car chases of *Breathless* (1960). *Week End*'s alienating traffic jam epitomizes a society, characterized by France's adoption of American-style consumerism, in which Godard sees no hope of progression.

What, then, should we make of *Wild at Heart*'s last scene, in which Sailor traverses dozens of cars stuck in an extensive queue before finally reaching Lula and Pace? Road movies face an inherent difficulty in ending their tales of travel, especially when such motions are often predicated on the lack of an ultimate destination. Brutal death has proved to be one popular method of curtailing the action, as demonstrated by *Bonnie and Clyde*, *Pierrot Le Fou* and *Easy Rider* (dir. Dennis Hopper, 1969). In *Wild at Heart*, Lynch halts the motions of the reel in a different manner: a traffic jam. The camera moves quickly along the congested vehicles, including one smoking wreck next to a telegraph pole, in an abbreviated version of *Week End*'s legendary sequence (Plate 37). Godard brought his cars to a standstill in the French countryside, as if to emphasize how the nation's rural arteries were becoming clogged by mindless leisure. Lynch uses the low-rise, low-density sprawl of El Paso, a city full of chain-fences, railroad trappings, pylons and warehouses, as the backdrop to his traffic jam—a stark contrast to the empty and frequently exhilarating rural landscapes of the Deep South. There are far fewer obstructions "out in the middle of it."

In fact, Lynch's roads are rarely so gridlocked. The "motorized stasis" that Kay sees as the burden of modern America is almost never depicted in Lynch's films, where the flow of movement is interrupted only by a single intrusion, such as the accident that begins *Mulholland Drive* or the road-rage incident in *Lost Highway*. In this way, Lynch's roads mimic his homes, which are invaded at a precise juncture by a specific force (for example, Bob crawling in through Laura's window in *Fire Walk With Me* or Jeffrey stealing into Dorothy's apartment in *Blue Velvet*).

Lynch's worlds, their architecture tightly constructed, are conventionally vulnerable to solitary incursions rather than collective endeavor. As noted, crowded urban scenes are also scarce in his work, so the conclusion of *Wild at Heart* represents an additionally unusual scenario. It appears to be an unashamedly happy ending, nevertheless, with Sailor and Lula reunited in the prospect of marriage—in direct contrast to Gifford's novel, which finishes with their parting.[36] Perhaps, though, there is a more ambivalent way to read Lynch's alteration. After all, Sailor and Lula's relationship is defined by sex and adventure on the road. Marriage, *Wild at Heart* suggests, comes with "motorized stasis." The question of what movements, if any, await the couple in the future remains distinctly uncertain—Lynch's camera circles them without moving forwards. The traffic jam at the end of *Wild at Heart* is the spatial rendering of a story, and a relationship, with nowhere else to go. A film that began with the image of a burning match is effectively burnt out by its final images.

America at Five Miles an Hour: *The Straight Story*

"In a way, nobody designs anything," Lynch once claimed, in a statement redolent of Frank Lloyd Wright. "All these shapes are found in nature."[37] Lynch's father was a research scientist for the federal Department of Agriculture and a desire to investigate the relationship between natural substances and man-made materials has characterized his own career—from the buzzing lights and mounds of dirt in *Eraserhead* to the taxidermy of *Twin Peaks*. Even *Dune*, with its complex interplanetary competition for energy resources, questions the extent to which humans might draw upon their natural environment, with one particular location—the Atreides imperial home—where the wooden interiors and Mayan touches owe a clear debt to Wright. Wright himself once claimed that the "land is the simplest form of architecture."[38] Similarly, Lynch refuses to draw strict distinctions between the processes of nature and the structures of the built environment. Unlike Wright, though, Lynch's most potent spaces often express a dangerous fusion of organic and inorganic elements.

As its title suggests, *The Straight Story* attends to form. The film parades the shapes of modern America, and the interactions between human design and nature. Indeed, despite critics constantly praising *The Straight*

Story's humanity—Colin Odell and Michelle Le Blanc, for example, have written: "*The Straight Story*'s Alvin is universal. He has failings but shows that humanity can triumph and that redemption is possible"—humans are the least interesting feature of the film.[39] Alvin's episodic encounters, in which he imparts folksy wisdom to young and old alike, lack the tension or excessive qualities that characterize Lynch's usual dialogue. Much more intriguing is the film's representation of Mid-Western spatial forms. In this regard, we can place *The Straight Story* in a long lineage of cinematic attempts to capture and celebrate agricultural movements, following films such as Eisenstein's *The General Line* (1929).

The geometric patterns that concern Lynch in *The Straight Story* are exemplified by one early scene. As Alvin begins his first, subsequently aborted, attempt to journey across the Mid-West, a familiar image materializes: a yellow line, inscribed on asphalt, rolls down the center of the frame. Similar close-ups of repetitive road markings previously appeared in *Blue Velvet*, *Wild at Heart* and *Lost Highway*. Here, though, the pace is noticeably slower: the line flows in a gentle fashion, as opposed to the frenetic streaming of previous versions, exposing the mottled texture of the surface. As the camera lifts and a vehicle appears on the road, an explanation emerges: we are traveling at Alvin's pace—that is, the speed of a second-hand lawn-mower, with a trailer attached, as it hugs the shoulder of the highway. To borrow a description from the film's script, this is "America at five miles an hour."[40] Lynch previously explored stasis, in the festering urban forms of *Eraserhead*, as well as unruly speed in *Wild at Heart*, but *The Straight Story* marked a new pace for his cinema.

Alvin's measured progress is not our only concern, however. During the scene in question, the camera continues to rise, revealing that this simple two-lane road runs directly through rows of corn and green verges, in perfect accord with its surroundings. Telegraph poles line the route until the horizon provides a perpendicular counterpoint, against a backdrop of distant trees. The abrasive settings of *Wild at Heart*—hot and sexy, discordant and ready to overflow at any point—have been superseded by a gentle American landscape in which each element is calmly delineated. The escalating image extends skyward, before pausing on some cosy clouds lit by soft sunshine. Eventually, we are smoothly lowered to see Alvin's slow motions through the lines and angles that shape this tale (Plate 38). The American road, the scene emphasizes, must be considered within a broader spatial context. The harmonious framework of demarcations we are presented with seem to affirm Wright's claim that the "land is the simplest form of architecture."

The Straight Story, then, is a very different kind of road movie, not least because this cheerful tale contradicts a genre dominated by dystopian views of America.[41] Whereas, in *Wild at Heart*, Sailor and Lula set off with only the vague idea of heading west, Alvin has a single-minded mission: to visit his sick brother Lyle, by traveling east from Laurens, Iowa to Mount Zion, Wisconsin—a distance of over three hundred miles. While the juvenile exuberance of *Wild at Heart* remains utterly in keeping with the traditions of the road movie—from *It Happened One Night* (dir. Frank Capra, 1934) to *Natural Born Killers* (dir. Oliver Stone, 1994), this is a genre that has associated movement with youth—*The Straight Story* is based on the real-life journey of a seventy-three-year-old man perched upon a thirty-year-old lawn-mower. The elderly are not barred from the road movie—a final journey can be the catalyst for self-reflection, as in Bergman's *Wild Strawberries* (1957)—but a lack of "giddy exhilaration" does engender alternate forms of architecture. In *The Straight Story*, there are no seedy motels, perky gas stations or neon signs. Such hyperactive "roadside eclecticism" is replaced by a quiet succession of small towns, farming apparatus and immense landscapes. As Robert Fish explains, cinema's close relationship to urban space, in terms of both production and exhibition, has often led to filmic implications that "the countryside is outside of, and lost to, modernity."[42] Yet, the rural scenery of *The Straight Story* emphasizes modern architectonic practices. Indeed, the Mid-West's division into agricultural grids, transportation routes and communication networks confirms that, above all, America's spatial history constitutes a straight story. As a character in Don DeLillo's *Americana* (1971), another tale of travel across the nation, concludes: "It's what we are. Straight lines and right angles."[43]

Flyover States

Alvin Straight is a quintessentially American traveler. Lynch describes him as "a lot like a cowboy" and his protagonist displays a stubborn self-reliance recalling the classic images of frontier riders.[44] Alvin is familiar with the road, too. Although we learn only fragments about his past, he does confess: "I've been traveling most of my life." Consequently, if we were to share Lawrence's suspicions about American travel, we might wonder what it is that Alvin has been trying "to get *away*" from for so long. The question of Alvin's past has promoted at least one speculative take on *The Straight Story*, with Tim Kreider and Rob Content arguing: "This movie is about how a mean drunk named Alvin Straight lost his daughter's children to the state because he let one of them get burned in a fire."[45]

Certainly, Alvin's belligerence emerges when the topic of public transport is raised: "I don't like someone else driving the bus," he complains. Instead, he prefers to assemble his own vehicle and shelter with a blowtorch and a saw. Both Alvin, and his daughter, Rose, who builds bird houses, employ the kind of independent craftsmanship that deeply appeals to Lynch, who has often constructed his own sets and continues to make furniture. There is a raw, highly personal feel to many of Lynch's home-made interiors, especially Henry's apartment in *Eraserhead* and the multiple rooms of *Inland Empire*. The director admits, "I'm such a frustrated shed builder!"[46]

Again, though, Alvin's American ingenuity feels infused with a European antecedent. Specifically, Lynch has outlined his admiration for Fellini's *La Strada* (1954)—"one of my favorite films!" he claims—in which a motorcycle and makeshift trailer tour rural Italy.[47] *La Strada* and *The Straight Story* are road movies where home, in its most humble form, is towed along for the ride. They are also, *contra* Virilio, automotive audiovisual feasts without a windshield in sight. In Lynch's case, his camera is freed by the absence of a car's structuring frame. Whereas *Wild at Heart* focused on Sailor and Lula within the borders of their vehicle, *The Straight Story* is distinguished by spiraling aerial images, shot from a helicopter, of the Mid-Western landscape. Lacking a windshield and the contours it provides, *The Straight Story* does not maintain the suffocating intensity of other Lynchian worlds. The stifling socio-spatial boundaries that characterize many of the director's most fraught environments are absent. Instead, *The Straight Story* features borders between fields, roads, homes and industry that are neatly, though never excessively, ordered— thresholds that peacefully exist without threat of disturbance. Social relations in the film are, accordingly, also harmonious.

In addition to Alvin's unusual mode of transport, *The Straight Story* is attentive to other methods of American travel. In the course of his trip, Alvin encounters roaring lorries, a coach filled with ageing tourists, a break-down truck, a pregnant hitchhiker, a fleet of competing cyclists, a commuting car and a tractor. It is the unseen helicopter, however, that is the real star of the film, enabling shots that highlight the geometry of the landscape, the demarcations of agriculture and the textures of autumnal processes. The horizontal expanses of Iowa's cornfields are tilted into surprising formations. Yet, Lynch's utilization of numerous aerial shots holds a neat irony. The dismissive term "flyover states," which describes those American regions often seen from a plane traveling between the East and West Coasts, includes the fields and farms of Iowa and Wisconsin that Lynch's camera also flies over.[48] These are the vast spaces Hitchcock imbued with such terror during the crop-dusting sequence in *North by Northwest* (1959). Lynch is aware of the potential for nervous isolation in a region where, as he points out, there are only a few farmers "and a great amount of land."[49] Moreover, natural forms in his work are often imbued with either a sense of abjection, in the manner of *Eraserhead*'s mounds, or palpable terror, exemplified by the woods in *Twin Peaks*. Despite the airborne perspective, however, there is little hint of arrogance or anxiety in Lynch's presentation of the Mid-West. We hear of such unfashionable locales as Des Moines, West Union, Hawkeye, Mason City and Prairie du Chien, yet the towns and the surrounding landscape depicted are much more welcoming than the sweltering shacks and barren sprawl of *Wild at Heart*. In fact, Alvin's journey is best appreciated from the air, admired for the scale of its ambition and the beauty of its setting, rather than the banal homilies it frequently provokes at ground level.

Mirroring Alvin's slow motions—fittingly, his doctor warns him about "circulation problems"—*The Straight Story* travels at a pace that promotes deliberate contemplation of Mid-Western landmarks. "It's an amazing thing what you can see when you're sitting," says Alvin. Sure enough, from a secure cinematic seat, we encounter within *The Straight Story* a more diverse series of architectural forms than we might expect. The town of Laurens, where the film begins, features a traditional American main street filled with family stores alongside rows of wooden-framed houses. These rather unremarkable features are overlooked by an enormous water tower emblazoned with the town's name (a Pop monument reminiscent of Archigram's imaginings) and the hulking cylinders of a grain elevator (the stuff of Le Corbusier's dreams). We might also note how Laurens differs from Lumberton in that no fences divide neighbors here. The shared plots indicate a society less obsessed with social division.

The grain elevator, located right at the heart of Laurens, deserves particular attention, as an example of a typology that holds a critical place in architectural history. Such giant American vessels, with their pure forms, rippling façades and enormous storage capacities, provoked great excitement among European observers. In *Towards a New Architecture*, Le Corbusier declared America's grain elevators to be "*the magnificent FIRST-FRUITS of the new age*" amid several bold images of industrial sheds.[50] In 1924, Erich Mendelsohn visited cavernous granaries in upstate New York and was moved to recall: "Everything else so far now seemed to have been shaped interim to my silo dreams, everything else was merely a beginning."[51] Banham, in outlining the impact of American industrial forms on European modernism, criticizes the absence of such structures from architectural history. Americans, Banham states, owe silos and factories "the same degree of respect they award other native arts that have affected the rest of the world, such as the Hollywood film, dance theatre, and jazz."[52] Just as Venturi, Scott Brown and Izenour attributed considerable value to the hot-dog stands and neon signage along America's roads, Banham considered grain elevators worthy of more rigorous attention.

In *The Straight Story*, Lynch exhibits a similar reverence towards the Mid-West's grain elevators and combine harvesters (Plate 39). He shares with Le Corbusier, Mendelsohn and Banham a deep respect for the aesthetics of industry. Indeed, one nocturnal shot of a large loft suggests Lynch too maintains "silo dreams." A sense of the sublime permeates *The Straight Story*'s numerous images of agricultural processes, as machines (we rarely see their human drivers) force the landscape into grids, channels and productive units. At a John Deere dealership, Lynch lingers on an array of shimmering machines ready for action. Such images confirm that the real designers of the Mid-West, forming shapes that seem to be "natural," are these mechanized instruments of human will. American land is not quite the simple form of architecture that Wright suggested; it is as structured and planned as the American highway system. With their streamlined forms, *The Straight Story*'s industrial structures also maintain a futuristic resonance. Alas, they are not so much "*magnificent FIRST-FRUITS of the new age*," as stubborn remnants of past utopian aspirations. For *The Straight Story* is filled with reminders of death and ageing. As well as his own declining health and his brother's hospitalization, Alvin also meets a coach party of elderly women, rests in an old cemetery and discusses the victims of war. Decay is always of interest to Lynch and *The Straight Story* suggests we are witnessing a region in permanent decline—another industrial zone where reproduction has faltered.

Nonetheless, Lynch continues to uncover the Mid-West's most intriguing feats of engineering. He briefly captures the Grotto of the Redemption in West Bend, Iowa (Plate 40). Begun in 1912 by a German-born priest and architect, and subsequently constructed over half a century, this assemblage of precious stones and minerals forms a series of paths and archways depicting biblical scenes. It looks like a vast mythical city, another ruined monument in the region. That Alvin passes by the Grotto, a feat of patience to surpass his own epic journey, adds further Christian iconography to a film already laden with religious themes (such as redemption and pilgrimage). Indeed, Alvin himself describes his brotherly estrangement as "a story old as the Bible." It remains architecture, though, that provides Alvin with his most divine moments. Sheltering in a barn while it rains, Alvin enjoys a moment of grace. Later, when crossing the Black Hawk Bridge from Iowa into Wisconsin, he is awed by the cantilevered structure looming over the Mississippi. There is a tangible harmony between him, his primitive vehicle, the magnificent bridge and the mighty river below. Furthermore, the bridge's latticed iron framework rhymes with the regular crop patterns and asphalt geometry seen elsewhere in the film. Alvin's language is peppered with admiration for nature ("the sky is sure full of stars tonight"), as well as quasi-religious agricultural metaphors ("I know to separate the wheat from the chaff"), yet it is mechanical processes, from lawn-mowers to grain elevators, that envelop his journey. For all its apparent engagement with the natural landscape, *The Straight Story* demonstrates how man and machinery have comprehensively conquered American space. Alvin's heartiest meal, we should note, is a deer killed by a motorist.

The incident involving the deer represents the first of two occasions when one of Lynch's trademark interruptions threatens to disturb Alvin's slow motions. While the camera focuses on Alvin's agitated response, we hear a car horn, the skid of brakes and a metallic thud. Lynch delays revelation of the accident for a short while longer, until finally we are presented with the outcome of those ominous sounds: a dented car and a dead deer. In *Wild at Heart*, this kind of scenario provoked Lynch into assembling outrageous scenes of pain and destruction. Here, though, the camera is much more restrained, even respectful, and resists the opportunity to create a gruesome tableau. The woman's angry yet comic response is more typical of Lynch's work—"I have hit thirteen deer in seven weeks driving down this road, mister [...] and I *love* deer!"—but Alvin's subsequent meal, when he turns his back on some model animals as he barbeques venison, pivots on easy sentimentality. One longs for Frank Booth, Mr Eddy or a Reindeer-led conspiracy to inject some life into these gentle events. Moreover, the real-life Alvin Straight caused "a massive traffic jam" in New Hampton, Iowa during the course of his trip, yet Lynch chose to ignore such ripe material in favor of more docile motions and emotions.[53]

Similarly, the sequence following the deer incident has the potential to be a classic Lynchian scenario. We initially see a burning house—an image that features in both *Wild at Heart* and *Lost Highway* as a symbol of domestic torment—which is quickly revealed to be a controlled exercise for firemen, and a spectacle for the locals, who sit watching with snacks as if at the movies. We could, perhaps, see the blaze as a reflection of the destructive flames that continue to rage within the Straight family. Indeed, Kreider and Content use the burning house, which remains framed in the background as Alvin recovers from his speedy ordeal, as evidence that the fire that injured his grandson continues to haunt him.[54] Alvin himself approaches the scene at unusual speed because his brakes have failed on the sharp incline into the town. The shots of his unstoppable lawn-mower tearing down the hill, with the asphalt beneath and the adjacent landscape blurring, are the only instant of "giddy exhilaration" in the film. When machinery malfunctions, Lynch's cinematic instincts peak. The incident is soon brought to a sudden and safe conclusion, however, and precipitates further opportunities for Alvin to dispense sentimental advice to those around him. In fact, Alvin's folksy wisdom seems to contradict everything interesting Lynch has offered about family life and social relations in the past. Notably, this is the only one of his feature films in which Lynch is not credited as a writer.

"A road," Lynch claims, "is a moving forward into the unknown, and that's compelling to me." He continues, with a pertinent comparison: "That's also what films are—the lights go down, the curtain opens and away we go, but we don't know where we're going."[55] *The Straight Story* never generates such uncertainty, the enveloping tension that characterizes Lynch's most successful cinematic journeys. There is a rare moment of doubt at the film's conclusion, as Alvin's long trip reaches its final destination—another isolated shack at the end of Lynch's narrative trails. Lyle's home is a simple wooden structure that fulfills Bachelard's innocent hopes ("A hermit's hut. What a subject for an engraving!") and provokes a sense of timeless American dwelling. Upon reaching the house, Alvin calls out, but no greeting is returned. Instead, the camera zooms in on an empty chair on the porch, intimating that Alvin has arrived too late to see the stroke-afflicted Lyle. However, this instant of anxiety is relieved by Lyle's sudden shout and the brothers are reconciled in a reserved fashion. Critics have almost universally praised this ending, with Odell and Le Blanc describing it as "unbearably moving."[56] It is certainly appropriate for a film that has privileged the understated; the excessive emotion Lynch conjures in *Twin Peaks* and *Mulholland Drive*, not to mention *Wild at Heart*, would clearly be misplaced here. Indeed, perhaps *The Straight Story* is best read in binary opposition to *Wild at Heart*: the barren landscapes of the Deep South becoming the fertile fields of the Mid-West; dizzying speed becoming contemplative slowness; youth replaced by age; mother–daughter strife replaced by a new element in Lynch's representation of family life: underlying affection.

Still, for all its thematic and emotional consistency, *The Straight Story*'s ending confirms why the film represents a minor addition to Lynch's canon. The Mid-Western landscape is again beautifully depicted in the scene, but Lynch's best films thrive on spatial tension, strange juxtapositions and uncertain borders. Here, there are no reverberations within the image and few challenges to conventional thinking. Unlike *Fire Walk With Me*, this is a lodge in the woods without disturbing connotations. Lynch's roads, at their most compelling, move forward "into the unknown." The slow motions and restrained emotions of *The Straight Story* are, by contrast, a cinematic dead end.

4 STAGE

I liked looking on at other people in crucial situations.
SYLVIA PLATH, *THE BELL JAR* (1963)[1]

The Enclosures of Modernity

The twentieth century can be mapped out in stages, literally. Platforms, arenas and rostrums—spaces that have been delineated and elevated—have dominated modern political and cultural life. From the Nuremberg rallies to the Nuremberg trials, from the Iron Curtain to the launch-pad, a proliferation of orchestrated oratory and stage-management has enveloped the world. Through Loos' domestic theaters, Le Corbusier's pilotis and Wright's Fallingwater to Brutalist walkways, streets in the sky and highway interchanges, modern architectural forms have also exhibited a fascination with decks, ramps and dramatic podiums. Moreover, from Bacon's fraught frames to the rise of installation art, and from the crooked rooms of German Expressionism to the eerie zone of Tarkovsky's *Stalker* (1979), artists and film-makers have created their own meticulous stages for scripted performance and immersive experience. As Heidegger famously noted at the mid-point of the century, "A boundary is not that at which something stops but, as the Greeks recognised, the boundary is that from which something *begins its presencing*." Once a structuring line appears, unplanned action becomes possible; new modes of being emerge. Whether defined by curtains or concrete, the enclosures of modernity are not neutral locales. Rather, their borders, deliberately made visible, generate a certain notion of space. In Heidegger's words, "Space is in essence that for which room has been made, that which is let into its bounds."[2]

The work of David Lynch is characterized by a succession of formal stages. His films make room for delineated space to create a struggle between the contained and the unlimited, the anxieties of claustrophobia versus the threats of boundlessness. His stages offer, paradoxically, a form of restricted infinity—they are sharply structured environments in which anything appears possible. His cinema is filled with viewing platforms, such as Merrick's theater box in *The Elephant Man*, and carefully choreographed performances, like Dorothy's show at the Slow Club in *Blue Velvet* or Betty's audition at Paramount Studios in *Mulholland Drive*. These arenas are built and filmed in anticipation of something essential beginning—a transformation, a confrontation or a revelation. Stages occupy a privileged position in his architecture, often existing within a central chamber at the heart of the film, as the patterned podium in *Eraserhead* demonstrates. The defining features of these spaces— thick curtains, raised platforms and compelling music—have become emblematic of Lynch's work as a whole. Indeed, as they provoke multiple associations and often devastating affect, it is these complex spaces that most explicitly display Lynch's engagement with the designs of the twentieth century. It is to Lynch's variety of stages, the spatial tensions they house, and their connections with a range of architectural and artistic forms that this chapter will attend. Initially, the focus will extend across his career, to consider the numerous clubs, theaters, cinemas and studio sets that litter his films, before a final section that deals exclusively with his most distinctive stage of all: the Red Room in *Twin Peaks*.

Some guidance is essential, however, before we navigate this tricky terrain. Although Lynch's stages are impossible to ignore, critics have struggled to define them, in a manner that suggests no single term or context can (or should) fully explain these spaces. There is yet to be a comprehensive survey of their status, though Chion does highlight the theater as a distinctive Lynchian setting, "a world which, although placed under the enchanted auspices of the night, can be controlled."[3] This not only emphasizes the nocturnal aspect of the spaces under examination; it also recognizes the tension, which underpins all Lynch's stages, between uninhibited actions and closely directed performance. Ultimately, we must consider whose hand is pulling the strings and to what end. Žižek, moreover, talks of "a series of hellish places in Lynch's films, places in which one encounters the final (not truth but) fantasmatic lie."[4] This again underlines how mechanisms of illusion are explicitly in play here, although it negates the heavenly aspect of Lynch's stages: these are platforms of pleasure, as well as pain. McGowan reminds us of our own position as spectators in these scenarios: "To watch a David Lynch film properly is to touch the screen, to find oneself bereft of the safe distance that the very architecture of the cinema seems to promise."[5] Thus, Lynch's on-screen stages, which heavily depend upon cinematic features, such as thick curtains, intense darkness and shafts of light, bleed into the conventional surroundings of the movie theater. The boundaries between the screen and the audience, and between communal experience and individual subjectivity, are placed in question. Chion suggests that the audience shares with Lynch's characters doubts and urges provoked by the spectacle. When watching these stage shows, "we cannot content ourselves with remaining spectators. Sooner or later, we have to go up there ourselves."[6] Performance, then, is key to these worlds. Another important boundary emerges here, too. As the protagonist of Kafka's *Amerika* (1927) learns when he comes across a theater company, one world exists on the stage, but there is "quite a different world on the other side of the curtain."[7]

Kafka is also a frequent reference for Deleuze in his analysis of Francis Bacon's work, notably when he equates "the ring, the amphitheatre, [and] the platform" that the painter employs with "the theatre of Oklahoma" in *Amerika*.[8] As our prior investigation into Lynch's homes demonstrated, these three figures—Kafka, Bacon and Lynch—share an approach to architecture in which perilous performance is a vital factor. In particular, Bacon's predilection for platforms contained within geometric frames or flowing drapes is a critical influence on Lynch's cinematic stages. Bacon's work combines a fascination with public spectacle and political power—oratorical apparatus, such as microphones and rostrums, regularly appears in his paintings—with an interest in Greek theater. His images also maintain a vision of private activity, especially sex, as an additional arena for performance. Like Lynch's films, Bacon's paintings continually make room for places of enactment.

Furthermore, Lynch inherits from Bacon a tension between the narrative and non-narrative elements of an image. Bacon was adamant that he wanted to avoid any narrative significance or symbolism being attached to his work: "the moment the story is elaborated," he explained, "the boredom sets in; the story talks louder than the paint."[9] This is not dissimilar to Lynch's notorious reluctance to attach specific meanings to his films. Bacon was determined to disrupt thoroughly the traditions of pictorial narrative by using frames that would isolate his figures. Despite their apparent confinement, these bodies are, in some respects, liberated from a broader context: they constitute pure movement or visceral emotion. In this way, a space beyond narrative begins to make its presence felt at the painting's internal boundaries. Of course, Bacon's framing devices often produce the opposite response, adding a mysterious element to the drama that increases narrative tension and raises political or historical associations. In cinema, the demand for a coherent narrative is even stronger. Yet, Lynch's stages stand apart for their refusal to be included in conventional narrative design. To a significant extent, arenas like Club Silencio and the Red Room exist independently of their narrative surroundings. These are isolated sequences within the larger frame of a film or a television series, where Lynch feels liberated to express concentrated bursts of emotion. That is not to say they are solely aesthetic experiences, void of wider narrative significance, but they are distinct interruptions into the flow of events around them.

In this regard, we might view Lynch's stages and the performances they host in the context of the spaces seen in post-war art. As Nieland points out, Lynch began his studies at the Pennsylvania Academy of the Fine Arts in Philadelphia in 1965 during an era when American artists were developing new modes of aesthetic production. These included the staging of semi-improvised events or "Happenings," the creation of three-dimensional spaces for a visitor to explore, and other multimedia experiments.[10] Lynch's stages hold much in common with the environments, situations, spaces and installations—to use the categories Julie H. Reiss uses to define installation art—which have moved from the margins to the center of the art world over the last fifty years.[11] Indeed, locations such as Club Silencio or the Red Room feel like works of installation art inserted into the framework of a film. Contemporary artists have reciprocated this gesture. The Polish-born, US-based artist Christian Tomaszewski, for instance, has created a series of works inspired by the sets of *Blue Velvet*, such as *On Chapels, Caves and Erotic Misery* (2006), a large-scale installation involving architectural elements from Lynch's film in various sizes and forms (including Dorothy's closet and kitchen, the corridor in Deep River Apartments, and the Lumberton town billboard) all housed within a cardboard and MDF structure that visitors can traverse (Plates 41 and 42). More recently, Tomaszewski created *ERASED* (2012), a video installation featuring footage from *Blue Velvet* with the actors and dialogue removed, so that architecture becomes the work's central character. Furthermore, Philippe Parreno constructed a billboard saying "Welcome to Twin Peaks" to greet visitors entering the labyrinthine spaces of the seminal group exhibition *No Man's Time* in Nice in 1991.

All of which leads us to an additional, and suitably open, source of theoretical illumination. Michel Foucault's suggestive and much debated piece "Of Other Spaces," based on a 1967 lecture but first published in English in 1986, has developed particular resonance in architectural circles, especially for its emphasis on complexity and difference. Foucault is attracted to certain sites "that have the curious property of being in relation with all the other sites, but in such a way as to suspect, neutralize, or invert the set of relations that they happen to designate, mirror, or reflect." These are places that maintain links with their surroundings, yet at the same time contradict or complicate them. Similarly, the spaces examined in this chapter cut across the symbolic locations that form the crux of Lynch's cinematic worlds. Lynch's stages are not wholly independent of the towns, cities, homes and roads previously discussed—Club Silencio, for instance, is part of downtown Los Angeles, and the theater in *Eraserhead* is found within a domestic radiator—but they do maintain a distinct atmosphere challenging the world outside them. In this respect, they call to mind the "heterotopias" that Foucault identifies. Heterotopias, Foucault proposes, are "counter-sites" that remain "outside of all places, even though it may be possible to indicate their location in reality."[12] This is a useful statement to consider when we enter one of Lynch's immersive theatrical arenas. Suddenly, our broader bearings are confused, conventional geography is scrambled and a new spatial logic emerges.

For Foucault, heterotopias maintain the ability to juxtapose "in a single real place several spaces, several sites that are in themselves incompatible."[13] It is this characteristic that has led other critics, notably Antony Easthope and David Harvey, to cite heterotopias when discussing *Blue Velvet*.[14] Lumberton, as we have seen, exemplifies the coexistence of sharply differing spaces within one Lynchian world. Given the diverse spaces and binary oppositions present within each of his locations, it is thus tempting to label all Lynch's cinematic worlds as heterotopias. Boris Groys adopts this position, suggesting Lynch's films maintain "a space that outwardly resembles American reality" but which also prompts "a feeling of having been displaced to a different, parallel space."[15]

However, a more precise association between heterotopias and Lynch's stages emerges when we consider Foucault's examples of spaces housing incompatible sites. Foucault highlights the theater (where a series of different places share the same stage) and the cinema (where three-dimensional spaces are projected onto a two-dimensional screen) as typifying a heterotopia's ability to hold contradictory impulses. As this chapter will argue, the spatial possibilities of both the theater and the cinema are continually exploited by Lynch. Moreover, Foucault explains that heterotopias, despite their status "outside of all places," also retain a functional affiliation with other spaces. There are two polarities within this relationship, both of which have implications for Lynch's stages. First, Foucault suggests heterotopias function as "a space of illusion that exposes every real space"—the role played by Club Silencio in exposing Diane Selwyn's Hollywood fantasies in *Mulholland Drive*. Indeed, the sense that a fundamental encounter is taking place, that something revelatory is occurring, is common to Lynch's stages. Second, Foucault states that heterotopias may act as spaces of compensation, in creating an environment that is as "meticulous" as our world is "messy, ill constructed, and jumbled."[16] Perhaps, the eerie order of *Twin Peaks'* Red Room might, in this light, be seen as compensation for the chaotic relations in the rest of the town. Indeed, we might read all of Lynch's stages as artistic compensation for the messy and jumbled world of film production, with its boundaries, limitations and compromises.

It Is Happening Again:
The Perils of Performance

Where do Lynch's characters, living such tense lives, find pleasure? What forms of entertainment do they seek out? They head straight to places where, like Sylvia Plath's heroine in *The Bell Jar*, they like to look on "at other people in crucial situations." These range from circuses and nightclubs to movie theaters and studio sets. What unites them is performance, usually by women, in a semi-public arena. Yet, how should we approach these spaces? For these are neither private nor wholly public sites. Rather, they necessitate a somewhat oblique approach. If classical notions of public space emphasize comprehensive access, then entrance to Lynch's communal yet isolated stages is more complex. Here, Foucault's definition of the heterotopia is again prescient, specifically how these spaces "always presuppose a system of opening and closing that both isolates them and makes them penetrable." This is true of Lynch's stages, which are theoretically open to all, but which remain somewhat concealed. Thus, to enter a heterotopia, as Foucault explains, "one must have a certain permission and make certain gestures."[17]

These strange locations have links with conventional amusements, as *The Elephant Man* reveals. Lynch's second film provides three preliminary examples—the circus, the pub and the theater—that develop into more intriguing scenarios later in his work. Lynch's vision of Victorian London begins with the patterns and sounds of a circus. Amid the fireworks and crowds, Frederick Treves stands out in his elegant clothing and self-assured manner. He is clearly our guide to this disorientating terrain, the figure who shares our appetite for spectacular and sordid sights. In fact, the men who navigate Lynch's stages, such as Treves, Jeffrey Beaumont and Dale Cooper, continue to maintain a certain distance from the spectacle. They are allowed to roam, even to participate occasionally, but they are rarely fully exposed. Lynch's female explorers, like Laura Palmer, Betty Elms or Nikki Grace, have a much more intimate relationship with the stage: they must perform, as well as observe.

The circus offers Treves many opportunities for entertainment, from fairground rides to animal shows, yet the doctor is drawn to the tent advertising freaks. Ignoring the "No Entry" sign above its curtained entrance, he crosses into a world of exhibits displayed within canvas-lined passageways—a labyrinthine architecture that resembles the final forms of the Red Room in *Twin Peaks*. Treves' social position, his bourgeois confidence, is permission enough to penetrate this multiplex of forbidden pleasure. The displays include a bearded lady and a deformed fetus in a jar, aberrant forms that both remind us of *Eraserhead*'s grotesque baby and anticipate the arrival of John Merrick. The obvious cinematic antecedent here is *Freaks* (dir. Tod Browning, 1932), especially when Lynch highlights the camaraderie among circus performers. Moreover, the circus allows Lynch to unite the voyeuristic clamor of Victorian society, Treves' intense curiosity (which his medical interests fail to justify), and our own appetite for sensational images. *The Elephant Man* immediately emphasizes the power of spectatorship, especially in terms of the human body—a theme that constantly returns in Lynch's stages. Here, it is inferred that the Victorian freak show, where abnormalities are paraded for pleasure and profit, is a precursor to cinematic logic. The circus briefly returns to Lynch's cinema in *Inland Empire*, in scenes filmed with the famous Cyrk Zalewski in Poland. Once again, it is portrayed as a European phenomenon, a spooky form of Old World entertainment with a hypnotic undertone that foreshadows the experience of cinema. For Lynch, film maintains the spirit of archaic forms, past devices and historic attractions.

The circus in *The Elephant Man* is an explicitly working-class environment, as is the public house. The pub's cramped, noisy conditions, with a curtain leading into the main bar, pre-empt the decadent clubs of *Wild at Heart* and *Fire Walk With Me*. There is also a portent of future performances in the porter's routine, as he publicizes Merrick's whereabouts to the pub's customers. Such public recitals have several cinematic functions. They allow news to spread speedily among many characters and are an indirect method of informing the audience of plot developments. They also enable us to see how a particular community responds to an incident, as demonstrated by the recurrent meetings, funerals and parties in *Twin Peaks* and the climactic rally (with its echoes of Nuremberg) in *Dune*. In *The Elephant Man*, the circus and the pub are directly contrasted with sedate bourgeois pursuits, such as afternoon tea and the theater. Towards the end of the film, Merrick is taken to a performance of *Puss in Boots* and is enraptured by the spectacle, a further display of Victorian design excess. In a hint of later interactions in Lynch's work between the stage and the audience, Merrick's presence in the theater is announced and attention turns to his position in the theater box. That the auditorium's architecture holds the potential for disturbing reversal is plain to see. Unlike later scenarios, however, *The Elephant Man* is content to resist the traumatic potency of the occasion. There is no danger or vibrancy in this scene, only a sentimental flourish.

In fact, the scene in *The Elephant Man* that most strongly prefigures the rest of Lynch's stages takes place in a lecture theater. Treves presents Merrick to his medical colleagues, acting as a master of ceremonies, but Lynch withholds a clear perspective on the latter's deformities. Instead, he is depicted in silhouette only while housed within a portable curtained arena (Figure 4.1). Lynch makes us wait until thirty minutes into *The Elephant Man* to have a clear view of Merrick, a delay that creates greater self-consciousness regarding the act of spectatorship. In concluding the lecture sequence with a close-up of the mechanical lighting used in the spectacle, Lynch ensures cinematic practices are again placed in a wider history of theatrical performance.

The communal pleasures of the Victorian circus, pub and theater are transformed by Lynch in his depiction of modern American entertainment. Indeed, to adapt Groys' argument, Lynch's bars and clubs outwardly resemble American reality, but also bring to mind "a feeling of having been displaced to a different, parallel space." Music is a critical feature of these settings, through an unusual combination of 1950s pop,

FIGURE 4.1 *The Elephant Man*: Merrick displayed in the lecture theater.
Credit: *The Elephant Man* (dir. David Lynch, 1980), © Brooksfilms.

heavy metal and jazz. In *Wild at Heart*, Sailor and Lula are part of a crowd furiously dancing to the band Powermad, as red strobe lighting flashes across the scene. Suddenly, Sailor takes control of the entire atmosphere of the club. First, he halts the band to confront a rival. Then, in victory, he croons an Elvis song against a backdrop of artificial screams. This fantasmatic scene moves from raw guitars to bubble-gum pop without a pause. The crowd in the club accepts the radical changes in mood and music, while the distance between the stage and the dance floor, and between those who perform and those who observe, shrinks. Through a series of rapid musical switches, this single cinematic space fluctuates violently, allowing it to play host to seemingly incompatible emotions.

Jazz defines the intense club scene in *Lost Highway*. At the Luna Lounge—announced by a neon sign streamlined like a 1950s car or movie theater—Fred Madison plays a frenzied saxophone solo. Here, the strobe lighting is white, the curtains are black and the music is extraordinarily loud, reaching a level at which volume holds its own logic. Just as Lynch's rooms are characterized by sharp light and deep darkness, his soundscapes, especially in *Lost Highway*, oscillate between low-pitched humming and concentrated bursts of immersive noise. Lynch pays close attention to music because our experience of cinematic space is dependent on aural, as well as visual, elements. To emphasize this, *Fire Walk With Me* features a nightclub scene dominated by the pulsating groove of the band on stage. Indeed, the music here is so loud the film's dialogue is impossible to comprehend without the subtitles provided. Thanks to the pounding music, the club feels like a secret world of debauchery, in which Laura Palmer performs excessive teenage rebellion. Beams of red light, some streaming through a hole in the ceiling, add to the theatrical, highly sexual atmosphere; clothes are shed as if, in the words of Jacques Renault, "there's no tomorrow." Furthermore, when we inhabit the perspective of a drugged Donna, the room warps and sways alarmingly. The scene finishes with a brilliant tracking shot of the dance floor covered in smoldering cigarettes and empty beer bottles: the aftermath of uninhibited pleasure.

Fred's jazz solo in *Lost Highway* is a rare example of a man performing upon one of Lynch's highly gendered stages. Habitually, the director prefers female club performances. In *Blue Velvet*, we are taken to the Slow Club, sign-posted in pink neon below glowing antlers. Inside this single-story roadside dive, the atmosphere is almost cosy, with an array of age groups enjoying beer and music. Given the surroundings, Dorothy's glamorous act feels utterly incongruous, just as she herself seems out of place in Lumberton. Introduced as "the blue lady," she is joined by an all-male backing band (including Angelo Badalamenti on piano) and performs, with an outmoded microphone, in front of deep-red curtains and kinks of blue neon (Plate 43). Her appearance is remarkably similar to that of Yvonne Marquis in Kenneth Anger's film *Puce Moment* (1949), a short tribute to Hollywood glamor laced with the sadness and unease that characterizes Anger's work. What is it, though, about the stage design at the Slow Club, repeated with subtle variations throughout his cinema, that so appeals to Lynch?

Perhaps the most crucial element is the curtains, which have become an intrinsic part of Lynch's architecture. Like Loos and Neutra, Lynch has continually exploited the architectural qualities of drapery. In fact, curtains remain a somewhat forgotten element of modernism, their ability to generate sensual, ambiguous structures often neglected amid the white walls and pilotis. Mies van der Rohe, for example, is famed for his steel and glass curtain walls, but thick drapery lined the interiors of the Barcelona Pavilion, Farnsworth House in Illinois and the Neue Nationalgalerie in Berlin. As Lynch's stages confirm, the presence of such curtains signifies that something vital is about to take place. They are a symbolic gesture to attract attention and to imbue the impending performance with an alluring edge. They provide a partition that can be penetrated, unlike walls of glass or steel, but, as well as being an entrance, Lynch's curtains also act as a boundary, in Heidegger's terms, "from which something *begins its presencing*." Tensions are generated by the mere appearance of such borders. Curtains create a pressurized divide—between what we see in front (the performance) and what occurs behind (backstage, where illusion is manufactured, is "a different world," as Kafka wrote). Sometimes, as *The Wizard of Oz* reveals, drapery shields us from the paucity of the puppet-master. Moreover, the curtain also contains hidden spaces within itself, elaborate folds and recesses implying depth, concealment and even boundlessness. A curtain is never fully exposed to us: it maintains a rippled disposition and refuses to settle. Here, architectural meaning is simultaneously created, obscured and deflected. It provokes, like the frames of Bacon's paintings, a tension between narrative and non-narrative elements. In the Red Room in *Twin Peaks*, Lynch's ultimate curtained arena, the entire space is defined by flowing walls of red velvet, so that veiled meaning forms the very material of this uncertain zone. Thus, curtains may possess an impurity antithetical to narrow conceptions of modernism, yet as a structural expression they speak as frankly of their function as a framework of exposed steel.

Lynch, of course, grew up in the age of the Iron Curtain. Reverberations from this most symbolic post-war partition can be felt throughout his work, which is structured around the kinks, slippages and deferred meanings generated by apparently indestructible divides. Yet, before international relations were split between melodramatic realms of good and evil (or White and Black Lodges, to adopt the terms of *Twin Peaks*), the iron curtain was itself a theatrical device—a metal sheet designed to stop fires spreading throughout theaters. Rather neatly, the first location to fit this (ultimately unsuccessful) safety measure was the Theatre Royal, Drury Lane, where Joseph Merrick, the real-life "Elephant Man," once attended a performance of *Puss in Boots*.[18] Patrick Wright, who has mapped the development of this concept in detail, concludes: "The theatrical origins of the Iron Curtain would largely be forgotten in the Cold War decades, yet many of the characteristic attitudes of the new division were directly inherited from its predecessor."[19] Indeed, from a small town in the Mid-West (Churchill's famous 1946 speech denouncing the Iron Curtain was made in Fulton, Missouri) to Central Europe, the Cold War's theatrical politics would play out on suburban televisions, in exhibition kitchens and even within outer space.

At the Roadhouse in *Twin Peaks*, bright red curtains herald the performance of another female singer. This is a three-story, wooden-paneled, colonial-style building, with a front car park that provides a handy space for surveillance. In red neon, complete with a firing gun, it is labeled the "Bang Bang Bar." Lynch clearly admires these buzzing electric signs, and how their graphic exuberance and primary colors intrude on the night sky. Like his curtains, the signs are another spectacle that speaks of disturbed flow and changing states. Inside the Roadhouse, there are more neon signs advertising beer alongside wooden tables and leather booths. Again, the crowd is mixed, ranging from teenagers to truckers, confirming that Lynch's nocturnal spaces offer a broad communal experience. The audience faces a stage that plays host to Julee Cruise's delicate performances.

The most evocative of these shows comes during episode fourteen of *Twin Peaks* and marks perhaps the high point of the entire project. Lynch gathers numerous figures from the town in the Roadhouse, where the atmosphere grows increasingly tense. Cruise is singing with her band, bathed in golden light, when suddenly they fade from the screen to be replaced by a giant, lit by a single spotlight (Plate 44). The world appears to pause momentarily, though only Cooper seems to witness this extraordinary rupture in space and time. There is a precise, almost stately, formality to these shots, to emphasize that a fundamental event is imminent. The giant solemnly announces: "It is happening again. It is happening again." (Everything must be duplicated in *Twin Peaks*, a world built on repetition and re-enactment.) With this, Lynch cuts to the Palmer household, where Madeleine Ferguson is brutally murdered by Leland. Their actions are also lit by a bright spotlight, intimating a relationship between this domestic theater and the public stage. We return to the Roadhouse, where the giant fades from the stage and Cruise reappears. Now, a palpable grief is present, an incredible collective intuition that something terrible has occurred, as if Leland's actions have been sensed by the entire community. As Roger Luckhurst observes, such outbursts complicate the notion that *Twin Peaks* might be an ironic pastiche: "what impresses is the wrenching *authenticity* of the emotional spectacle of the series."[20] Through the conduit of the stage, private trauma has generated public tremors and the town's sorrow has been distilled into a single chamber. Lynch has taken the idea that public space is an arena in which news can be shared, manifest in a more prosaic form in *The Elephant Man*, and extended it into an overwhelming scenario.

In *Eraserhead*, public space has been eroded by a malfunctioning economy. Left alone in these urban wastelands with only his deformed baby for company, Henry seeks compensation and salvation in a fantasmatic counter-site. Lynch slowly zooms in on Henry's radiator, as if it holds the answer to all his problems, until its iron railings open up to designate a new space. Inside, there is a stage with checkered flooring, encircled by earth and a series of light bulbs, with ornate curtains behind and classical columns framing the action—a set built in an outdoor laundry pit next to Greystone Mansion in Beverly Hills. The atmosphere here, thanks partly to the organ we hear, feels akin to a music hall. This, however, is clearly a private world, in which the show—performed by a gentle girl with swollen cheeks—is solely for Henry's benefit. "In Heaven, everything is fine," she reassures him. Yet, this crafted spectacle is a peculiarly vulnerable space— its initial meticulousness soon follows Philadelphia into mess and jumble. Henry's on-going fears concerning reproduction are played out on the stage, with sperm-like objects raining upon its surface. The singer seems to hold divine powers, yet Henry is ultimately decapitated (or castrated, perhaps) within her theatrical home. Once penetrated, this stage becomes a catastrophic scene of blood and soil (Figure 4.2). Any promise imbued by the lady in the radiator is finally obliterated.

Lynch's depiction of female singers demands further consideration. It is easy to suggest from whence this obsession emanated. The insertion of a musical performance into a cinematic narrative is a common maneuver in Classical Hollywood, in films like *Gilda*, and for European directors such as Fellini and Godard—twin spheres of influence for Lynch. In Mulvey's landmark analysis, scenes involving a female stage performance allow the cinematic spectator's gaze to fuse with that of male characters

FIGURE 4.2 *Eraserhead*: the stage as catastrophe.
Credit: *Eraserhead* (dir. David Lynch, 1977), © David Lynch and the American Film Institute for Advanced Studies.

in the film. Consequently, "For a moment the sexual impact of the performing woman takes the film into a no-man's land outside its own time and space."[21] This is often the case in Lynch's cinema, most graphically in *Lost Highway* when Alice is forced to strip before a ring of gangsters controlled by Mr Eddy—an image Jean Nouvel chose to adorn a room in The Hotel Luzern. For Lynch, female performance, often explicitly directed by a man, ruptures narrative equilibrium. There are almost no examples of these power relations being reversed in his work (except, perhaps, when Dorothy initially threatens Jeffrey in *Blue Velvet*), although Lynch's heterotopian counter-sites are not exclusively generated through the routines of women, as the singing of Sailor in *Wild at Heart* demonstrates.

In Club Silencio, however, the symbolic power of female performance is heightened to such an extent that destabilization inevitably follows. *Mulholland Drive*'s central space combines the quasi-cinematic atmosphere of an abandoned downtown movie theater with the physical stage movements of a live recital—to create something akin to a late-night avant-garde club. Rebekah del Rio's performance, in front of dark-red curtains, is so haunting that the "no-man's land" it produces is a space of pure, almost unbearable affect. Betty's streaming tears in response to the act recall the climactic concert in Hitchcock's *The Man Who Knew Too Much* (1956), when Doris Day grows increasingly distraught within the Albert Hall. In both cases, female characters convulse at the implications of a stage performance, as a public show provokes the most intimate fears.

In *Mulholland Drive*, though, the singer's collapse explicitly questions the nature of cinematic performance, especially in terms of gender (Plate 45). In updating Mulvey's argument, Kaja Silverman has outlined how "the *female* voice is as relentlessly held to normative representations and functions as is the female body." Specifically, Silverman claims, Classical Hollywood "pits the disembodied male voice," which is omniscient, omnipotent and often invisible, against "the synchronized female voice," which remains closely identified with the body.[22] *Mulholland Drive* offers a startling reversal of Silverman's argument, in a scene filmed, as previously noted, within the Tower Theater in Los Angeles—a venue of historical significance when it comes to sound and cinema. Rebekah del Rio's voice continues after she is carried from the stage, in a manner that undermines the conventional bodily spectacle seen on stages like the Slow Club. Cinema's typical synchronization of sound and image, and of the female body with the female voice, offers Lynch the opportunity for traumatic disruption. Thus, our own emotions feel as manipulated as those of the spectators within Club Silencio when the symbolic pressure placed on female performance, by Lynch among others, finally shatters. In this sense, the scene works against the director's previous films: we are so accustomed to Lynch's slick female performances that this interrupted routine comes as an upsetting jolt. In *The Last Tycoon* (1941), F. Scott Fitzgerald used a similar trope to highlight the artifice of Hollywood: "Outside the window the singer came to the climax of *I love you only*, held it a moment and then, I swear, started it over again. Or maybe they were playing it back to her from the recording machine."[23] Yet, in *Mulholland Drive*, Lynch presents us with the shocking spectacle of a disembodied voice right before our eyes. He exposes the pretension, but the performance retains an immense impact. In her analysis of the Club Silencio scene, Elena del Río argues that the lip-synching exemplifies "Lynch's insight into the affective value and power of the false."[24] It is the symbolic configuration of the stage, a venue we (and the film's characters) expect to host certain modes of performance (especially from women), which makes this shocking affect possible.

The Other Side of the Cameras

Club Silencio reinforces the idea that the movie theater has had a significant impact on Lynch's spatial consciousness. Cinemas hold the potential for infinite escape within a perfectly bounded arena, an immersive experience with another frame at the center. The flowing curtains, lucid sounds, intense darkness and isolated light that characterize cinematic experience constantly return throughout Lynch's stages. Moreover, in *Mulholland Drive* and *Inland Empire*, the interiors of two classic Los Angeles cinemas—the Tower Theater and the Orpheum Theater—stage uncanny confrontations. The cinema, then, is an essential space for Lynch: an environment constitutive of more than just film spectatorship.

What is more, the architecture of cinematic production has become a guiding force in Lynch's recent work. Studio sets, boardroom meetings, rehearsal rooms and audition booths appear throughout *Mulholland Drive* and *Inland Empire*. While housing a series of platforms for performance, the film studio represents a somewhat different form of

Lynchian stage. In essence, his last two films display the worlds "on the other side of the curtain." As such, there are fewer physical stages and less drapery on display. Instead, the construction of fictional performance is the main concern, with architecture a critical component.

Specifically, it is the Paramount Studios lot on Melrose Avenue in Los Angeles that holds Lynch's attention. Paramount moved there in 1926, when the company was known as Famous Players-Lasky, having purchased the site from United Artists.[25] The advantages this location provides Lynch are three-fold. First, it is the only major studio in Los Angeles whose location allows for a shot juxtaposing the Hollywood sign and a cinematic soundstage—the creepy sequence that appears early in *Inland Empire*. The most potent symbol of cinema, an advertising hoarding precariously balanced on a mountainside, is thus placed alongside the elaborate machinery that underpins it. Second, the Paramount lot lies adjacent to the Hollywood Forever Cemetery. Lynch literalizes this geographical proximity: ghostly detritus—images and phrases from film history that refuse to rest in peace—haunts *Mulholland Drive* and *Inland Empire*. Cecil B. DeMille is one of the many famous Hollywood figures buried in the cemetery, and the making of DeMille's epic *Samson and Delilah* (1949) features in another Paramount production, *Sunset Boulevard*. Wilder's film is the third and most important factor in Lynch's decision to base his interrogations of film-making at the Paramount lot.

Wilder and Lynch share a fascination with the architecture of the film studio. Betty Schaefer, in *Sunset Boulevard*, is thrilled by the constructions of the Paramount lot: "Look at this street: all cardboard, all hollow, all phoney, all done with mirrors. You know, I like it better than any street in the world." Architectural authenticity is at its most vulnerable in Hollywood, where the same spaces play host to ersatz versions of global locations. Here, though, Betty suggests that openly acknowledging the fake and flimsy fittings of the studio lot might allow us to appreciate its other delights—pure imagination and a utopian commitment to visual pleasure without the restrictions of everyday urbanism.

Betty Elms, in *Mulholland Drive*, is another idealist who gasps at the Paramount gate famously featured in *Sunset Boulevard*. Her visit to the studios is more problematic because she fails to understand the "cardboard" nature of the environment and its inhabitants. As with Club Silencio, our assumptions are also in flux here. Initially, Betty's audition at Paramount is a resounding success. Lynch crowds an assortment of agents and assistants around her performance, which is so sincere it lifts the banalities of the script to unexpected emotional heights. As George Toles has noted, the surprising affect this performance generates jolts the audience, removing any assumption of ironic superiority over the characters: the distance between the screen and the spectator is again narrowed via a Lynchian stage.[26] Notably, Betty is offered the enigmatic directorial advice: "Don't play it for real until it gets real". At Paramount Studios, though, Betty cannot grasp which elements of the place are "all hollow, all phoney, all done with mirrors" and which are "real". Her elation following the audition is swiftly shattered by gossip that the director will "never get that picture made." Betty is then taken to a soundstage where auditions for *The Sylvia North Story* are taking place against a cardboard backdrop of the Hollywood Hills (Plate 46). Further artifice emerges in the form of two lip-synched pop performances inside gaudy booths, before Betty exchanges an intense look with the director Adam Kesher. Yet, in the midst of all this pretence, how "real" is their connection? We certainly sense something important, but Betty's fantasy is abruptly exposed in the final stages of the film, when Diane Selwyn, standing in front of another cardboard urban scene, watches Adam seduce Camilla Rhodes instead.

The difference between Wilder's Betty and Lynch's Betty pivots on their respective roles in the movie business. *Mulholland Drive* distorts the failed ambitions of an actor who craves the spotlight. In *Sunset Boulevard*, Betty Schaefer is an aspiring screen-writer, who happily admits: "What's wrong with being on the other side of the cameras? It's really more fun." It is Norma Desmond, another actor who has problems distinguishing the "phoney" from the "real," whom Lynch's Betty takes after. In Lynch's films, the male architects of performance, such as Mr Reindeer in *Wild at Heart* or Mr Eddy in *Lost Highway*, enjoy pulling the strings and observing the spectacle. Those who must perform upon the stage, like Betty Elms or Laura Palmer, struggle with their allocated roles. In front of the cameras and the curtains, their position is much more vulnerable. The film spectator, however, cannot observe these crucial situations from a safe distance. The dynamics of the Lynchian stage ensure we are implicated in the performance, its boundaries extending beyond the screen to encompass the auditorium around us.

Sections of *Sunset Boulevard* were filmed in soundstage 18 at Paramount Studios. This is the same building in which Hitchcock assembled the world of *Rear Window* and in which Marlon Brando directed *One-Eyed Jacks* (1961), which would later give its name to a brothel in *Twin Peaks*. It is these endless coincidences—the ability of a soundstage to juxtapose, in Foucault's terms, "several sites that are in themselves incompatible"—that so appeals to Lynch. By contrast, Baudrillard, while captivated by Los Angeles, was left unimpressed by Paramount Studios: "Where is the cinema? It is all around you outside, all over the city, that marvellous, continuous performance of films and scenarios. Everywhere but here."[27] For Lynch, though, Paramount Studios epitomizes the strange shared spaces of cinema. These "phoney" sets contain distinct historical reverberations, which Lynch seeks to capture through the literal imposition of certain architectural features, such as the Paramount gate or Norma Desmond's car. They also provide the perfect stage for an exploration of fantasy. Despite their thin materials, "phoney" studio sets constitute a distinct architectural scenario, a series of tangible, inhabited spaces. Likewise, *Mulholland Drive* emphasizes a physical and highly visceral experience of fantasy. Indeed, Betty's fantasmatic Hollywood is a much more alluring world than Diane's miserable existence.

By *Inland Empire*, the divisions between psychological space and physical reality have all but evaporated. Notably, the world of *On High in Blue Tomorrows*, one of the many films within *Inland Empire*, is created inside soundstage 4 at Paramount. Connected by an alleyway to soundstage 18, soundstage 4 is also clearly visible when entering through the studio's famous gate—the threshold traversed by Norma Desmond and Betty Elms. In effect, Lynch traces a literal pathway through cinematic history, taking us from *Sunset Boulevard* to *Mulholland Drive* and *Inland Empire*, as if these worlds were somehow linked. Moreover, the half-finished studio sets that litter all these films, alternate worlds that were never fully constructed, are both a reminder of Hollywood's unrealized projects and a stark metaphor for the psychological effects of ruined careers. As the next chapter demonstrates, *Inland Empire* places a whole geography of cinema under one roof. In a sense, soundstage 4 at Paramount Studios is the room in which the incompatible spaces of Southern California and Central Europe, Classical Hollywood and its transatlantic neighbor, are all housed. This hulking heterotopia, totalling over 13,000 square feet, contains multiple, endlessly changing worlds.

Yet, even warehouses like this are not perfectly sealed worlds. Jean Renoir once told Bernardo Bertolucci to welcome the unexpected events that occur in film-making via an evocative metaphor: "You must always leave the door of the set open because you never know what might come in."[28] In *Inland*

Empire, Lynch literalizes this idea in an uncanny fashion, by having Nikki creep into the back of soundstage 4 to disturb rehearsals for her own film. "The stage is supposed to be ours and ours alone," complains Kingsley, the director of *On High in Blue Tomorrows*. As ever, though, certain gestures allow unexpected performers to penetrate the Lynchian stage. Thus, the "other side of the cameras" cannot remain a safe and sealed world—it, too, is heterotopian in nature. In a permanent mode of performance, Nikki continues her remorseless search for psychological stability, behind the curtains, in front of the cameras and in the alleyways that join them.

Inside a Labyrinth: The Red Room

To date, the most famous world Lynch has built and filmed is the Red Room in *Twin Peaks*. The first appearance of its distinctive red drapes and patterned floor has been described by Marc Dolan as "unlike almost any scene that had ever been depicted on television."[29] Yet, what is this iconic space? Where is it located and what does it symbolize? What architectural, cinematic and theoretical revelations might we discover?

There are many possibilities. Lynch himself has described the Red Room as a place where "anything can happen [...] a free zone, completely unpredictable and therefore pretty exciting but also scary."[30] By this account, the Red Room is distinctly heterotopian in nature, a place of contradictory impulses and inverted relations, capable of maintaining Black and White Lodges within its bounds. Martha Nochimson brands the Red Room "a possible site of vision, truth, and reality for the seeker," which emphasizes its revelatory potential within the confusing terrain of *Twin Peaks*.[31] Perhaps, then, we might consider this "site of vision" to be a version of the "Aleph" described in Jorge Luis Borges' famous story. The "Aleph" is "one of the points in space that contains all other points"—that is, a space in which, simultaneously, all other places are and can be seen, without overlapping.[32] Inhabitants of the Red Room certainly have a privileged perspective on events elsewhere in Twin Peaks, while the arena itself disturbs spatial and temporal logic. Borges' concept has frequently inspired urban theorists, especially Edward Soja. In using the Argentine writer to explicate his concept of "Thirdspace," Soja himself offers another potential category for Lynch's Red Room, a space where everything "comes together" with an "all-inclusive simultaneity." Like Soja's "Thirdspace," the Red Room functions, for the residents of Twin Peaks, as a place "simultaneously real and imagined," a chamber where all the town's stories coalesce.[33] It is, to extend this reading, a kind of control suite or, as John Orr puts it, a sublime "director's editing room."[34] The Red Room is where Lynch can oversee his master plan.

For such a famous location, the Red Room actually appears on screen for a relatively brief amount of time. It hosts two substantial sequences in *Twin Peaks*, in the second and last episodes, and then three shorter scenes in *Fire Walk With Me*. These appearances at the beginning and end of the project confirm its special status, while avoiding over-familiarity. What is more, among *Twin Peaks'* diverse collaborators, Lynch alone directs sequences in the Red Room, implying a particularly personal relationship with the space. Jeff Johnson has complained that "the action in the Red Room seems superfluous, doing little to advance the story," but this ignores the most basic premise of Lynch's stages: something is clearly experienced here, in a location specifically demarcated for affect.[35] There is a radical simplicity to this logic: for Lynch, curtains and a stage are sufficient to generate immersive drama. After all the confusing conversations and wild theories about Black and White Lodges, as well as the cave drawings, maps of Tibet and unexplained portals, both the series and the film return to the Red Room at their conclusions.

Let us, then, consider each of the Red Room's main appearances in turn. It first emerges as part of an elaborate dream experienced by Cooper in a Surrealist intervention at the end of *Twin Peaks'* second episode (Plate 47). Instinctively, this set-up recalls Dalí's dream sequence in Hitchcock's *Spellbound* (1945), which also features a curtained room and classical sculpture. Perhaps, Lynch suggests, the contents of Cooper's dream will prove, after rigorous analysis, to hold the key to the entire narrative. Within the Red Room, it is evident that Cooper has aged dramatically, as if thrust into the future, and time remains unstable in this arena. The sound here is distinct, too—a warped, highly sensitive acoustics in which speech runs backwards. A sensuous mixture of styles characterizes the décor, with three Art Deco armchairs and two free-standing lights joined by a Greek statue and a globe. Further spotlights, from an unseen source, focus on the thick red curtains that enclose the space, creating an opulent bunker. The floor, composed of jagged lines, resembles electric shockwaves—a design also found in the lobby of Henry's apartment block in *Eraserhead*. Intriguingly, Lynch's first film was released in France as *Labyrinth Man* and this floor pattern, a typically Lynchian form of distorted repetition, implies a dangerous but consistent pathway. Perhaps, there is a figure in this carpet, a solution to our many unanswered questions, if we follow it to the end. The Red Room's flooring also recalls the terrazzo sidewalk patterns that architects such as S. Charles Lee placed outside movie palaces to entice spectators, so that cinematic design spilled into the street.[36] Here, attention would be drawn to the geometry of illusion, with the ground beneath visitors becoming a platform for urban performance. In the initial Red Room sequence, Cooper is joined by a dwarf in a red suit (the Man from Another Place, according to the credits), who dances and offers cryptic remarks, as well as a woman whom he describes as looking "almost exactly like Laura Palmer." Alongside the disturbances to space, time, sound and speech, identity is rendered volatile within the Red Room.

Despite these fluctuations, though, the Red Room maintains an atmosphere of perverse calm. Its formal arrangement, combining classical and modern motifs, feels like an eccentric living room or, like Club Silencio, a kind of avant-garde club. The space could easily sit within a contemporary gallery as a piece of installation art. Indeed, we can see a close resemblance to the Red Room in works such as Cildo Meireles' *Red Shift* installations (1967–84), which include a room furnished with ordinary domestic fittings coated in red paint, and Juan Muñoz's *The Prompter* (1988), where a platform patterned with a geometric design is overseen by a papier-mâché dwarf. Spectators can walk through Meireles' installation, surrounded by the exuberant color, though for Muñoz's piece an audience can only look at the stage without stepping onto it. It is precisely this tension between immersion and distance, common throughout installation art, that faces characters entering Lynch's stages. Lynch's drawing and installation in the Fondation Cartier exhibition operated along similar lines.

The Red Room also calls to mind one of Le Corbusier's strangest and least-discussed creations: the Beistegui Apartment in Paris (Figure 4.3). Situated on the Champs-Élysées, this was a home designed for lavish entertainment, "a frame for big parties," as Colomina puts it, with a sound-proof projection booth included.[37] Specifically, it is the rooftop garden and terraces that prompt comparison with Lynch's architecture, not least because of their combination of natural elements with mechanical interventions. Here, Le Corbusier designed hedges controlled by hydraulics and a periscope that functioned as a *camera obscura*. The overall effect, Dorothée Imbert claims, is "a nearly perfect example of the garden as viewing platform."[38] Indeed, perception is constantly

FIGURE 4.3 Appartement de M. Charles de Beistegui in Paris.
Credit: Copyright FLC/ADAGP, Paris and DACS, London 2014.

manipulated from an elevated position so that the terrace operates as an editing suite in which Paris is the raw footage. At the highest point of the structure, Le Corbusier wilfully inhibits views of the Arc de Triomphe and instead creates an enclosed solarium—a chamber turning spectatorship inwards in defiance of the celebrated cityscape. Within tall white walls, this outdoor arena maintains the trappings of interior space: a false fireplace and ornate furniture, decorated in the baroque style favored by the owner, lie upon a carpet of grass.

Like the Red Room, Le Corbusier's solarium is a minimalist stage containing disparate motifs, and is a delineated space held apart from the rest of the community. Both spaces maintain extravagant touches within a simple framework, a form of impure modernism with Surrealist overtones. The playful, unearthly sensations generated by these environments have an idyllic quality, too. The Man from Another Place tells Cooper: "Where we're from, the birds sing a pretty song and there's always music in the air," before soft jazz soaks the Red Room. Le Corbusier described his ideal terrace in similar terms: "At night people dance to the music of a gramophone. The air is pure, the sound is muffled, the view distant, the street far away. If trees are nearby, you are above their canopy."[39] These are transcendent conceptions of space. In spite of its dangers, the Red Room is a form of Lynchian utopia, "a free zone" where the director's imagination is not restrained by narrative concerns.

Furthermore, while the Red Room on its initial manifestation seems to be a completely enclosed arena, later appearances demonstrate that here, as with Le Corbusier's solarium, the division between interior and exterior space is complicated. The final episode of *Twin Peaks* reveals that the Red Room is accessed via a circle of twelve sycamore trees, known as Glastonbury Grove, within the local woods. When Cooper enters this space, whose name hints at Arthurian legends, the vegetative cloak becomes a screen of red velvet into which the detective disappears. It is an incredible, Surreal image, with additional echoes of the draped figure in Bacon's *Study from the Human Body* (1949). How or why particular individuals are able to cross this threshold is never fully explained. All we can deduce, to follow Foucault, is that "one must have a certain permission and make certain gestures." Nonetheless, the gateway links the natural world of Ghostwood Forest with the Red Room's architectural flourish, again implying that the woods are Twin Peaks' most potent force. Akira Mizuta Lippit has written evocatively of Lynch's obsession with secret passages connecting different buildings or realms, and the director admits his excitement at the idea that "a little opening could exist and we could go somewhere else."[40] Notably, *Twin Peaks* was a series originally entitled *Northwest Passage*.

In *Twin Peaks'* remarkable finale, Cooper navigates an endless series of chambers and corridors within the Red Room (Figure 4.4). The spaces begin to blur, with Lynch overlaying images in hypnotic fashion. Cooper encounters a range of characters and their apparent doppelgängers, including his own double (Plate 48). At one point, the Man from Another Place tells him, "This is the waiting room," suggesting a space of permanent transition, never to be settled. Soon enough, physical metamorphosis, duplication and injury abound; all matter is disrupted, as coffee switches from liquid to solid; lights flash wildly. Though the tranquillity of its earlier incarnation has gone, these Red Room scenes still maintain a studied quality, enhanced by the exaggerated sound of Cooper's footsteps and shots extended far beyond the televisual norm. Finally, the episode and the series conclude with an evil version of Cooper escaping from his confines to reach the Great Northern Hotel. Another Lynchian world has leaked beyond its prescribed boundaries.

FIGURE 4.4 The Red Room set on the final day of filming for *Twin Peaks* (1991). Credit: Copyright Richard Beymer. Photograph by Richard Beymer, with thanks to Rob Wilson.

What this final episode implies is that the Red Room is a network of interlinked spaces—corridors and chambers that loop endlessly. A series initiated by cartography ends with a lesson in way-finding inside a total architectural experience. Perhaps, then, what underpins the Red Room is the mythology of the labyrinth—one of architecture's founding stories. Built to house a monstrous hybrid of human and animal desires in need of frequent sacrifice (the Minotaur/Bob), by an acclaimed architect (Daedalus/Lynch) commissioned by higher powers (King Minos/the television bosses), the Red Room seduces an intrepid explorer from distant parts (Theseus/Cooper), inspired by a woman (Ariadne/Laura Palmer), to enter its dangerous walls. In this reading, Lynch's placement of Greek sculpture within the Red Room acts as a nod to Knossos.

There is certainly evidence to suggest a broader obsession with the labyrinth in recent years. Theodore Ziolkowski talks of a modern "labyrinthomania," with 5,000 structures created worldwide since 1970.[41] According to Kathryn Milun, there are now 1,800 labyrinths in the United States alone, located in public spaces outside churches, parks and museums, and within hospitals, prisons and teenage centers. Walking through a labyrinth—a rational space rather than a disorientating maze—has become a therapeutic technique, which Milun places within the history of responses to agoraphobia (a condition from which Lynch has suffered). With the emphasis it places on concentration and awareness, a labyrinth is "a little training ground, a safe space in which to experiment with recovering the public self." Against the *horror vacui* of the modern American city, which *Eraserhead* depicts so memorably, "the labyrinth offers contours where there was once only empty space."[42]

Twin Peaks cannot be understood in quite so straightforward a fashion. The series is full of false pathways, dead ends and cul-de-sacs. Strictly speaking, it maintains an architecture more akin to a maze than a coded labyrinth, although these terms are often conflated. If you continue along the elongated route of a labyrinth, you will eventually find the satisfaction of the center. In Milun's analysis, this journey reveals a coherent "public self." *Twin Peaks* resists such logic. However, to adapt her argument, the series' concluding episode does offer contours as an answer to narrative abyss. When Lynch returned to direct this last installment, he was faced with a daunting web of disparate storylines. He chose neither total resolution (that is, forming all the various threads into a coherent pattern), nor absolute ambiguity (leaving these threads twisted without explanation). Instead, we are led around the series' own internal labyrinth where the central chamber provokes an impossible encounter: Cooper meets himself. There is no therapeutic comfort to be gained from this experience, just as benign notions of community, public space and subjectivity are thwarted throughout Lynch's work. In fact, Cooper ends the series in a kind of exuberant madness, gazing into a mirror that reveals the Minotaur in himself.

Assessing the Red Room within the history of cinema's engagement with the labyrinth offers further explication. Nicholas Christopher focuses on *film noir*, a genre where labyrinthine processes operate on three levels. First, the American city becomes distorted and claustrophobic, full of shadows, stairwells and alleyways. Second, *noir* plots twist around complex human interactions and metaphysical conundrums. Third, *noir* protagonists face an interior struggle.[43] This offers a useful framework for *Twin Peaks*, which plays with many *noir* tropes (such as social corruption, a flawed detective and the *femme fatale*). Lynch, though, translates these conventions into an unfamiliar rural context, so they take on stranger undertones alongside woods, waterfalls and family homes. Furthermore, his worlds refute the cynicism of *noir* fictions for the "wrenching *authenticity*," as Luckhurst put it, of intense emotional performance.

More intriguing comparisons lie in Stanley Kubrick's work. The final scenes of *2001: A Space Odyssey* (1968) depict a prototypical Lynchian chamber, when the astronaut Bowman encounters ageing and fetal versions of himself within a white bedroom clad in eighteenth-century décor. As with the Red Room, this space establishes dream-like spatial co-ordinates for temporal subversion. The symbolic weight of neoclassical architecture, with its formal arrangement of space, contrasts with the fluid movements of identity that follow. There is less sensuality in Kubrick's architecture, which is also more glossy and poised than Lynch's structures, yet the directors share a sense of mood and pacing that prioritizes disturbing affect. The stark, windowless rooms at the heart of *2001* and *Twin Peaks* are built and filmed for concentrated expression.

In *The Shining* (1980), the Red Room is anticipated by a tale of "REDRUM." Both Kubrick and Lynch display a fascination with mirroring effects, placing the rhythms of speech and performance in reverse as part of a larger engagement with duality. Like *Twin Peaks*, *The Shining* is full of replication and disturbing doubles. Just as Cooper battles his own doppelgänger, Jack Torrance is a study in darkness and light, although his patriarchal violence suggests a more fitting comparison with Leland Palmer (who also inhabits the Red Room). For both Kubrick and Lynch, the monstrous form inside the family, the Minotaur in the living room, is the father himself. *The Shining* plays out its familial conflicts utilizing a succession of mazes. Labyrinthine patterns flood Kubrick's imagery—in carpets, wall-coverings and a model maze inside the hotel. Within these complex designs, Jack's own physical features come to resemble a bull, as Pallasma has noted.[44] The film ends with a nocturnal chase sequence around a large maze in the hotel's grounds, with spotlights adding a peculiar sense of theater. Again, we see a narrative avoiding absolute resolution by threading itself through physical corridors and chambers, deferring any concrete meaning by constructing endless internal prisons—including a final photographic frame for Jack's image, which anticipates Laura Palmer's captivity in media. Like the Red Room, *The Shining's* maze may not be a strict labyrinth in its avoidance of rational pathways, but it certainly manipulates the symbolic potency of the myth.

In both *Twin Peaks* and *The Shining*, the mirror is the object through which decisive communications are translated. Bob's deathly presence within Leland and Cooper, as well as the murderous intentions of Jack

Torrance, are revealed by reversed images that mediate between the conventional world and the horrors of another, labyrinthine zone. For Foucault, mirrors offer a "mixed, joint experience" that leaves them poised between utopias and heterotopias.[45] Further cinematic evidence of mirrors bridging disparate zones comes in the shape of Cocteau's *Orphée*, where they act as portals between everyday life and the underworld. Indeed, we learn "the secret of secrets" from the film's ominous chauffeur: "Mirrors are the doors by which Death comes." Here, another precursor to the Red Room emerges, one that has been implied before without sustained explanation. For instance, John Alexander claims, "Orpheus is the underlying myth to the *Twin Peaks* narrative" and it is easy to see Cooper as the legendary figure who negotiates a curtained underworld in search of a woman.[46]

In Cocteau's version of the myth, the upper reaches of Orpheus' home contain an editing suite, with messages transmitted from an attic space accessed via a trapdoor. Within this room, admission to the underworld takes place through a mirror laid upon a textured floor patterning almost identical to that of the Red Room (Figure 4.5). Shot from above, this distorted design acts as the launch-pad for Orpheus' subterranean exploration. Again, certain gestures must be made (gloves are essential) and rational thought is discouraged ("You don't have to understand. You just have to believe"). The visual tricks employed in this maneuver and

FIGURE 4.5 *Orphée* (dir. Jean Cocteau, 1949): Orpheus enters "the zone."
Credit: *Orphée* (dir. Jean Cocteau, 1949), © Andre Paulve Film, Films du Palais Royal.

throughout *Orphée*—the sudden disappearance of characters, reversed movements and the emergence of strange spaces—all seem somewhat primitive now, but are exactly of the type still favored by Lynch, who remains content to leave his artifice ungilded by more elaborate special effects.

Once he has passed through the portal, Orpheus enters into "the zone"—a "no-man's land" between life and death composed of "memories and the ruins of human habit." Within these battered walls, Orpheus' movement is distorted; the usual co-ordinates of space and time have been completely disrupted. This is a place, to return to Soja's terms, that is "simultaneously real and imagined." It has a distinct physical reality, yet dreams are also constitutive. In a phrase reminiscent of those uttered by Lynch's Log Lady, Cocteau's Princess of Death tells Orpheus: "The role of the dreamer is to accept his dreams." This, of course, is a key legacy of Surrealism—an architecture created from random association and unconscious inconsistencies. *Orphée* also presents a space of specific historical detritus. At the heart of the labyrinthine underworld lies a courtroom, composed of the ruins of Nuremberg and the *Épuration légale*. This is a final chamber of judgment, combining heterotopian ambiguity with bureaucratic certainty. Participants in *Orphée's* legal performances, who symbolize the twentieth century's collaborators, conspirators and bystanders, are all told: "There is no maybe here."

Cocteau's architecture of death—the passages of the underworld and the ghoulish workings of mirrors—remind us that ultimately the Red Room functions as Laura Palmer's tomb. This is the lingering impression of *Fire Walk With Me*. The film reveals that, like Cooper, Laura first encountered the Red Room in a dream, inspired by a painting on her wall. This is a space that must be imagined before it can be fully inhabited. At the end of the film, we return to the Red Room, where initially it is Leland and a ferocious Bob who hold sway. Yet, Lynch does not allow the Minotaur(s) to have the last word. Instead, the camera hovers over an empty version of the stage, allowing us to enjoy its jazzy flooring and red drapery free from bodily disturbance. However, our horizontal progress also mirrors the journey of Laura's plastic wrapping as it floats towards the shore, confirming the Red Room to be in dialogue with action outside in the town.

Finally, we are presented with Laura herself, her face flooded by blue light (from the flickering television screen that brought her to life, perhaps). An angel appears and the Red Room becomes, in Orr's words, a "celestial antechamber."[47] Proceedings here maintain spiritual connotations throughout *Twin Peaks*, although it is difficult to define whether this "waiting room"—replete with angels and demons—represents heaven, hell or purgatory. Laura is evidently moved by the spectacle, while the soundtrack's soaring synthesizers imbue the scene with further emotion. As the camera tilts upwards, leaving her to be comforted by Cooper, the distorted floor pattern forms a final backdrop, before the image is submerged by blinding white light. The curtain has fallen on Laura's epic performance and the "waiting room" has become an eternal resting place.

5 ROOM

All the rooms in this house are in one room.

**THE SCARECROW (DIR. BUSTER KEATON
AND EDWARD F. CLINE, 1920)**

The Logic of Simultaneity

Inland Empire is David Lynch's most radical work. Indeed, it is one of the most challenging American films to have appeared in a generation. Although its thematic and structural antecedents can be seen in Lynch's previous work, particularly *Lost Highway* and *Mulholland Drive*, there is an unequivocal chasm between those films, which maintain a level of narrative convention, and the montage of sounds, images and spaces we encounter in *Inland Empire*. Perhaps unsurprisingly, *Inland Empire* alienated many critics. David Edelstein complained, "*Inland Empire* is way, way beyond my powers of ratiocination," and Carina Chocano confessed: "I found myself pining for *The Elephant Man*."[1] Even a sympathetic reviewer like Michael Atkinson emphasized *Inland Empire*'s singularity, claiming that "roping it into any category with other movies seems a dubious labour."[2] *Inland Empire*, then, sits in a room of its own.

Rather, however, than defining it purely as an aberrant addition to the Lynch canon, we are better served in considering *Inland Empire* as the culmination of past obsessions, as well as a decisive transformation of them. In particular, it extends the heterotopian notions of space previously expressed in Lynch's stages, so much so that the film feels like it takes place in one giant Red Room. If, as Soja famously suggested, "it all comes together in Los Angeles," then *Inland Empire*—a title that encompasses a region in the Pacific Northwest where Lynch grew up and an area in Southern California, as well as implying the heartlands of Central Europe—is where it all comes together for David Lynch.[3] This is a film about Old and New Worlds, symbolic territories that clash, merge and overlap. Its three-hour depiction of Nikki Grace's struggles is organized around spatial concepts that again call to mind Bachelard: "If one were to give an account of all the doors one has closed and opened, of all the doors one would like to re-open, one would have to tell the story of one's entire life."[4] *Inland Empire*, then, is the Lynch film with the most to teach us about cinematic architecture.

The film does, however, necessitate a different approach. To this point, my analysis of Lynch's architecture has itself adopted a spatial structure. A strictly chronological investigation of his films has been sidelined in favor of chapters drawn up around archetypal locations. With *Inland Empire*, this critical method is impossible. The film revises our usual understanding of cinematic space by prohibiting isolated discussion of its individual settings. Parveen Adams highlights the way in which different times and spaces adhere to each other in the film, through a formal "stickiness."[5] This indicates how the layers of the film refuse to be separated coherently, how marks and traces are left in each location. In short, *Inland Empire* demands, impossibly, that we consider it all, all at once. Of course, the act of criticism entails examples and sequences. As Soja notes, any geographical description faces the conundrum that, while language dictates "a linear flow of sentential statements," the spaces we see remain "stubbornly simultaneous."[6] Cinema, grounded on the accumulated unfurling of images, faces a similar problem. Something different is taking place in *Inland Empire*, requiring our analysis of the film to be distilled into a single chapter.

Further explication of this methodological change is both necessary and instructive. Lynch's films are usually set within one clear location, such as London, Lumberton or Los Angeles. Even *Wild at Heart* and *The Straight Story* progress along a specific channel—the American highway. *Inland Empire* is different: it switches between various unexplained spaces, denying the spectator any geographical confidence. Cinematic space, Stephen Heath reminds us, is heavily dependent on the establishing shot. Conventionally, directors provide "an overall view, literally the 'master-shot' that will allow the scene to be dominated in the course of its reconstitution narratively as dramatic unity."[7] *Inland Empire* denies us the establishing shots critical to the creation of secure space. The only "overall view" given in the film is a brief shot of the Hollywood sign, which pans down to Paramount Studios. Otherwise, Lynch's handheld camera remains claustrophobically close to the action. The scale and layout of our surroundings remain murky; we must rely on changes in lighting, furnishings or even language for a sense of navigation.

What is more, while Lynch's later films turn on an incident of narrative rupture, such as Fred Madison morphing into Pete Dayton in *Lost Highway* or Betty Elms awakening as Diane Selwyn in *Mulholland Drive*, there is no single transformative moment in *Inland Empire*. We might see Lynch's *Inland Empire* as exhibiting a form of total rupture—a shattering of all "dramatic unity"—but this does not correspond with the emotional coherence it maintains. As Daniel Frampton points out, "we understand what the film is about, even if we don't think we do."[8] For François-Xavier Gleyzon, *Inland Empire* is not so much a journey like other Lynch films, but more of a "dynamic, a series of comings and goings and curves."[9] It is more useful, then, to consider *Inland Empire* as a film structured around simultaneity.

Some examples are useful to flesh out a logic of simultaneity. First, consider Buster Keaton's home in *The Scarecrow*, where living, dining and sleeping take place within the same space, thanks to ingenious technical adjustments. The layout is explained in an on-screen cue card: "All the rooms in this house are in one room." The description tells us something vital: the relationship between architecture and film is structured around delineated rooms. All cinematic locations are contained within the identical geometry of the screen—a flat surface imbued with limitless depth and a Pandora's box that houses the world of the film. Cinematic space is, in this regard, fully conterminous. If the action is always framed in the same manner, then these images are also received within the standard arrangement of the cinema itself—another heterotopian room able to house multiple desires. The architecture of cinematic production, in the form of film studios, encourages an additional notion of shared space. Catherine Coulson, later to become the Log Lady in *Twin Peaks*, was a camera assistant on *Eraserhead*. In that film, she explains, "All these rooms were the same space with different sets built in it."[10] To adapt the description of Keaton's home, all the rooms in *Eraserhead* were in one room.

Of course, a contrary approach to cinematic architecture also holds true. Early practitioners such as Eisenstein and Pudovkin were excited by the possibilities of montage. Rather than creating several different environments within the same space, Lev Kuleshov's experiments with spatial continuity demonstrated that unity could emerge from disparate sites. Five shots, taken in five separate locations, could construct one continuous "place": this was cinema's "creative geography."[11] Yet, as Vertov noted, in a passage highlighted at the beginning of this book, montage also establishes "an extraordinary room." The walls may have originated in different parts of the globe, but together they create "a film-phrase which is the room." Thus, all the rooms from this disconnected footage form one room.

Inland Empire literalizes the fascinating possibilities of cinematic architecture, with an eye on the cultural and psychological implications they raise. In so doing, Lynch unites the two locations most commonly discussed in studies of film and architecture—Central Europe in the early twentieth century and contemporary Los Angeles. The final moments of the film, in which the Polish Lost Girl races around, in a single journey, a series of corridors, sets and rooms seen throughout the film, suggests something akin to the design of Keaton's house. From the Californian suburbs to the streets of Łódź: all these locations, we might deduce, are simultaneously housed within the same structure. Earlier, when Nikki is rehearsing within soundstage 4 at Paramount Studios, her melodramatic scene comes to a premature close with the line: "Look in the other room." At this point, the performance is halted for fear of trespassers on the set. Yet, the search for "the other room," for a passage or alleyway into a different world, haunts *Inland Empire*. Polish gangsters discuss an "opening," while Nikki herself burns holes through silk underwear. Ultimately, though, Lynch shows us that, in the world of the film, there is no "other room." All the rooms in cinema are in one room. To capture the temporal dimension of this situation, we should tweak the giant's words from *Twin Peaks*. In *Inland Empire*, it is not "happening again." Rather, it is happening *now*, over and over again, in the same place, at the same time—despite the superficial appearance of separate locations, eras and characters. As such, it is impossible for anyone in the film to remember, in the words of Nikki's neighbor, "if it's today, two days from now, or yesterday."

"Space," Michael Dear remarks, "is nature's way of preventing everything from happening in the same place."[12] True enough, but what if we cannot rely on spatial delineation, the disturbing scenario that unfolds in *Inland Empire*? Then, a new definition of space becomes essential. Here, Foucault remains a compelling voice:

> The present epoch will perhaps be above all the epoch of space. We are in the epoch of simultaneity: we are in the epoch of juxtaposition, the epoch of the near and far, of the side-by-side, of the dispersed. We are at a moment, I believe, when our experience of the world is less that of

a long life developing through time than that of a network that connects points and intersects with its own skein.[13]

Inland Empire, in Lynch's idiosyncratic fashion, is an attempt to grapple with the implications arising from this "epoch of simultaneity." However, the vast "network" Lynch presents, described by one character as "an ocean of possibilities," is again founded on a binary opposition. The most symbolic product of American sprawl, Los Angeles, meets its spatial predecessor: the centripetal European industrial city, the urban model that has provoked such suspicion in the United States. Southern California, habitually regarded as immense, open and untainted, is haunted with ghostly Polish ancestry; Hollywood is twinned with HollyŁódź. This is Lynch's logic of simultaneity.

Before beginning a detailed investigation into *Inland Empire*, we should return to Frampton's intriguing statement, a claim that might also, paradoxically, contribute to our understanding of how Lynch "un-learns" a desire "to get it." If, as Frampton states, "we understand what the film is about, even if we don't think we do," then what is *Inland Empire* about? In search of a critical opening to this dense world, one incident early in the film acts as a useful entry-point. The Hollywood actor Nikki Grace, married to a possessive Polish man, is visited by a spooky woman with a distinct Central-European accent. A neighborly knock at the door always signals a dangerous (and potentially exciting) intrusion into a Lynchian world—from the woman across the corridor who seduces Henry in *Eraserhead* to the echoing sounds that terrorize Diane in *Mulholland Drive*. In *Inland Empire*, the strange pronouncements of the visitor seem to shape the rest of the film.

First, the visitor introduces herself to Nikki as "your new neighbor"—a category, as we saw in *Blue Velvet*, that prompts suspicion in Lynch's work, given its fraught symbolic border. "I think that it is important to know one's neighbors," she adds, pointedly, placing us firmly in Foucault's "epoch of juxtaposition." Of course, our definition of neighborly status is based as much on social or historical factors, as geographical proximity. Who, or what, then, might be considered as "neighbors" in *Inland Empire*?

Second, the visitor asks Nikki about her latest film role. "Is it about marriage?" she asks. "Your husband, he's involved?" Marriage is perhaps the most palpable theme in *Inland Empire*, a film brimming with deceit and wrath, jealousy and lust, clandestine meetings and unplanned pregnancies. Fidelity is certainly at stake here, but fidelity to whom, or, rather, to what? For *Inland Empire* is a story as concerned with geographical relations as personal affairs, with spatial as well as sexual couplings. At the heart of its transatlantic pairings is the unexpected "marriage" of Łódź and Los Angeles. Nikki becomes increasingly disorientated by the European intrusion into her Californian idyll, particularly as her lavish Hollywood lifestyle is brutally called into question by unidentified claims from the past. When her "new neighbor" begins to talk of "an unpaid bill," we must move beyond financial matters to consider the spatial and cultural debts involving Central Europe and the United States.

Lastly, Nikki's excruciating encounter comes to a close with the visitor recounting "an old tale" and its "variation." The latter story not only sends reverberations through *Inland Empire*, but is also highly suggestive in terms of Lynch's career as a whole:

> A little girl went out to play. Lost in the marketplace, as if half-born. Then, not through the marketplace—you see that, don't you?—but through the alley behind the marketplace. This is the way to the palace. But it isn't something you remember.

The notion of "an old tale" could be applied to many of *Inland Empire*'s threads: the adultery, prostitution and domestic abuse occurring throughout the film; the recycling of myths and scripts that underpins the narrative; and the connections between Europe and America, especially the architectural and cinematic traces littering Southern California, that Lynch emphasizes. Something else, however, is to be found in the visitor's strange story. In the final section of this chapter, we will enter "the alley behind the marketplace" to see what insights concerning Lynch's career might be lurking there. For now, we should proceed with other evocative terms in mind—neighbors and marriages, old tales and unpaid bills—as they offer vital co-ordinates to *Inland Empire*'s multi-layered geography.

An Old Tale: The Marriage of Łódź and Los Angeles

Łódź and Los Angeles might seem a perverse pairing. When news emerged that Frank Gehry and Lynch were involved in Łódź's regeneration plans—a partnership that saw Gehry project an image from *Inland Empire* on the façade of his proposed cultural center, while Lynch expressed his interest in establishing a film studio next to it—the *New York Times* felt compelled to ask, in rather patronizing terms, "What could they possibly see in the so-called Manchester of Poland?"[14] After all, both Gehry and Lynch are famed for their work in Los Angeles, where the suburbs, freeways and beaches once led Baudrillard to conclude: "Europe has disappeared."[15] Los Angeles has defined itself in opposition to the crowded industrial metropolis. Łódź, with its cobbled streets and cotton mills, represents the antithesis of California's centrifugal landscape (Plate 49). The capital of the Polish textile industry, the site of a prominent Jewish ghetto in World War II and a staunch socialist stronghold—how could Łódź's past possibly speak to the history of Los Angeles? Do they share any spatial or cinematic language? These puzzles are at the heart of *Inland Empire*. Yet, the initial improbability of this pairing, and perhaps the complexity of the film as a whole, has led most critics to neglect analyzing the Polish sections of *Inland Empire* in any depth—an additional surprise, given how rarely Lynch has shot outside of the United States in the rest of his career.

Lynch's interest in Łódź, Poland's third-largest city, began on a visit to its cinematography festival in 2000. In late 2003, he returned to take over 1,400 photographs, focusing on Łódź's decaying industrial apparatus, as well as various openings—doorways, staircases and courtyards—in the urban fabric. Assessing these initial trips, Žižek made the telling point that Lynch feels "very much at home" not in "the Romantic Poland" of Chopin or the Solidarity movement, but in the "ecologically ruined Poland of industrial wasteland." According to Žižek, this confirms "Lynch's extraordinary sensitivity," as such rotting zones of the "*Second World*" constitute "history, threatened with erasure between the posthistorical First World and prehistorical Third World."[16] Łódź, in this reading, seems to sit in an alley behind the marketplace.

Certainly, Lynch's initial mapping exercise confirms his continued fascination with industrial debris and particularly the interaction between mechanical and organic processes. It is Łódź's decay that caught his attention, especially the deterioration of its factories, where historical tribulations are inscribed on mottled beams and in peeling paint. Thirty years after illustrating Philadelphia's decline in *Eraserhead*, Lynch found a familiar home within Europe's own "Rust Belt." There remains a distinct historicity to the Łódź we see in *Inland Empire*, although here more romantic traces appear. Indeed, many of the film's Polish scenes, where snow-lined streets are traversed by horse-drawn carriages, appear to take place in a much earlier era to the sequences in Southern California. This again brings to mind Lynch's first perceptions of Europe, generated by his 1965 trip: "it felt like way more of the last century was manifest at that time." Central Europe, therefore, offers Lynch the opportunity for strange historical synthesis.

Prior representations of Łódź offer further guidance as to why it has appealed to Lynch. Joseph Roth's novel *Hotel Savoy* (1924) takes place in an unnamed city, clearly based on Łódź, at "the gates of Europe." Set in the aftermath of World War I, the city is described in terms comparable to the smoking chimneys, roaring furnaces and bubbling mounds of *Eraserhead* and *The Elephant Man*:

> The town, which had no drains, stank in any case. On grey days, at the edge of the wooden duckboards, one could see in the narrow, uneven gullies, black, yellow, glutinous muck out of the factories, still warm and steaming. It was a town accursed of God. It was as if the fire and brimstone had fallen here, not on Sodom and Gomorrah.
>
> God punished this town with industry. Industry is God's severest punishment.

A similar attention to the lush textures and fertile emissions of industry pervades Lynch's work. What is more, Roth suggests how fantasmatic desires might arise from this grim urban environment. "In this town," his protagonist states, "nothing is more needed than a cinema." The fraught juxtapositions of centripetal urbanism and the compressed leisure produced by industrial time-keeping require release in the form of the movie theater. Later in *Hotel Savoy*, "cheats and braggarts" from the film industry arrive in the city, anticipating Łódź's development as the capital of Polish cinema.[17] After World War II, the city became home to one of the most prestigious film schools in Europe, which includes Roman Polański and Krzysztof Kieślowski among its alumni. It also grew into a major site of cinematic production, earning the inevitable nickname HollyŁódź. As Orr points out, Łódź forms part of Central European cinema's own inland empire, along with Berlin, Vienna and Budapest, a "topographic nexus that has existed alongside Hollywood in the years of classical cinema and beyond."[18] Łódź, then, might be seen as Los Angeles' transatlantic twin. At the end of *Hotel Savoy*, however, Roth's narrator leaves this "accursed" city while dreaming of America, just as Neutra imagined California to be the antidote to Europe's "extreme squalidness."[19] For a continent torn apart by warfare, the United States increasingly functioned as the promised land.

When Andrzej Wajda, another graduate of the National Film School in Łódź, immortalized an earlier period in the city's development, the title of *The Promised Land* (1975) maintained an ironic tinge. Wajda's film is an incredible vision of industrial urbanism at the end of the nineteenth century, when Łódź was one of the fastest-growing cities in the world. In 1840, the population of Łódź was only 20,000, yet by 1900 it had reached 315,000.[20] Wajda depicts enormous factories and grand palaces surrounded by black smoke and pools of effluence. While rich industrialists enjoy homes filled with baroque décor and evenings watching sumptuous stage performances, workers are condemned to filthy streets and cramped accommodation. "The machines don't need you," one tycoon reminds a pleading employee. Another scene, in which a mangled body lies inside a large cotton loom, provides graphic evidence of industry's brutal consequences. As in *The Elephant Man* and *Eraserhead*, *The Promised Land* reveals the troubled marriage of man and machinery. Łódź's textile industry also provides an appropriate metaphor for the fabric of *Inland Empire*, where numerous cultural and historical threads are woven together to form a continuous cloth. (Neatly enough, the Polish word for factory is *fabryka*.) Furthermore, nineteenth-century Łódź, as *The Promised Land* confirms, hosted a rich congregation of cultures, including Poles, Germans, Russians and a substantial Jewish community, the kind of heterogeneous intertwining of nationalities and customs that would later emerge in Los Angeles during the twentieth century. Both these cities, then, have acted as regional meeting-points, where rampant commerce has provoked a patchwork of identities.

One final example confirms why Lynch, with his "extraordinary sensitivity" for symbolic locations, should be drawn to this particular Polish city. Daniel Libeskind, who was born in Łódź, returned to his hometown to find a vivid, distinctly Lynchian atmosphere:

> So familiar and yet so strange. [. . .] Uncanny and magnificent, yet full of sadness. That's how Łódź felt to me. The city appeared to be made of cardboard, a decaying set for a movie that wrapped long ago.[21]

Libeskind's remarks imply that manufacturing decline has created cinematic affect. Indeed, his characterization of Łódź recalls the qualities often attributed to Los Angeles and its own "cardboard" film studios (the architecture praised by Betty in *Sunset Boulevard*). Thus, Łódź's unreal environs, imbued with traumatic undercurrents, seem a prime target for Lynch's camera. In *Inland Empire*, moreover, he sets out to demonstrate that, when Łódź meets Los Angeles, the encounter will feel strangely familiar. In order to better understand this "marriage," we should examine in detail the powerful locations Lynch utilizes in the film.

An Unpaid Bill: *Inland Empire*

First, let us consider Nikki's home (Plate 50). Her baroque Hollywood mansion is full of mirrors and columns, ornate furnishings and *trompe l'oeil* effects. She lives like an aristocrat, with an arched entrance gate framed by statues of lions. This lavish display of wealth and status, maintained by an array of staff, is set within an exclusive, leafy district. The house also bears a striking resemblance to the location that immediately precedes it in *Inland Empire*. Just before we encounter Nikki's Hollywood mansion, we see two Polish men talking in another luxurious room. Here, shimmering surfaces, opulent paneling, thick drapes and rococo flourishes again dazzle (Plate 51). The two interiors are so similar they might easily be assumed to lie within the same house. Yet, this room is not part of a fashionable Californian development, but—in reality—sits within the Pałac Herbsta in Łódź (Plate 52). Designed by Hilary Majewski and completed in 1877, this grand villa, set alongside an enormous cotton factory and streets of workers' housing, is part of the vast empire created by Karl Scheibler, one of Europe's most ambitious industrialists of the nineteenth century. Indeed, *Inland Empire* contains other scenes in which we might assume Nikki is in her Californian home—when, for instance, she talks to her husband's parents—though she is actually in the Pałac Herbsta in Łódź. Shots of the exterior of her home do not match, in a strict geographical sense, the interiors she inhabits. Following Vertov, this film "room" is composed of "various parts of the world."

In *Inland Empire*, disparate places begin to speak to one another; unexpected bonds are formed. Nikki's "new neighbor" may outline "the way to the palace," but the film presents us with two concurrent versions: a Hollywood mansion and a tycoon's Polish villa. In both instances, the spaces pursue a form of luxury deeply indebted to European aristocratic traditions. During their rapid periods of growth, made possible by the absence of land and labor restrictions, Łódź and Los Angeles generated an assortment of architectural styles, often crudely distorted from their origins. Montage was a perennial urban feature. In Wajda's *The Promised Land*, one Łódź businessman leads a colleague around his palatial home. "This is our Spanish room," he declares. His daughter disagrees: "Papa's wrong—it's our Mauritian room." Later, she adds, "Every proper palace has a Chinese or Japanese room." This is exactly the kind of stylistic assemblage that prompts severe criticism of Los Angeles—the "truly monstrous" range of domestic designs satirized by Nathanael West. As we have seen, Lynch is compelled by such deviant products, whether they are generated by factories or the film industry. The golden palaces of Łódź and Los Angeles are extravagant examples of abnormal urbanism.

Let us turn to a second example of how Lynch marries these two cities. Later in *Inland Empire*, Nikki finds herself wandering among the down-and-out population of Hollywood Boulevard (Plate 53). It seems the only pedestrians in car-dominated Los Angeles are those "lost in the marketplace"—that is, prostitutes and the homeless. Suddenly, in the middle of the scene, the action cuts to a snowy evening in Łódź. A parallel line-up of women emerges, consisting of the same actors we saw in America, but now dressed in wintry fashions of the 1920s (Plate 54). Once again, the Polish scenes in the film act as a ghostly double to the accompanying Hollywood story. American actions are placed alongside European doppelgängers, as if the New World were re-enacting scenes that have previously occurred across the Atlantic. This, for some, is a terrifying prospect. "I wouldn't do a remake," says Devon Berk, Nikki's co-star.

The Polish version of Hollywood's red-light district is conspicuously archaic, with horse-drawn carriages and outmoded cars riding through the streets. Perhaps, this stark temporal shift is deemed appropriate for what is so often deemed the oldest profession in the world. Yet, other episodes in Łódź also contain candles and séances, intimating that the city represents another era, as well as a parallel space to Los Angeles. In Lynch's eyes, Łódź is stuck in its industrial heyday, unable to respond to contemporary concerns—a piece of vinyl still spinning in a digital age. Seemingly, the old Polish folk tale said to be haunting Nikki's new film is playing out before our eyes.

This folk tale, we learn, was previously the subject of an aborted film adaptation entitled *Vier Sieben* ("Four Seven"). The exact meaning of these numbers, which later appear on the door housing the "Rabbits" sitcom, is never explained in *Inland Empire*, although they allow for maddening speculation. Might *Vier Sieben* be a reference to Minnelli's *The Band Wagon* (1953), a film about remaking a theatrical show for a star's big comeback in which the central party scene—involving songs mixing English and German—takes place in a hotel room numbered 47? Does *Vier Sieben* have any connection with Bacon's painting *The End of the Line* (also from 1953), which features a spooky hut and a railway signal bearing the number 47? The latter suggestion becomes more intriguing when we consider Martin Harrison's claim that the building in Bacon's painting is based on a photograph of Thomas Edison's Black Maria—the wooden hut that housed America's first film studio.[22] Of course, such speculation traces a path as convoluted as Nikki's journey through Central Europe and Southern California. Nonetheless, it remains evocative to imagine the very heart of *Inland Empire* containing the architectural origins of American cinema, re-conceived by a European artist.

The history of cinema is certainly pertinent to the scenes of prostitution in *Inland Empire*. In Lynch's sudden geographical switch, Hollywood Boulevard is paired with Plac Zwycięstwa in Łódź, one of the city's oldest squares. In reality, these Polish women line up adjacent to the city's current Museum of Cinematography, as if searching for celluloid immortality (Plate 55). In fact, this alley, which lies opposite a former market-ground, also leads to a palace, for the museum is located inside another former home of Karl Scheibler. The interiors of this neo-renaissance structure, first erected in 1855, are now filled with antique film equipment, but were previously utilized as a set for Wajda's *The Promised Land*. Such abundant associations are a perennial feature of *Inland Empire's* locations, further confirming its director's "extraordinary sensitivity" to place. Elsewhere in the city, HollyŁódź even has its own walk of fame, commemorating the likes of Wajda, Polański and Kieślowski along Ulica Piotrkowska, the longest street in Poland (Plate 56). These golden stars, slightly distorted as if to indicate a more angular approach to cinema, replicate the famous icons on Hollywood Boulevard.

Lynch alludes to this dual cinematic heritage by having Nikki eventually collapse upon a Hollywood Boulevard plaque commemorating Dorothy Lamour. Lamour became a Paramount regular in the 1930s, the decade in which Hollywood Boulevard supplanted Broadway as the home of Los Angeles cinema by hosting the industry's most glamorous premieres. Now, however, as *Inland Empire* emphasizes, the street is as decayed as Łódź's factories, but corrosion again arouses Lynch's curiosity. Nikki crosses the famous intersection of Hollywood and Vine, where Neutra designed an office for Universal-International Pictures in 1933 adjacent to a restaurant designed by Rudolph Schindler (Plate 57). This corner, like the junction next to Winkie's diner in *Mulholland Drive*, was another location where budding actors would congregate in anticipation of stardom. Yet, a route to the palace remained impossible for most pretenders. For Lynch, such urban sites, in both Łódź and Los Angeles, constitute the alleys behind the marketplace, the murky spaces beyond the cinematic frame where dreams become nightmares.

After being stabbed by a rival, Nikki eventually "dies" on Hollywood Boulevard opposite the Pantages Theatre, home to the Academy Award ceremonies of the 1950s. In an uncanny move, the camera retracts, revealing this "death" to be yet another Oscar-worthy performance: what we are actually witnessing is a film-shoot within soundstage 4 at Paramount Studios. This shift from location shooting to a studio environment feels shocking, as if Lynch is taunting a spectator's architectural assumptions. Can you tell the difference between a real city and a cardboard set? the film seems to ask. If so, how much do these differences matter? A similar maneuver is employed earlier in *Inland Empire*, when Nikki opens the door to a wooden studio construction—previously shown to be merely a façade—only to enter a physical home elsewhere in California. All these environments, in Łódź or Los Angeles, in the studio or the suburbs, seem to exist simultaneously.

Inland Empire creates a series of uncertain regions between the supposedly ethereal world of film and the traditional materiality of the built environment, undermining regular conceptions of both cinema and architecture. It is a film filled with unexpected depth. There is, Kingsley tells Nikki and Devon, "something inside the story." Thus, what should be two-dimensional—a studio façade or a film script—proves to be three-dimensional. Libeskind's memoir offers a poetic defense of architecture's solidity, its role as "the eternal witness testifying mutely that the past we imagine is not illusory. I really did walk this street long ago, really did knock on that door."[23] Jeremy Till has also outlined the extent to which control, order and coherence have been at the center of architecture's self-conception from Vitruvius to Le Corbusier.[24] Such reassurances are exploded by Nikki's bewildered travels through California and Poland, in which her most common request is: "look at me, and tell me if you've known me before." Here, the physical presence of the buildings around her is shown to be worthless—there is no guarantee such structures are not the temporary creations of a cinematic world. In *Inland Empire*, architecture is less of an "eternal witness" and more like an unreliable narrator. The logical restrictions of place and continent seem effortlessly traversable. Libeskind believes architecture "expresses, stabilizes, and orients in an otherwise chaotic world."[25] Nikki, however, cannot calculate whether she really did "walk this street" or "knock on that door." For her, architecture itself forms a "chaotic world."

If *Inland Empire* forces us to confront the consequences of losing the reassuring solidity architecture is supposed to provide, then Lynch simultaneously emphasizes the highly physical qualities involved in the production of cinematic images. The architecture of cinema—lights, cameras, sets, movie theaters and projection rooms—as well as the sheer materiality of the film reel, are the building blocks of Lynch's fiction. What was begun in *Eraserhead* and *The Elephant Man*, films in which industrial practices are shown to have unintended effects on the city and its inhabitants, is carried to a conclusion in *Inland Empire*. Rather, however, than workshops erasing individuals or factories generating deformities, it is the psycho-spatial conflicts produced by the film industry that unite Los Angeles and Łódź.

The creepy sequence on Hollywood Boulevard maintains a powerful sense of physical loss. Indeed, *Inland Empire*'s digital images embody a distinct mourning for film and for the urban spaces that accompanied cinema's triumph. Nikki's scripted death, on such a symbolic street, is as traumatic as the staged events at Club Silencio, shot inside an abandoned downtown cinema: something beyond individual suffering is clearly at work here. In fact, just as Łódź's crumbling factories caught his eye, the fertile ruins of the film industry act as inspiration for *Inland Empire*. For Barber, the "mass-cultural experience of film and of cinema-going accumulated such pervasiveness within human gesture and perception [. . .] that its eventual dissolution necessarily possessed a correspondingly deep, sensorial and corporeal crash."[26] Nikki's own "corporeal crash"— and "crash" is the perfect term for a digitally shot collapse—occurs on a dilapidated strip of urban history to be captured first on 35mm film (for *On High in Blue Tomorrows*, the film she is making) and then by Lynch's digital camera (for *Inland Empire*). From this makeshift Hollywood Boulevard housed within Paramount Studios, Nikki wanders into an empty cinema—the Orpheum Theater on Broadway—via a red curtain indicating the heterotopian nature of the space (Plates 58 and 59). There, passing marble columns that add glamor to this tale of cinematic decay, she encounters her past, present and future movements on the screen, in another vivid representation of temporal simultaneity. Furthermore, the Kafkaesque figure (named, we should note, Mr K in the credits), who previously acted as an interviewer or analyst for one of Nikki's performances, now seems to be a cinema usher, leading Nikki towards a metallic control room filled with clocks and dials. These sites of neglect and desertion reverberate with the collected memories of cinematic urbanism, yet the looping celluloid city has been replaced by the logic of a new medium. As Tom McCarthy recognizes, the inter-connected rooms, streets, sets and screens of *Inland Empire* constitute a "digital" architecture constructed around "information storage, relay and configuration."[27]

Within its own digital images, *Inland Empire* remains haunted by the ghostly arrangements of other technologies. From radios and gramophones to CCTV monitors, *Inland Empire* is inhabited by competing media. We might even locate a plausible explanation for the film's narrative complexities via a Polish television screen. At the beginning and end of *Inland Empire*, we see a young woman inside a plush hotel room watching a variety of images on television, including sequences from the rest of the film. These scenes were shot inside Łódź's Hotel Grand—designed, like the Pałac Herbsta, by Hilary Majewski—which was originally a factory before its conversion (Plate 60). On the street below the hotel are the plaques honoring Poland's cinematic stars, while the suite Lynch utilized commemorates Arthur Rubinstein, the famous Łódź pianist who fled to Beverly Hills during World War II (and who now has his own star on the Hollywood Walk of Fame on Vine Street). This evocative setting provides an intriguing stage for scenes that some critics claim hold the key to *Inland Empire*. For example, McGowan believes the various worlds we encounter "all emanate from the Lost Girl who appears at the beginning of the film" and Joshua Gonsalves agrees: "The crying whore is imagining a variety of scenarios that will allow her to attain resolution."[28] By this reading, the Rubinstein suite at the Hotel Grand is one of Lynch's central chambers or control rooms, a venue from which filmic action is manipulated. Łódź, with its industrial apparatus and cinematic history, is certainly a suggestive spot for the operation of Hollywood drama. However, in *Inland Empire*, where space and time function under the logic of simultaneity, where identities fuse and the boundaries between the real and the filmic dissolve, such a didactic interpretation of the film's various subjectivities seems reductive. The approach of McGowan and Gonsalves is better suited to *Lost Highway* and *Mulholland Drive*, where a governing force (Fred Madison and Diane Selwyn, respectively) drives the distorted narratives.

One last example from *Inland Empire* demonstrates how a wider set of geographical registers, from within and beyond the cinematic screen, underpin the marriage of Łódź and Los Angeles. The Polish Lost Girl, as abused by men as her American counterpart Nikki, recites the words (in Polish): "Cast out this wicked dream that has seized my heart." This is a line once uttered by Gloria Swanson in *Queen Kelly* (1929), directed by the Austrian-born, Hollywood-based Erich von Stroheim, and produced by Swanson with financing by Joseph Kennedy. *Queen Kelly* is a famously unfinished film, of which several versions with differing endings exist. Lost in the marketplace for decades, it only received a full theatrical release in 1985. It is a tale set in an ancient Middle-European kingdom involving palaces, brothels and suicide.[29] The line "Cast out this wicked dream that has seized my heart" also appears on-screen in *Sunset Boulevard*, as Norma Desmond (played by Swanson again) relives her past glories, aided by a faithful butler (played by von Stroheim). Furthermore, before making his mark in Hollywood, *Sunset Boulevard*'s director, Billy Wilder, was born in an area of Austria-Hungary that is now part of Poland. *Sunset Boulevard*, Lynch claims, "is in my top five movies, for sure."[30] Indeed, when he first moved to Los Angeles, Lynch spent several days cruising suburban neighborhoods in search of Norma Desmond's home, further indicating his obsessional approach to cinematic architecture.[31]

Many implications arise from the unraveling of this complex sequence. First, it contradicts the notion that *Inland Empire* operates beyond comprehension or conceivable inspiration. For instance, Atkinson's claim that the film displays "no visible marks" of either "influence" or "homage" is rendered void.[32] In fact, the film is constructed around the physical traces of cinematic history, including those parts left on the cutting-room floor. More importantly, by imposing such a fertile quotation into *Inland Empire*, Lynch draws upon its multifaceted genealogy and geography. He suggests an inter-continental, inter-generational network of female actors, all seized by the "wicked dream" of cinematic stardom (though male violence remains "an old tale," too). The scene also stresses that the histories of Central Europe and Southern California are deeply intertwined, that the two regions are, in some sense, married. And, as

Nikki's Polish husband reminds Devon, "the bonds of marriage are real bonds."

For Lynch, Los Angeles—famed for its easy-going attitude, the absence of social restrictions and a plenitude of fresh land—remains inhabited by the moods, spaces and spirits of its ancestors. Lynch himself is particularly indebted to the incredible range of talent that moved from Europe to America in the 1920s and 1930s, the era in which many of the Polish scenes in *Inland Empire* appear to take place. Directors such as Wilder, Preminger and Sirk, as well as architects such as Neutra and Mies van der Rohe, have all exerted a significant influence on his life and on his films. The emigration of so many crucial cultural figures is one of the defining geographical movements of the twentieth century. According to Richard Pells, for Europe it represented "a haemorrhage of talent and intellect from which the Continent never recovered."[33] Perhaps, then, we might see *Inland Empire* as Lynch's oblique acknowledgment that his career and the rise of the Classical Hollywood cinema that inspired him, as well as the development of the Californian architectural modernism he so admires, all constitute an "unpaid bill" to European creditors. Moreover, the fact that many of these significant creative figures emigrated in response to Nazism lends additional resonance to Lynch's use of Łódź—the site of enormous suffering during World War II, when it was renamed Litzmannstadt. Indeed, the sisters of Kafka (whom Lynch, we must remind ourselves, regards as "the one artist I feel could be my brother") were among the hundreds of thousands who died in the Łódź Ghetto. Luckhurst rightly points out that Lynch "is interested less in specific, historical *losses* than in general, structural *absences*—that is, the foundational trauma of what it means to be a subject rather than any locatable historical condition."[34] Nevertheless, the unsettling atmosphere underpinning the Polish elements of *Inland Empire* certainly implies a great historical trauma—an "old tale" that refuses to fade away.

Adam Thirlwell has suggested: "Think about it. Everyone, always, is living in central Europe." The countless tragedies and endless translations tied to the region not only provoke this universal status, a form of global simultaneity that *Inland Empire* promotes; but, for Thirlwell, they also refresh creative energies so that "old ideas of form and content are replaced by messier concepts—junk, or kitsch, or defeat."[35] *Inland Empire* involves the radical reworking of symbolic material into a raw, chaotic, emotionally compelling whole. For Lynch, Europe functions as a privileged site of mourning and memory, the site of recurring anxieties and suspicions, with particular connotations for the film industry. After all, European cinema has traditionally feared the dominance of Hollywood; in turn, Hollywood has frequently depicted Europe as a source of sophisticated malevolence (see, for example, Mr Reindeer in *Wild at Heart*). Yet, *Inland Empire* positions the marriage of Łódź and Los Angeles as an "old tale" with more universal overtones. The film begins with the announcement of "the longest-running radio play in history" and ends with the apocalyptic fervor of Nina Simone's "Sinnerman," where the judgments on good and evil simultaneously occur "all on that day."

At the end of *Inland Empire*, there is a tumultuous collision of people and places. As the Lost Girl sprints through the film's various corridors, sets and rooms, all these locations are revealed to be simultaneously housed within the same structure: the marriage of Łódź and Los Angeles is complete. Indeed, here the film itself feels like a fairground funhouse, containing unexpected connections and cheap special effects. It is as if nineteenth-century entertainment, cinema's precursor, has returned, and the Lost Girl—like Treves in the circus in *The Elephant Man*—becomes a figure capable of navigating its contours. *Inland Empire* culminates in perhaps the most joyous scene in Lynch's cinema, when the film's female characters congregate in a celebratory union in direct contrast to the violence, confusion and terror that has preceded it. Like a Renaissance drama, the conflicting emotions and intricate action of the past 170 minutes are brought to a close with a final ceremony. The scene has an important spatial dimension, too. After exposing us to so many settings, Lynch ends the film in the marble ballroom in Nikki's Hollywood mansion. All the rooms in *Inland Empire* have led to this room. The prostitutes and the actors have finally found their way to the palace.

The Alley Behind the Marketplace

Inland Empire's last scene feels like the end to more than just one film. It seems to signal definitive closure—a triumphant departure, a final dramatic statement and an epic celebration. While he continues to be an active painter, photographer and musician, among other activities, at the time of writing, Lynch has yet to return to feature-length film-making. If it remains too early to state that *Inland Empire* is Lynch's farewell to cinema, and rumors about new projects continue to circulate, the film certainly represents the culmination of many of his most potent themes. To again extend the logic of Keaton's home in *The Scarecrow*, it is as if all Lynch's films are somehow housed within *Inland Empire*. The heightened finality of its ending further encourages us to assess the career that led to this point.

One of the most suggestive phrases from *Inland Empire* frames these broader considerations. The "variation" on "an old tale" that Nikki's neighbor recounts at the start of the film culminates in the evocation of an "alley behind the marketplace." This, Nikki is told, "is the way to the palace," although "it isn't something you remember." These terms not only help us to understand *Inland Empire*; they also provide a productive spatial metaphor through which we can read Lynch's six decades of filmmaking.

First, we might consider what associations are prompted by the thought of an "alley." Beyond its primary meaning as a narrow passage, the *OED* outlines a specifically American definition of the term: "A backlane running parallel with a main street." The symbolic power of dark corridors, tight channels and claustrophobic spaces has been manipulated by Lynch throughout his career. His domestic environments are constantly accessed through side entrances or windows (consider Merrick's attic in *The Elephant Man*, Laura's bedroom in *Fire Walk With Me* and Diane's apartment in *Mulholland Drive*). Rarely do Lynch's characters approach their surroundings from a straightforward angle, while his camera frequently thrusts into unexpected openings (within a radiator in *Eraserhead* and a lawn in *Blue Velvet*). As such, Lynch covers the same symbolic territory as more conventional directors, including urban life, family homes and road trips, while occupying his own "alley" parallel to the main street.

This approach has led Lynch to discover compelling spaces in neglected landscapes—the field "behind Vista" in *Blue Velvet*, for instance, or the garbage area behind Winkie's diner in *Mulholland Drive*. In *Inland Empire*, a physical representation of "the alley behind the marketplace" appears in the form of a small lane full of rusting cans and graffiti—a place where Nikki parks when she needs groceries (Plate 61). Critically, this passage is shown to lie next to soundstage 4 at Paramount Studios and houses a doorway into its famous sets. Fittingly enough, since 2010, the tight passage linking soundstages 4 and 18 at the Paramount Studios lot has been known as "The Alley." Encompassing, in the words of Paramount's promotional material, "200 Feet of Urban Flexibility," this area can be dressed for different city scenes. "Let's face it," the studio's website concludes, "shooting a scene in a real downtown alley is expensive, dirty and time consuming."[36]

For Lynch, "the alley behind the marketplace" epitomizes an artistic route that runs adjacent to the major sites of filmic production—an approach that enters these powerful locations on occasion, but which does so from an askew angle. What is more, an "alley" implies a distinct connection between two places, via a passage unseen by most observers. Hence, *Inland Empire*'s marriage of Łódź and Los Angeles is one of the many spatial systems in Lynch's cinema that pivots on surprising combinations and unsettled histories. Likewise, *Blue Velvet*'s Lumberton sits somewhere between the 1950s and 1980s, and *Eraserhead*'s Philadelphia festers anxiously amid competing industrial eras. The simultaneous presence of incongruent elements, the strange protrusions and fraught juxtapositions produced by places caught in conflict, all emerge under Lynch's microscopic examination. Critical inquiries into these alleys expose architectural meanings situated beyond the conventional "marketplace."

That *Inland Empire*'s "alley" lies behind a "marketplace" should lead us to think more closely about the commercial pressures to which Lynch's cinema often obliquely returns. His directorial career initially hinged on leaving Philadelphia, a city in the midst of severe economic troubles, for the fertile terrain of Southern California. Through Henry's uneasy relationship with public space, as well as his unemployment, *Eraserhead*'s vision of urban decline offers a graphic representation of agoraphobia—a condition, in its Greek origins, defined as fear (*phobos*) of the marketplace (*agora*). Lynch followed this independent debut with two major studio productions, the second of which, *Dune*, left him distinctly wary of the economic forces driving Hollywood. The curtailment of *Twin Peaks* and the failure of the *Mulholland Drive* television project have added to his disdain for contemporary commercial logic. Thus, the "marketplace" has always troubled Lynch. A parallel zone "behind" this frustrating and terrifying environment offers a degree of safety and artistic control, while still providing access to the stars (such as Laura Dern and Jeremy Irons) and facilities (including Paramount Studios) of mainstream cinema. This is a potentially unstable position to inhabit, however. One crew member claimed that *Lost Highway*, like many of Lynch's works, occupies "a sort of middle ground between an art film and a major studio release. This is a hard niche to work in. It's an economically fragile niche, you could say."[37] Lynch's work often feels like a strange collision between avant-garde forms (particularly evident in *Eraserhead* and *Inland Empire*) and mainstream commercial enterprises (*Twin Peaks* comes to mind here), so much so that one definition of "Lynchian" might be a scene or an entire work that operates in "the alley behind the marketplace."

Moreover, Lynch may have had his struggles with feminist critics, but *Inland Empire* outlines specific concern for the women "lost in the marketplace." Indeed, from Norma Desmond to Betty Elms and Nikki Grace, the film industry's destructive treatment of female actors, as well as the multiple performances required of all women, have become prime concerns for Lynch. Hollywood's own alleys "behind the marketplace" are darker realms where prostitution, as *Inland Empire* demonstrates, and the porn industry, highlighted in *Lost Highway*, operate. One observer has also placed *Inland Empire*'s transatlantic journeys in the context of sex trafficking.[38]

The explicit reward of "the palace" further complicates these interpretations. This destination not only suggests a Hollywood mansion or a Polish villa, with their connotations of European royalty; it also hints at the classic American movie palace, with all its democratic hopes. If the "alley" is understood in the more menacing sense of prostitution or pornography, then Lynch implies that these activities, which actors might not care to "remember," are what ultimately leads to cinematic stardom. Furthermore, the desolate movie palace Nikki enters in *Inland Empire* suggests that film-making can no longer attract its required customers. Alternatively, if we consider the "alley" in terms of a creative space carved out adjacent to the numbing demands of mainstream cinema, then Lynch insinuates that only this avenue can lead to artistic fulfillment. The "alley behind the marketplace" might, therefore, symbolize the "unrestricted space and the means to overcome those limitations" that Nouvel defined as the shared goal of the film-maker and the architect, faced with a world governed by compromise. The "palace," by this account, becomes a place of artistic satisfaction rather than financial achievement. In *Inland Empire*, Nikki's "new neighbor" may be encouraging the actor to abandon her literal "palace" for more challenging (and less well-paid) acting roles.

In following "the alley behind the marketplace," Lynch has rallied against the historical tendency for American space to be propelled into grids and straight stories; not for nothing have his last four films been overseen by Asymmetrical Productions. From Lynch's skewed perspective, symbolic spaces are approached from a passage parallel to the main street; uncanny encounters are staged. Thus, "the alley behind the marketplace" is a distinctly self-conscious piece of dialogue. It is a reminder to a director, struggling to fulfill his creative ambitions, of the methods he has used in the past. Amid such reflexivity, *Inland Empire's* multiple stories, recurring phrases and overlapping images function as confrontations between the film and itself. Just as Nikki wanders into an empty cinema to find herself on-screen, Lynch wants to challenge his own images while he creates them. This is a further element of the film's logic of simultaneity, and a rigor designed to ensure the final product avoids being "lost in the marketplace." Lynch, it seems, wants to be in the same room as the exalted names of cinematic history, yet he wants to access this space via an unfamiliar route.

With its industrial heyday now past, and persistent poverty remaining, Łódź currently finds itself in one of the uncertain zones Lynch has often manipulated. Presently, it is concerned with reinventing itself as a post-industrial assemblage of conference centers and hotels, shopping malls and aqua parks, universities and media outlets—an urban model pioneered by Los Angeles and the kind of rebranding exercise designed to catch the attention of the *New York Times*. Recent plans for the city have included Lynch's desire to create a film studio inside an old power station in the EC1 area of the city, adjacent to the site for which Gehry designed a new cultural center (Plate 62). However, both Lynch and Gehry have found their projects stalled amid severe funding problems. Apparently, another "unpaid bill" haunts Łódź.

Lynch, of course, is not known for aiding smooth changes in identity, on an individual or urban scale. In fact, the reasons why he was drawn to Łódź—its raw industrial forms and richly symbolic history, especially in cinematic terms—are now increasingly packaged into bland tourist simulacra, epitomized by the city's Manufaktura complex. With *Inland Empire* in mind, Gehry's appropriation of Lynch's film might seem like a supplementary vow to Łódź's marriage with Los Angeles. It would be easy to conclude that the building and the film share a similar architecture, with Gehry's jarring forms reflecting the irregular narrative of *Inland Empire*. Certainly, the range of meanings to be drawn from Lynch's work provides a welcome change from the insipid ambitions of images often projected into the public realm. At the same time, *Inland Empire* feels ill-suited for assimilation into a glossy regeneration project. That Gehry's plans remain unrealized seems rather more in keeping with the architecture of Lynch's film.

Notably, Hal Foster has recently examined with skepticism a number of strands running through the celebrated creations of contemporary architects, including the work of Gehry and Nouvel. In particular, Foster criticizes "environments that confuse the actual with the virtual"— buildings that, instead of activating our senses, tend to "subdue us." Such buildings, Foster argues, provoke a "stunned subjectivity." He specifically cites Nouvel's Fondation Cartier in Paris, the building that housed Lynch's art exhibition in 2007, because its extensive glass panels are designed "to dazzle or confuse, as if the paragon of architecture might be an illuminated jewel or mysterious ambiance."[39]

By contrast, Lynch's architecture is a constant provocation. Rather than producing the "stunned subjectivity" Foster identifies as a common response to contemporary design, the worlds Lynch has built and filmed force us to confront the strange forces involved in urban change, the social relations architecture constitutes, the uneasy feelings of being at home, the dynamics of spectatorship, and the presence of the past in the spaces of the present. Through his extreme awareness of the symbolic pressures attached to certain archetypal structures, the manner in which architectural meaning is produced through cultural and psychological associations, Lynch encourages us to reassess and redesign the everyday forms that shape our lives. In "the alley behind the marketplace," he has located an artistically profitable perspective on American life. This approach has, for Lynch, been the way to the palace. It is something more film-makers, not to mention architects, should remember.

ACKNOWLEDGMENTS

The author and publisher gratefully acknowledge the permission granted to reproduce the copyright material in this book.

This book was written in London, Lisbon and Berlin, and has involved research trips over the last seven years to Paris, Los Angeles, Łódź and Philadelphia. The project began life as a PhD thesis at the London Consortium—a collaborative doctoral program based at Birkbeck, University of London. My research benefited enormously from the faculty and students at the Consortium, and especially from its director, Steven Connor, and my two supervisors, Barry Curtis and Tom McCarthy, all of whom were enthusiastic and encouraging about the project from the outset. Stephen Barber and Matthew Gandy, who examined the final thesis, have continued to provide guidance and support, while comments from Parveen Adams, Marko Daniel, Roger Luckhurst and Matthew Taunton greatly improved my work. I am extremely grateful to the Arts and Humanities Research Council for a doctoral award and for providing additional funding for my trip to Los Angeles.

In Los Angeles, Karen Kice compensated for my lack of driving skills with an expert tour, while in Łódź I was deeply indebted to Piotr Strzelecki's knowledge of the city. It was a pleasure to work with Yana Stoimenova, who took a wonderful series of photographs of Los Angeles for the book, and with Craig Ritchie, who shot locations in London. I also extend my thanks to the many copyright holders who allowed me to reproduce images here. The generosity of Docomomo UK, who awarded me the John Bancroft Memorial Grant to cover the costs of the illustrations, is greatly appreciated, and to have the book associated with such a distinguished architect brings me particular pleasure.

At Bloomsbury, I have been lucky to find highly professional support for the book, with thanks to Simon Cowell, Simon Longman, Rebecca Barden and, in particular, Abbie Sharman. I am especially grateful for the thoughtful and perceptive comments provided by the anonymous reviewers of both the proposal and the manuscript.

Arguments in the book were rehearsed in presentations at Tate Modern, London; the University of Nottingham; the Rothermere American Institute, University of Oxford; Oxford Brookes University; the University of Central Lancashire; the Lisbon Summer School for the Study of Culture; the University of Kent; and the Technische Universität Dortmund. My thanks to the organizers of all the events for the opportunity to share my work, and to the participants who offered such useful feedback.

A section of Chapter 1 was previously published in *European Journal of American Culture*, Vol. 32, Issue 3 (2013), while an early version of Chapter 5 appeared in *49th Parallel: An Interdisciplinary Journal of North American Studies*, Vol. 25 (Spring 2011). My thanks to the journal editors for permission to reproduce material here.

For too long my friends and family have listened to me talk about this project. I have shared ideas constantly with Nick Dobson, Jonathan Gross and Alex Stein, who remain the most inspiring friends. Lucy Scholes generously read large chunks of the text, offered brilliant insights and was always eager to talk about movies, old and new. The friendship of Miles Wilkinson, Ozlem Koksal, Ben Dawson, Adam Kaasa, Richard Daniels, Christien Garcia and Dietmar Meinel has sustained me during the research and writing. The love and support of my parents, Sharon and Graham Martin, was vital throughout.

The book is dedicated with love to Alice Honor Gavin, who made it possible in more ways than I can ever acknowledge, and to Seba Davies, for being its most eager and reliable champion.

NOTES

Prologue: Three Journeys

1   Jean Baudrillard and Jean Nouvel, *The Singular Object of Architecture*, trans. Robert Bononno (Minneapolis: University of Minneapolis Press, 2002), p. 8.
2   Conway Lloyd Morgan, *Jean Nouvel: The Elements of Architecture* (London: Thames and Hudson, 1999), p. 151.

Introduction: Mapping the Lost Highway

1   Le Corbusier, *Towards a New Architecture*, trans. Frederick Etchells (New York: Dover, 1986), p. 73.
2   Michel Chion, *David Lynch*, trans. Robert Julian (London: BFI, 2006), p. 170.
3   Arie Graafland and Jaspar de Haan, "A Conversation with Rem Koolhaas," in *The Critical Landscape*, ed. Michael Speaks (Rotterdam: 010 Publishers, 1996), pp. 227–8.
4   Steven Jacobs, *The Wrong House: The Architecture of Alfred Hitchcock* (Rotterdam: 010 Publishers, 2007), p. 138.
5   For brevity and clarity, I will refer to the television series as *Twin Peaks* and the 1992 film version, *Twin Peaks: Fire Walk With Me*, as simply *Fire Walk With Me*.
6   Gaston Bachelard, *The Poetics of Space*, trans. Maria Jolas (Boston: Beacon Press, 1994), p. 127.
7   "(Why) is David Lynch Important? A *Parkett* Inquiry," *Parkett*, No. 28 (1991), pp. 153–62.
8   John Powers, "Getting Lost is Beautiful: The Light and Dark World of David Lynch," *LA Weekly*, 19–25 October 2001.
9   Kathrin Spohr, "The World Reveals Itself," in *David Lynch: Interviews*, ed. Richard A. Barney (Jackson: University Press of Mississippi, 2009), p. 168.

10 *Lynch on Lynch*, ed. Chris Rodley (London: Faber and Faber, 2005), p. 110.

11 Ibid., p. 2.

12 Ibid., p. 33.

13 Greg Olson, *David Lynch: Beautiful Dark* (Lanham, MD: Scarecrow Press, 2008), p. 22.

14 *Lynch on Lynch*, p. 36.

15 Chion, *David Lynch*, p. 10.

16 Slavoj Žižek, *The Art of the Ridiculous Sublime: On David Lynch's Lost Highway* (Seattle: Walter Chapin Simpson Center for the Humanities, 2002); Todd McGowan, *The Impossible David Lynch* (New York: Columbia University Press, 2007).

17 Justus Nieland, *David Lynch* (Urbana: University of Illinois Press, 2012), pp. 3–4.

18 Vitruvius, *The Ten Books on Architecture*, trans. Morris Hicky Morgan (New York: Dover, 1960), pp. 5–12.

19 Bruno Taut, "Artistic Film Program," in *Film Architecture: Set Design from Metropolis to Blade Runner*, ed. Dietrich Neumann, trans. Almuth Seebohm (Munich: Prestel, 1996), p. 183.

20 Katherine Shonfield, *Walls Have Feelings: Architecture, Film and the City* (London: Routledge, 2000), p. 173.

21 Wim Wenders, "Find Myself a City to Live In," in *On Film: Essays and Conversations* (London: Faber, 2001), p. 384.

22 Paul Smith, "The Eisenman–Haneke Tapes," *Icon*, No. 55 (January 2008).

23 *Jean Nouvel 1987–2006*. Special Issue of *Architecture and Urbanism*, ed. Nobuyuki Yoshida and Ai Kitazawa (April 2006), p. 148.

24 Laura Barnett, "Portrait of the Artist: Nigel Coates, Architect," *The Guardian*, 12 October 2010.

25 Michelangelo Antonioni, "A Conversation with Michelangelo Antonioni," in *The Architecture of Vision: Writings and Interviews on Cinema* (New York: Marsilio, 1996), p. 135.

26 Spohr, "The World Reveals Itself," p. 169.

27 Hans Dieter Schaal, *Learning from Hollywood: Architecture and Film*, trans. Michael Robinson (Stuttgart: Axel Menges, 1996), p. 54.

28 Spohr, "The World Reveals Itself," p. 169.

29 Dziga Vertov, *Kino-Eye: The Writings of Dziga Vertov*, trans. Kevin O'Brien (London: Pluto Press, 1984), p. 17.

30 *Lynch on Lynch*, p. 74.

31 Sergei Eisenstein, "Montage and Architecture," trans. Michael Glenny, *Assemblage*, No. 10 (December 1989), p. 117; Giuliana Bruno, *Atlas of*

Emotion: Journeys in Art, Architecture and Film (New York: Verso, 2002), p. 68.

32 Baudrillard and Nouvel, *The Singular Object of Architecture*, pp. 6–7.

33 Morgan, *Jean Nouvel*, pp. 97; 101.

34 Reyner Banham, *A Concrete Atlantis: U.S. Industrial Building and European Modern Architecture, 1900–1925* (Cambridge, MA: MIT Press, 1986), p. 9.

35 *Jean Nouvel 1987–2006*, p. 152.

36 Baudrillard and Nouvel, *The Singular Object of Architecture*, p. 5.

37 Fredric Jameson, *Postmodernism, Or, The Cultural Logic of Late Capitalism* (London: Verso, 1993), p. 113.

38 *Lynch on Lynch*, p. 275.

39 *Jean Nouvel 1987–2006*, p. 140.

40 Tom Conley, *Cartographic Cinema* (Minneapolis: University of Minnesota Press, 2007), p. 18.

41 Juhani Pallasmaa, *The Architecture of Image: Existential Space in Cinema*, trans. Michael Wynne-Ellis (Helskini: Rakennustieto, 2007), pp. 18; 33.

42 Baudrillard and Nouvel, *The Singular Object of Architecture*, p. 12.

43 Tim Bergfelder, Sue Harris and Sarah Street, *Film Architecture and the Transnational Imagination: Set Design in 1930s European Cinema* (Amsterdam: Amsterdam University Press, 2007), p. 13.

44 Baudrillard and Nouvel, *The Singular Object of Architecture*, p. 12.

45 Ibid., p. 6.

1: Town and City

1 Henry Ford, "The Farmer—Nature's Partner," in *Ford Ideals: Being a Selection from "Mr. Ford's Page" in the Dearborn Independent* (Dearborn, MI: Dearborn Publishing Company, 1922), p. 127.

2 Jonathan Raban, *Soft City* (London: Picador, 2008), p. 11.

3 Morton and Lucia White, *The Intellectual Versus the City: From Thomas Jefferson to Frank Lloyd Wright* (Cambridge, MA: Harvard University Press, 1962).

4 Frank Lloyd Wright, *When Democracy Builds* (Chicago: University of Chicago Press, 1945), p. 116.

5 Jane Jacobs, *The Death and Life of Great American Cities* (New York: Vintage, 1992), pp. 220; 255.

6 Robert Beauregard, *Voices of Decline: The Postwar Fate of US Cities* (Oxford: Blackwell, 1993), p. xi.

7   Ibid., p. 118.

8   David Brodsly, *L.A. Freeway: An Appreciative Essay* (Berkeley: University of California Press, 1981), p. 33.

9   Raban, *Soft City*, p. 2.

10 Georg Simmel, "The Metropolis and Mental Life," trans. Kurt H. Wolff, in *Simmel on Culture: Selected Writings* (London: Sage, 2000), pp. 174–85.

11 Edward W. Soja, *Postmodern Geographies: The Reassertion of Space in Critical Social Theory* (London: Verso, 1994), p. 7.

12 Andrew Webber, "Introduction: Moving Images of Cities," in *Cities in Transition: The Moving Image and the Modern Metropolis*, ed. Andrew Webber and Emma Wilson (London: Wallflower Press, 2008), p. 1.

13 Henri Lefebvre, *The Urban Revolution*, trans. Robert Bononno (Minneapolis: University of Minneapolis Press, 2003), p. 57.

14 Kevin Lynch, *The Image of the City* (Cambridge, MA: MIT Press, 1960), pp. 87; 89.

15 Le Corbusier, *The City of Tomorrow and its Planning*, trans. Frederick Etchells (New York: Dover, 1987), p. 5; Michel de Certeau, *The Practice of Everyday Life*, trans. Steven Rendall (Berkeley: University of California Press, 1988), p. 93.

16 Judith R. Walkowitz, *City of Dreadful Delight: Narratives of Sexual Danger in Late-Victorian London* (London: Virago, 1992), p. 18.

17 Olson, *David Lynch*, p. 123.

18 Henry Ford, *My Life and Work* (Sydney: Cornstalk, 1924), p. 103.

19 Walter Benjamin, "The Work of Art in the Age of Mechanical Reproduction," in *Illuminations*, trans. Harry Zorn (London: Pimlico, 1999), pp. 211–44.

20 Le Corbusier, *Towards a New Architecture*, p. 57.

21 Jacobs, *The Death and Life of Great American Cities*, p. 54.

22 Ibid., pp. 105; 37.

23 Ibid., p. 171.

24 Richard Sennett, *The Conscience of the Eye: The Design and Social Life of Cities* (New York: W. W. Norton, 1992), pp. 47–8.

25 John C. Teaford, *The Metropolitan Revolution: The Rise of Post-Urban America* (New York: Columbia University Press, 2006), pp. 133, 138; Joseph S. Clark, Jr. and Dennis J. Clark, "Rally and Relapse, 1946–1968," in *Philadelphia: A 300-Year History*, ed. Russell F. Wigley (New York: W. W. Norton, 1982), p. 668.

26 Paul A. Woods, *Weirdsville USA: The Obsessive Universe of David Lynch* (London: Plexus, 2000), p. 32.

27 Henry James, *The American Scene* (London: Granville, 1987), pp. 196–204.

28 John Updike, *Rabbit, Run* (London: Penguin, 2006), pp. 23–4; John Updike, *Rabbit is Rich* (London: Penguin, 2006), p. 141; John Updike, *Rabbit at Rest* (London: Penguin, 2006), p. 281.

29 Olson, *David Lynch*, p. 26.

30 *Lynch on Lynch*, p. 43.

31 Michael Alan Goldberg, "There Goes the Eraserhood: Why Local Artists are Hoping to Preserve the Callowhill District's Gritty Past," *Philadelphia Weekly*, 11 July 2012.

32 McGowan, *The Impossible David Lynch*, pp. 26–48.

33 Peter Eisenman, "Architecture as a Second Language: The Texts of Between," in *Restructuring Architectural Theory*, ed. Marco Diani and Catherine Ingraham (Evanston, IL: Northwestern University Press, 1989), p. 70.

34 Edward Dimendberg, *Film Noir and the Spaces of Modernity* (Cambridge, MA: Harvard University Press, 2004), pp. 10; 255.

35 Ibid., p. 91.

36 Le Corbusier, *When the Cathedrals Were White: A Journey to the Country of Timid People*, trans. Francis E. Hyslop, Jr. (London: Routledge, 1948), p. 157.

37 Jameson, *Postmodernism*, p. 296; Marshall Berman, *All That is Solid Melts into Air: The Experience of Modernity* (London: Penguin, 1988), p. 330; John Updike, "Why Rabbit Had to Go," *New York Times*, 5 August 1990.

38 See, for example, Stanley Corkin, *Starring New York: Filming the Grime and the Glamour of the Long 1970s* (New York: Oxford University Press, 2011).

39 *Lynch on Lynch*, p. 279.

40 Paul Swann, "From Workshop to Backlot: The Greater Philadelphia Film Office," in *Cinema and the City: Film and Urban Societies in a Global Context*, ed. Mark Shiel and Tony Fitzmaurice (Oxford: Blackwell, 2001), pp. 88–98.

41 Sean Wilentz, *The Age of Reagan: A History, 1974–2008* (New York: Harper, 2008), p. 135.

42 The Epistle of Paul the Apostle to the Romans 13. 9.

43 Slavoj Žižek, Eric L. Santer and Kenneth Reinhard, *The Neighbor: Three Inquiries in Political Theology* (Chicago: University of Chicago Press, 2005), p. 5.

44 James T. Patterson, *Restless Giant: The United States from Watergate to Bush v. Gore* (Oxford: Oxford University Press, 2005), p. 129.

45 Entitled "Prouder, Stronger, Better," the commercial was originally screened on 17 September 1984 and can be seen at: http://www.livingroomcandidate.org/commercials/1984/prouder-stronger-better.

46 Emanuel Levy, *Small-Town America in Film* (New York: Continuum, 1991); Kenneth MacKinnon, *Hollywood's Small Towns: An Introduction to the American Small-Town Movie* (Methuen, NJ: Scarecrow Press, 1984).

47 Alec MacGillis, "Lost in Rural USA," *New Statesman*, 27 October 2008, p. 16.

48 Andrew Ross, *The Celebration Chronicles: Life, Liberty, and the Pursuit of Property Values in Disney's New Town* (London: Verso, 2000), pp. 18; 37.

49 Andres Duany, Elizabeth Plater-Zyberk and Jeff Speck, *Suburban Nation: The Rise of Sprawl and the Decline of the American Dream* (New York: North Point Press, 2001), p. xi.

50 Dolores Hayden, *Building Suburbia: Green Fields and Urban Growth, 1820–2000* (New York: Pantheon Books, 2003), p. 214.

51 Duany, Plater-Zyberk and Speck, *Suburban Nation*, p. 243.

52 Ada Louise Huxtable, *The Unreal America: Architecture and Illusion* (New York: The New Press, 1997), p. 42.

53 See, for example, Michael Atkinson, *Blue Velvet* (London: BFI, 1997).

54 Robert Beuka, *SuburbiaNation: Reading Suburban Landscape in Twentieth-Century American Film and Fiction* (New York: Palgrave Macmillan, 2004).

55 Beauregard, *Voices of Decline*, pp. 234–5.

56 Kenneth T. Jackson, *Crabgrass Frontier: The Suburbanization of the United States* (New York: Oxford University Press, 1985), p. 11.

57 Nieland, *David Lynch*, p. 6.

58 Ross, *The Celebration Chronicles*, pp. 4–5.

59 For more details on *One Saliva Bubble*, see David Hughes, *The Complete Lynch* (London: Virgin, 2003), p. 247.

60 Jonathan Rosenbaum, "Bad Ideas: The Art and Politics of *Twin Peaks*," in *Full of Secrets: Critical Approaches to Twin Peaks*, ed. David Lavery (Detroit: Wayne State University Press, 1995), p. 25.

61 Laura Mulvey, *Fetishism and Curiosity* (Bloomington: Indiana University Press, 1996), p. 153.

62 Leo Marx, *The Machine in the Garden: Technology and the Pastoral Ideal in America* (New York: Oxford University Press, 2000), p. 29.

63 Sigmund Freud, *Civilization and its Discontents*, trans. David McLintock (London: Penguin, 2002), p. 51.

64 McGowan, *The Impossible David Lynch*, p. 93.

65 Dean MacCannell, " 'New Urbanism' and its Discontents," in *Giving Ground: The Politics of Propinquity*, ed. Joan Copjec and Michael Sorkin (London: Verso, 1999), p. 118.

66 Slavoj Žižek, *Violence: Six Sideways Reflections* (London: Profile, 2008), p. 50.

67 Chion, *David Lynch*, p. 88.

68 William Burroughs, "Love Your Enemies," on *Dead City Radio* (Import Music Services, 1995).

69 Freud, *Civilization and its Discontents*, pp. 47–9.

70 Slavoj Žižek and Glyn Daly, *Conversations with Žižek* (Cambridge: Polity, 2004), p. 73.

71 Sennett, *The Conscience of the Eye*, p. 201.

72 McGowan, *The Impossible David Lynch*, p. 106.

73 Laura Mulvey, "Notes on Sirk and Melodrama," in *Visual and Other Pleasures* (Basingstoke: Macmillan, 1989), pp. 39–40.

74 Jacobs, *The Death and Life of Great American Cities*, p. 112.

75 Žižek, *Violence*, p. 50.

76 *Lynch on Lynch*, p. 1.

77 Paul Giles, *The Global Remapping of American Literature* (Princeton: Princeton University Press, 2011), p. 226.

78 Jonathan Raban, "Metronatural America," *New York Review of Books*, 26 March 2009.

79 *Lynch on Lynch*, p. 158.

80 David Gartman, *From Autos to Architecture: Fordism and Architectural Aesthetics in the Twentieth Century* (New York: Princeton Architectural Press, 2009), pp. 34–42.

81 Jacobs, *The Death and Life of Great American Cities*, pp. 444–5.

82 Bachelard, *The Poetics of Space*, p. 185.

83 Lynch, *The Image of the City*, p. 41.

84 Jacques Derrida, "Some Statements and Truisms about Neologisms, Newisms, Postisms, Parasitisms, and Other Small Seismisms," trans. Anne Tomiche, in *The States of "Theory": History, Art, and Critical Discourse*, ed. David Carroll (New York: Columbia University Press, 1990), p. 63.

85 Reyner Banham, *Los Angeles: The Architecture of the Four Ecologies* (Berkeley: University of California Press, 2001), pp. 5–6.

86 Beauregard, *Voices of Decline*, p. 75.

87 Mark Shiel, *Hollywood Cinema and the Real Los Angeles* (London: Reaktion, 2012), p. 116.

88 Brodsly, *L.A. Freeway*, p. 4.

89 Robert Bruegmann, *Sprawl: A Compact History* (Chicago: University of Chicago Press, 2005), p. 5.

90 Soja, *Postmodern Geographies*, p. 221; Charles Jencks, *Heteropolis: Los Angeles, the Riots and the Strange Beauty of Hetero-Architecture* (London: Academy Editions, 1993), p. 7.

91 Jencks, *Heteropolis*, pp. 9; 19.

92 Michael T. Dear, *The Postmodern Urban Condition* (Oxford: Blackwell, 2000), p. 256.

93 Thom Andersen, "Collateral Damage: Los Angeles Continues Playing Itself," *CinemaScope*, No. 20 (Autumn 2004).

94 Jean-Paul Sartre, "American Cities," in *Literary and Philosophical Essays*, trans. Annette Michelson (London: Hutchinson, 1969), p. 115.

95 Andersen, "Collateral Damage."

96 David Thomson, *The Whole Equation: A History of Hollywood* (New York: Alfred A. Knopf, 2005), p. 164; Shiel, *Hollywood Cinema and the Real Los Angeles*, p. 136.

97 David Lynch, *Catching the Big Fish: Meditation, Consciousness, and Creativity* (London: Penguin, 2006), pp. 31–2.

98 Shiel, *Hollywood Cinema and the Real Los Angeles*, pp. 229–30.

99 *Lynch on Lynch*, p. 273.

100 Gregory Paul Williams, *The Story of Hollywood: An Illustrated History* (Los Angeles: BL Press, 2005), p. 329; *Lynch on Lynch*, p. 277.

101 *Lynch on Lynch*, p. 277.

102 Banham, *Los Angeles*, pp. 183; 190.

103 Rem Koolhaas, *Delirious New York: A Retroactive Manifesto for Manhattan* (New York: Monacelli Press, 1994), p. 20; Sennett, *The Conscience of the Eye*, p. 48.

104 Koolhaas, *Delirious New York*, p. 20.

105 Sennett, *The Conscience of the Eye*, p. 55.

106 Nieland, *David Lynch*, p. 98.

107 Ibid., p. 96.

108 Tom McCarthy, "His Dark Materials," *New Statesman*, 11 January 2010, pp. 46–8.

109 Sennett, *The Conscience of the Eye*, p. 214.

110 Edward W. Soja, *Thirdspace: Journeys to Los Angeles and Other Real-and-Imagined Places* (Cambridge, MA: Blackwell, 1996), p. 18.

111 Cecilia Rasmussen, " 'Wall Street of the West' Had Its Peaks, Crashes," *Los Angeles Times*, 11 June 2000.

112 Shiel, *Hollywood Cinema and the Real Los Angeles*, p. 26.

113 J. Hoberman and Jonathan Rosenbaum, *Midnight Movies* (New York: Harper and Row, 1983), p. 220.

114 Maggie Valentine, *The Show Starts on the Sidewalk: An Architectural History of the Movie Theatre, Starring S. Charles Lee* (New Haven: Yale University Press, 1994), p. 56.

115 Stephen Barber, *Abandoned Images: Film and Film's End* (London: Reaktion, 2010), p. 11.

116 Shiel, *Hollywood Cinema and the Real Los Angeles*, p. 190.

117 Valentine, *The Show Starts on the Sidewalk*, pp. 53–69.

118 Sennett, *The Conscience of the Eye*, pp. 49–50.

119 Mike Davis, *City of Quartz: Excavating the Future in Los Angeles* (London: Verso, 2006), p. 30.

120 Banham, *Los Angeles*, p. 9.

121 Mike Davis, *Magical Urbanism: Latinos Reinvent the US City* (London: Verso, 2010), pp. 49; 1–2.

122 Godfrey Hodgson, *More Equal Than Others: America from Nixon to the New Century* (Princeton: Princeton University Press, 2004), pp. 128–9; 121.

123 Shiel, *Hollywood Cinema and the Real Los Angeles*, p. 12.

2: Home

1 Bachelard, *The Poetics of Space*, p. 6.

2 Ibid., pp. xix; 137.

3 Ibid., pp. 31; 4; 53.

4 *Lynch on Lynch*, p. 10.

5 Sigmund Freud, *The Uncanny*, trans. David McLintock (London: Penguin, 2003), pp. 124; 134; 144.

6 Anthony Vidler, *The Architectural Uncanny: Essays in the Modern Unhomely* (Cambridge, MA: MIT Press, 1992), pp. 10–11.

7 Panayotis Tournikiotis, *Adolf Loos* (New York: Princeton Architectural Press, 1996), p. 36.

8 *Lynch on Lynch*, pp. 72–3.

9 Kenneth Frampton, "Adolf Loos: The Architect as Master Builder," in Roberto Schezen, *Adolf Loos: Architecture 1903–1932* (New York: Monacelli Press, 1996), p. 18.

10 Beatriz Colomina, *Privacy and Publicity: Modern Architecture as Mass Media* (Cambridge, MA: MIT Press, 1994), p. 270.

11 Beatriz Colomina, "The Split Wall: Domestic Voyeurism," in *Sexuality and Space*, ed. Beatriz Colomina (New York: Princeton Architectural Press, 1992), p. 85.

12 Adolf Loos, "The Principle of Cladding," in *Spoken into the Void: Collected Essays 1897–1900* (Cambridge, MA: MIT Press, 1982), p. 66.

13 Colomina, "The Split Wall," p. 95.

14 Sylvia Lavin, *Form Follows Libido: Architecture and Richard Neutra in a Psychoanalytic Culture* (Cambridge, MA: MIT Press, 2004), pp. 24; 56; 129.

15 Joseph Rosa, *A Constructed View: The Architectural Photography of Julius Shulman* (New York: Rizzoli, 1994), p. 49.

16 *Lynch on Lynch*, p. 169.

17 Lynch, *Catching the Big Fish*, p. 133.

18 *Lynch on Lynch*, p. 57.

19 Gilles Deleuze, *Cinema I: The Movement-Image*, trans. Hugh Tomlinson and Barbara Habberjam (London: Continuum, 2005), p. 180.

20 *Lynch on Lynch*, p. 216.

21 Woods, *Weirdsville USA*, p. 159.

22 Barry Gifford, "Fuzzy Sandwiches, or There is No Speed Limit on the Lost Highway: Reflections on David Lynch," in Hughes, *The Complete Lynch*, p. ix.

23 Alan Ehrenhalt, *The Great Inversion and the Future of the American City* (New York: Alfred A. Knopf, 2012), pp. 146–7.

24 Koolhaas, *Delirious New York*, p. 25.

25 Franz Kafka, "The Burrow," in *Metamorphosis and Other Stories*, trans. Willa and Edwin Muir (London: Vintage, 1999), pp. 163; 129.

26 Merrick was treated at the Royal London Hospital in Whitechapel, but the exterior shots used in *The Elephant Man* are actually of the Eastern Hospital in Homerton (demolished in 1982). The scenes featuring the hospital's corridors and offices were filmed in the National Liberal Club on Whitehall Place.

27 Colomina, *Privacy and Publicity*, pp. 238; 48.

28 Franz Kafka, "Metamorphosis," in *Metamorphosis and Other Stories*, trans. Richard Stokes (London: Hesperus, 2002), pp. 31; 3; 24.

29 Ibid., pp. 22; 31; 16.

30 Bachelard, *The Poetics of Space*, pp. 102; 27.

31 *Lynch on Lynch*, p. 57.

32 Bachelard, *The Poetics of Space*, p. 161.

33 Geoff Andrew, *Stranger Than Paradise: Maverick Film-Makers in Recent American Cinema* (London: Prion, 1998), p. 48.

34 Kafka, "The Burrow," pp. 131; 147.

35 Kafka, "Metamorphosis," pp. 3; 46.

36 Woods, *Weirdsville USA*, p. 25.

37 Spohr, "The World Reveals Itself," p. 167.

38 Kafka, "Metamorphosis," p. 58.

39 *Lynch on Lynch*, p. 56.

40 Bachelard, *The Poetics of Space*, p. 123.

41 Louis Aragon, "On Décor," in *The Shadow and its Shadows: Surrealist Writings on Cinema*, ed. Paul Hammond (San Francisco: City Lights Books, 2000), pp. 50–2.

42 Thomas Elsaesser, "Tales of Sound and Fury: Observations on the Family Melodrama," in *Home is Where the Heart is: Studies in Melodrama and the*

Woman's Film, ed. Christine Gledhill (London: BFI, 1987), p. 61; Le Corbusier, *Towards a New Architecture*, p. 288.

43 Lavin, *Form Follows Libido*, p. 47.

44 Lynn Spigel, "The Suburban Home Companion: Television and the Neighbourhood Ideal in Postwar America," in *Sexuality and Space*, p. 188.

45 Lavin, *Form Follows Libido*, p. 129.

46 Spigel, "The Suburban Home Companion," p. 191.

47 William L. O'Neill, *American High: The Years of Confidence, 1945–1960* (New York: Free Press, 1986), p. 77.

48 Laura Mulvey, "Melodrama Inside and Outside the Home," in *Visual and Other Pleasures*, p. 63.

49 Steven Connor, "Rough Magic: Screens," in *Thinking Organization*, ed. Stephen Linstead and Alison Linstead (Oxford: Routledge, 2005), p. 184.

50 Spigel, "The Suburban Home Companion," p. 188.

51 Mulvey, "Melodrama Inside and Outside the Home," pp. 63–4.

52 Hughes, *The Complete Lynch*, p. 118.

53 Jacobs, *The Wrong House*, p. 4.

54 *Lynch on Lynch*, p. 279.

55 Ibid., p. 175.

56 Lynch, *Catching the Big Fish*, p. 15.

57 John Russell, *Francis Bacon* (Oxford: Oxford University Press, 1979), p. 152; Alan Jenkins, "No Bed for Francis Bacon," *Times Literary Supplement*, 3 December 2008.

58 Chion, *David Lynch*, p. 9.

59 David Sylvester, *Interviews with Francis Bacon* (London: Thames and Hudson, 2002), pp. 141; 199; 189; 21; 141.

60 *Lynch on Lynch*, p. 17.

61 Martin Harrison, *In Camera: Francis Bacon: Photography, Film and the Practice of Painting* (London: Thames and Hudson, 2005), p. 10.

62 Kenneth E. Silver, "Master Bedrooms, Master Narratives: Home, Homosexuality and Post-War Art," in *Not at Home: The Suppression of Domesticity in Modern Art and Architecture*, ed. Christopher Reed (London: Thames and Hudson, 1996), pp. 206; 208; 209.

63 Sylvester, *Interviews with Francis Bacon*, p. 120.

64 Harrison, *In Camera*, pp. 114–15.

65 Gilles Deleuze, *Francis Bacon: The Logic of Sensation*, trans. David W. Smith (London: Continuum, 2003), p. 100.

66 Jacobs, *The Wrong House*, p. 286.

67 Deleuze, *Francis Bacon*, pp. 2; xii.

68 Franz Kafka, *The Diaries: 1910–1923*, trans. Joseph Kresh, Martin Greenberg and Hannah Arendt (New York: Schocken Books, 2000), p. 32.

69 W. T. Lhamon, Jr., *Deliberate Speed: The Origins of a Cultural Style in the American 1950s* (Washington: Smithsonian Institutional Press, 1990), p. xiii.

70 Harrison, *In Camera*, pp. 114; 57; 186.

71 Michael Peppiat, *Francis Bacon: Anatomy of an Enigma* (London: Phoenix, 1999), p. 34.

72 Aldo Rossi, "Introduction," trans. Stephen Sartarelli, in Loos, *Spoken into the Void*, p. x.

73 Nicholas Royle, *The Uncanny* (Manchester: Manchester University Press, 2003), p. vii.

74 Colomina, *Privacy and Publicity*, p. 276.

75 Thomas S. Hines, *Richard Neutra and the Search for Modern Architecture* (New York: Rizzoli, 2005), pp. 18–19.

76 Dominique Vellay, *La Maison de Verre: Pierre Chareau's Modernist Masterwork* (London: Thames and Hudson, 2007), p. 11.

77 Jacobs, *The Wrong House*, pp. 200; 73.

78 Elsaesser, "Tales of Sound and Fury," p. 60.

79 Peter Wollen, *Paris Hollywood: Writings on Film* (London: Verso, 2002), p. 209.

80 Diane Stevenson, "Family Romance, Family Violence, and the Fantastic in *Twin Peaks*," in *Full of Secrets*, p. 77.

81 Walter Benjamin, "Paris, Capital of the Nineteenth Century," in *Reflections: Essays, Aphorisms, Autobiographical Writings*, trans. Edmund Jephcott (New York: Schocken Books, 1986), p. 155.

82 Laura Mulvey, "Pandora: Topographies of the Mask and Curiosity" in *Sexuality and Space*, p. 59.

83 *Lynch on Lynch*, p. 156.

84 Diana Hume George, "Lynching Women: A Feminist Reading of *Twin Peaks*," in *Full of Secrets*, p. 119.

85 Esther McCoy, *Vienna to Los Angeles: Two Journeys* (Santa Monica: Arts and Architecture Press, 1979), p. 113.

86 Hines, *Richard Neutra*, p. 44.

87 Jackson, *Crabgrass Frontier*, p. 179.

88 Nathanael West, *The Day of the Locust*, in *Miss Lonelyhearts and The Day of the Locust* (New York: New Directions, 1969), pp. 60–1; 184.

89 Shiel, *Hollywood Cinema and the Real Los Angeles*, pp. 169–70.

90 Davis, *City of Quartz*, p. 153.

91 David Foster Wallace, "David Lynch Keeps His Head," in *A Supposedly Fun Thing I'll Never Do Again: Essays and Arguments* (New York: Back Bay, 1998), p. 185.

92 Davis, *City of Quartz*, p. 223.

93 Setha Low, *Behind the Gates: Life, Security, and the Pursuit of Happiness in Fortress America* (New York: Routledge, 2003), p. 15.

94 Witold Rybczynski, *Home: A Short History of an Idea* (London: Heinemann, 1988), p. ix.

95 Joseph Rosa, "Tearing Down the House: Modern Homes in the Movies," in *Architecture and Film*, ed. Mark Lamster (New York: Princeton Architectural Press, 2000), pp. 159; 167.

96 Banham, *Los Angeles*, p. 81.

97 Colomina, "The Split Wall," p. 94.

98 Nieland, *David Lynch*, pp. 55–7.

99 *Lynch on Lynch*, p. 23.

100 Ibid., p. 102.

101 Nieland, *David Lynch*, pp. 32; 59.

102 Le Corbusier, *Towards a New Architecture*, p. 54.

103 Le Corbusier, *When the Cathedrals Were White*, p. 46.

104 Hines, *Richard Neutra*, pp. 69; 236.

105 Sigfried Giedion, *Building in France, Building in Iron, Building in Ferroconcrete* (Santa Monica: The Getty Center for the History of Art and the Humanities, 1995), p. 176.

106 Vidler, *The Architectural Uncanny*, p. 32.

107 Mikal Gilmore, "The Lost Boys," *Rolling Stone*, 6 March 1997.

108 Kafka, "The Burrow," pp. 138–9.

109 Žižek, *The Art of the Ridiculous Sublime*, p. 46, n. 25.

110 Paul Virilio, "The Third Window: An Interview with Paul Virilio," trans. Yvonne Shafir, in *Global Television*, ed. Cynthia Schneider and Brian Wallis (Cambridge, MA: MIT Press, 1988), p. 187.

111 An extended description for the Slow House, including the above quotations, is available at: http://www.dsrny.com/.

112 Colomina, *Privacy and Publicity*, pp. 14; 234.

113 Ibid., p. 250.

114 Nieland, *David Lynch*, p. 50.

115 *Desert America: Territory of Paradox*, ed. Michael Kubo, Irene Hwang and Jaime Salazar (Barcelona: Actar, 2006), p. 6.

116 Jean Baudrillard, *America*, trans. Chris Turner (London: Verso, 1988), p. 1.

3: Road

1 Simone de Beauvoir, *America Day by Day*, trans. Carol Cosman (London: Phoenix, 1999), p. 168.

2 Bruno, *Atlas of Emotion*, p. 172.

3 John Orr, *Hitchcock and Twentieth-Century Cinema* (London: Wallflower Press, 2005), pp. 14–15.

4 D. H. Lawrence, *Studies in Classic American Literature* (London: Penguin, 1971), p. 9.

5 Dimendberg, *Film Noir and the Spaces of Modernity*, p. 181.

6 Lewis Mumford, *The Highway and the City* (London: Secker and Warburg, 1964), p. 177.

7 Jane Holtz Kay, *Asphalt Nation: How the Automobile Took Over America, and How We Can Take It Back* (New York: Crown, 1997), p. 8.

8 Ibid.

9 Peter Blake, *God's Own Junkyard: The Planned Deterioration of America's Landscape* (New York: Holt, Rinehart and Winston, 1964), p. 109.

10 Robert Venturi, Denise Scott Brown and Steven Izenour, *Learning from Las Vegas: The Forgotten Symbolism of Architectural Form* (Cambridge, MA: MIT Press, 1977), pp. 8; 9.

11 Philip Roth, "Pictures of Guston," in *Shop Talk: A Writer and His Colleagues and Their Work* (London: Vintage, 2002), p. 135.

12 Vladimir Nabokov, *Lolita* (New York: Vintage, 1997), pp. 152–3.

13 Conley, *Cartographic Cinema*, p. 157.

14 Virilio, "The Third Window," p. 188.

15 Iain Borden, *Drive: Journeys Through Film, Cities and Landscapes* (London: Reaktion, 2013), p. 12.

16 Donald Appleyard, Kevin Lynch and John R. Myer, *The View from the Road* (Cambridge, MA: MIT Press, 1964), p. 4.

17 Jack Sargeant and Stephanie Watson, "Looking for Maps: Notes on the Road Movie as Genre," in *Lost Highways: An Illustrated Guide to the Road Movie*, ed. Jack Sargeant and Stephanie Watson (London: Creation, 1999), p. 6.

18 Iain Borden, "Driving," in *Restless Cities*, ed. Matthew Beaumont and Gregory Dart (London: Verso, 2010), p. 117.

19 David Greene, "Gardener's Notebook," in *Archigram*, ed. Peter Cook (New York: Princeton Architectural Press, 1999), p. 110.

20 McGowan, *The Impossible David Lynch*, p. 113.

21 Thanks to Alice Correia for suggesting this reading of *Twin Peaks'* narrative.

22 Woods, *Weirdsville USA*, p. 116.

23 Olson, *David Lynch*, p. 609.

24 Chion, *David Lynch*, p. 132.

25 Steven Cohan and Ina Rae Hark, "Introduction," in *The Road Movie Book*, ed. Steven Cohan and Ina Rae Hark (London: Routledge, 1997), p. 8.

26 Le Corbusier, *When the Cathedrals Were White*, p. 136.

27 Hughes, *The Complete Lynch*, p. 151.

28 Kay, *Asphalt Nation*, pp. 100; 14.

29 J. G. Ballard, "Introduction," in *Crash* (London: Harper Perennial, 2008), unpaginated.

30 Ballard, *Crash*, p. 33.

31 Karen Beckman, *Crash: Cinema and the Politics of Speed and Stasis* (Durham, NC: Duke University Press, 2010); Ricarda Vidal, *Death and Desire in Car Crash Culture: A Century of Romantic Futurisms* (Oxford: Peter Lang, 2013).

32 Deleuze, *Francis Bacon*, p. 77.

33 Owen Hatherley, *A Guide to the New Ruins of Great Britain* (London: Verso, 2010), pp. xxvii; xxviii.

34 McGowan, *The Impossible David Lynch*, p. 12.

35 Beckman, *Crash*, p. 227.

36 Barry Gifford, *Wild at Heart: The Story of Sailor and Lula* (London: Paladin, 1990), p. 159.

37 Woods, *Weirdsville USA*, p. 28.

38 Frank Lloyd Wright, *The Future of Architecture* (New York: Mentor, 1963), p. 41.

39 Colin Odell and Michelle Le Blanc, *David Lynch* (Harpenden: Kamera Books, 2007), p. 107.

40 John Roach and Mary Sweeney, *The Straight Story: A Screenplay* (New York: Hyperion, 1999), p. 50.

41 Cohan and Hark, "Introduction," p. 4.

42 Robert Fish, "What are these Cinematic Countrysides?" in *Cinematic Countrysides*, ed. Robert Fish (Manchester: Manchester University Press, 2007), p. 6.

43 Don DeLillo, *Americana* (London: Penguin, 2006), p. 118.

44 Woods, *Weirdsville USA*, p. 193.

45 Tim Kreider and Rob Content, "Reviews," *Film Quarterly*, Vol. 54, No. 1 (Autumn 2000), p. 26.

46 *Lynch on Lynch*, p. 91.

47 Ibid., p. 269.

48 See, for example, Stephanie Simon, "Words Don't Fail Iowans When Describing State," *Los Angeles Times*, 17 March 1999, in which the author drolly suggests "Iowa: The flyover state" as a regional slogan.

49 Woods, *Weirdsville USA*, p. 192.

50 Le Corbusier, *Towards a New Architecture*, p. 31.

51 Banham, *A Concrete Atlantis*, p. 6.

52 Ibid., p. 21.

53 Odell and Blanc, *David Lynch*, p. 107.

54 Kreider and Content, "Reviews," p. 29.

55 *Lynch on Lynch*, p. 269.

56 Odell and Le Blanc, *David Lynch*, p. 108.

4: Stage

1 Sylvia Plath, *The Bell Jar* (London: Faber and Faber, 2005), p. 12.

2 Martin Heidegger, "Building Dwelling Thinking," in *Poetry, Language, Thought*, trans. Albert Hofstadter (New York: Harper and Row, 1975), p. 154.

3 Chion, *David Lynch*, p. 183.

4 Žižek, *The Art of the Ridiculous Sublime*, p. 20.

5 McGowan, *The Impossible David Lynch*, p. 25.

6 Chion, *David Lynch*, p. 183.

7 Franz Kafka, *Amerika*, trans. Willa and Edwin Muir (London: Vintage, 2005), p. 225.

8 Deleuze, *Francis Bacon*, p. 10.

9 Sylvester, *Interviews with Francis Bacon*, p. 22.

10 Nieland, *David Lynch*, p. 4.

11 Julie H. Reiss, *From Margins to Center: The Spaces of Installation Art* (Cambridge, MA: MIT Press, 1999).

12 Michel Foucault, "Of Other Spaces," trans. Jay Miskowiec, *Diacritics*, Vol. 16, No. 1 (Spring 1986), p. 24.

13 Ibid., p. 25.

14 Antony Easthope, "Cinécities in the Sixties," in *The Cinematic City*, ed. David B. Clarke (London: Routledge, 1997), p. 129; David Harvey, *The Condition of Postmodernity: An Enquiry into the Origins of Cultural Change* (Cambridge, MA: Blackwell, 2008), p. 48.

15 "On the Art of David Lynch: A Conversation between Boris Groys and Andrei Ujica," trans. Elena Sorokina and Emily Speers Mears, in *David Lynch: The Air is on Fire* (Paris: Fondation Cartier pour l'art Contemporain, 2007), p. 381.

16 Foucault, "Of Other Spaces," pp. 25; 27.

17 Ibid., p. 26.

18 Patrick Wright, *Iron Curtain: From Stage to Cold War* (Oxford: Oxford University Press, 2007), pp. 67–70.

19 Ibid., p. 375.

20 Roger Luckhurst, *The Trauma Question* (London: Routledge, 2008), p. 199.

21 Laura Mulvey, "Visual Pleasure and Narrative Cinema," in *Visual and Other Pleasures*, pp. 19–20.

22 Kaja Silverman, *The Acoustic Mirror: The Female Voice in Psychoanalysis and Cinema* (Bloomington: Indiana University Press, 1988), pp. viii; 39.

23 F. Scott Fitzgerald, *The Last Tycoon* (London: Penguin, 2001), p. 30.

24 Elena del Río, *Deleuze and the Cinemas of Performance* (Edinburgh: Edinburgh University Press, 2008), p. 183.

25 Shiel, *Hollywood Cinema and the Real Los Angeles*, p. 153.

26 George Toles, "Auditioning Betty in *Mulholland Drive*," *Film Quarterly*, Vol. 58, No. 1 (Fall 2004), pp. 2–13.

27 Baudrillard, *America*, p. 56.

28 Bernardo Bertolucci, "Masterclass with Bernardo Bertolucci," in Laurent Tirard, *Moviemakers' Master Class: Private Lessons from the World's Foremost Directors* (New York: Faber and Faber, 2002), pp. 49–50.

29 Marc Dolan, "The Peaks and Valleys of Serial Creativity: What Happened to/ on *Twin Peaks*," in *Full of Secrets*, p. 38.

30 *Lynch on Lynch*, p. 19.

31 Martha P. Nochimson, *The Passion of David Lynch: Wild at Heart in Hollywood* (Austin: University of Texas Press, 1997), p. 97.

32 Jorge Luis Borges, "The Aleph," in *The Aleph and Other Stories, 1933–1969*, trans. Thomas di Giovanni (London: Jonathan Cape, 1971), p. 23.

33 Soja, *Thirdspace*, pp. 56–7; 11.

34 John Orr, *Contemporary Cinema* (Edinburgh: Edinburgh University Press, 1998), p. 151.

35 Jeff Johnson, *Pervert in the Pulpit: Morality in the Works of David Lynch* (Jefferson, NC: McFarland, 2004), p. 165.

36 Valentine, *The Show Starts on the Sidewalk*, p. xiii.

37 Colomina, "The Split Wall," p. 107.

38 Dorothée Imbert, *The Modernist Garden in France* (New Haven: Yale University Press, 1993), p. 170.

39 Ibid., p. 168.

40 Akira Mizuta Lippit, "David Lynch's Secret Passages," *Flow*, Vol. 15, No. 6 (2012); John Alexander, *The Films of David Lynch* (London: Letts, 1993), p. 173.

41 Theodore Ziolkowski, *Minos and the Moderns: Cretan Myth in Twentieth-Century Literature and Art* (Oxford: Oxford University Press, 2008), p. 80.

42 Kathryn Milun, *Pathologies of Modern Space: Empty Space, Urban Anxiety, and the Recovery of the Public Self* (New York: Routledge, 2007), pp. 238; 243; 251.

43 Nicholas Christopher, *Somewhere in the Night: Film Noir and the American City* (New York: Free Press, 1997), p. 17.

44 Pallasmaa, *The Architecture of Image*, p. 100.

45 Foucault, "Of Other Spaces," p. 24.

46 Alexander, *The Films of David Lynch*, p. 157.

47 Orr, *Contemporary Cinema*, p. 151.

5: Room

1 David Edelstein, "They Cut Glass. And Hands," *New York Magazine*, 3 December 2006; Carina Chocano, "*Inland Empire*," *Los Angeles Times*, 15 December 2006.

2 Michael Atkinson, "*Inland Empire*," *Sight and Sound*, Vol. 17, No. 4 (April 2007), p. 68.

3 Soja, *Postmodern Geographies*, pp. 190–248.

4 Bachelard, *The Poetics of Space*, p. 229.

5 Parveen Adams, "Sticking to the Plot," in *Urban Images: Unruly Desires in Film and Architecture*, ed. Synne Bull and Marit Paasche (Berlin: Sternberg Press, 2011), pp. 138–45.

6 Soja, *Postmodern Geographies*, p. 2.

7 Stephen Heath, *Questions of Cinema* (London: Macmillan, 1981), p. 41.

8 Daniel Frampton, "Sublime Confusion," *The Philosophers' Magazine*, No. 47 (October 2009).

9 François-Xavier Gleyzon, "Introduction: David Lynch's Seismograph," in *David Lynch in Theory*, ed. François-Xavier Gleyzon (Prague: Litteraria Pragensia, 2010), p. 3.

10 K. George Godwin, "Lynchland: David Lynch and the Making of *Eraserhead*," *Ciné-Fantastique*, Vol. 4, Nos. 4–5 (September 1984).

11 V. I. Pudovkin, *Film Technique and Film Acting: The Cinema Writings of V. I. Pudovkin*, trans. Ivor Montagu (London: Vision, 1954), pp. 60–1.

12 Dear, *The Postmodern Urban Condition*, p. 47.

13 Foucault, "Of Other Spaces," p. 22.

14 Monica Khemsurov, "Eastern Promises," *New York Times*, 26 September 2010.

15 Baudrillard, *America*, p. 81.

16 Slavoj Žižek, *The Parallax View* (Cambridge, MA: MIT Press, 2006), p. 159.

17 Joseph Roth, *Hotel Savoy*, trans. John Hoare (London: Granta, 2000), pp. 9; 77; 100; 107.

18 John Orr, "A Cinema of Parallel Worlds: Lynch, Kieślowski and *Inland Empire*," *Film International*, Vol. 7, No. 1 (February 2009), p. 29.

19 Roth, *Hotel Savoy*, p. 123.

20 Norman Davies, *God's Playground: A History of Poland, Volume II: 1795 to the Present* (Oxford: Clarendon Press, 1981), p. 171.

21 Daniel Libeskind, *Breaking Ground: Adventures in Life and Architecture* (London: John Murray, 2004), pp. 284–5.

22 Harrison, *In Camera*, p. 132.

23 Libeskind, *Breaking Ground*, p. 285.

24 Jeremy Till, *Architecture Depends* (Cambridge, MA: MIT Press, 2009), p. 28.

25 Libeskind, *Breaking Ground*, p. 285.

26 Barber, *Abandoned Images*, p. 76.

27 McCarthy, "His Dark Materials," p. 48.

28 Todd McGowan, "The Materiality of Fantasy: The Encounter with Something in *Inland Empire*," in *David Lynch in Theory*, p. 18; Joshua D. Gonsalves, " 'I'm a Whore': 'On the Other Side' of *Inland Empire*," in *David Lynch in Theory*, p. 128.

29 Darragh O'Donoghue, "Paradise Regained: *Queen Kelly* and the Lure of the 'Lost' Film," *Senses of Cinema*, Issue 27 (July 2003).

30 *Lynch on Lynch*, p. 71.

31 Olson, *David Lynch*, p. 53.

32 Atkinson, "*Inland Empire*," p. 68.

33 Richard Pells, *Not Like Us: How Europeans Have Loved, Hated, and Transformed American Culture Since World War II* (New York: Basic Books, 1997), p. 26.

34 Luckhurst, *The Trauma Question*, p. 198.

35 Adam Thirlwell, "Czech Mates," *New Statesman*, 17 May 2010, pp. 42–3.

36 See: http://www.paramountstudios.com/stages-and-backlots/the-alley.html.

37 Wallace, "David Lynch Keeps His Head," p. 184.

38 Gonsalves, " 'I'm a Whore'," pp. 118–19.

39 Hal Foster, *The Art-Architecture Complex* (London: Verso, 2011), pp. xii; 125.

LIST OF ILLUSTRATIONS

Plates

1 Camerimage Łódź Center, designed by Frank Gehry (2009). Credit: Image provided by Gehry Partners, LLP.

2 David Lynch, *Untitled* (drawing for an interior), undated, 6 × 12.7 cm. Credit: Collection Fondation Cartier pour l'art contemporain, Paris.

3 David Lynch, *Untitled*, installation designed for the exhibition *David Lynch, The Air is on Fire* (2007), adapted from *Untitled* (drawing for an interior). Credit: Collection Fondation Cartier pour l'art contemporain, Paris. Photograph by Fabrizio Marchesi.

4 Beverly Johnson House, designed by Lloyd Wright in 1963. Credit: Photograph by Yana Stoimenova.

5 Olga Neuwirth, who composed an operatic version of *Lost Highway*, inside a room inspired by the film in the Hotel Luzern, designed by Jean Nouvel. Credit: Copyright Priska Ketterer. Photograph by Priska Ketterer, with thanks to Betty Freeman and Olga Neuwirth.

6 Shad Thames, London. Credit: Photograph by Craig Ritchie.

7 Liverpool Street station. Credit: Photograph by Craig Ritchie.

8 Callowhill, Philadelphia—part of the "Eraserhood." Credit: Photograph by Richard Martin.

9 *Eraserhead* mural by Evan Cairo on the exterior of the Philadelphia Mausoleum of Contemporary Art. Credit: Copyright Eric Bresler. Mural by Evan Cairo. Photograph by Laura Jane Brubaker.

10 4th Street Bridge, downtown Los Angeles. Credit: Photograph by Yana Stoimenova.

11 Beverly Center, West Hollywood. Credit: Photograph by Yana Stoimenova.

12 *Blue Velvet*: the field behind "Vista." Credit: *Blue Velvet* (dir. David Lynch, 1986), © De Laurentiis Entertainment Group.

13 David Lynch, *Twin Peaks #1* (map). Credit: Copyright David Lynch.

14 *Twin Peaks*, pilot episode: the Packard Sawmill. Credit: *Twin Peaks*, pilot episode (dir. David Lynch, 1990), © Lynch/Frost Productions, Propaganda Films, Worldvision Enterprises, Inc.

15 Il Borghese apartment building, Hancock Park. Credit: Photograph by Yana Stoimenova.

16 *Mulholland Drive*: the Paramount Studios gate. Credit: *Mulholland Drive* (dir. David Lynch, 2001), © Studio Canal, Les Films Alain Sarde, Asymmetrical Productions.

17 *Mulholland Drive*: the space behind Winkie's diner. Credit: *Mulholland Drive* (dir. David Lynch, 2001), © Studio Canal, Les Films Alain Sarde, Asymmetrical Productions.

18 *Mulholland Drive*: skyscrapers in downtown Los Angeles. Credit: *Mulholland Drive* (dir. David Lynch, 2001), © Studio Canal, Les Films Alain Sarde, Asymmetrical Productions.

19 The back of the Palace Theatre, used by Lynch as the entrance to Club Silencio. Credit: Photograph by Yana Stoimenova.

20 The Tower Theater on Broadway. Credit: Photograph by Yana Stoimenova.

21 Richard Neutra, Kaufmann House, Palm Springs, California (1946).

Credit: Photograph by Richard Neutra. Kindly provided by Raymond Richard Neutra.

22 Joseph Merrick's model of Mainz Cathedral (c. 1886).

Credit: Courtesy of The Royal London Hospital Archives.

23 *Blue Velvet*: the final tableau in Dorothy's apartment.

Credit: *Blue Velvet* (dir. David Lynch, 1986), © De Laurentiis Entertainment Group.

24 Francis Bacon, *Two Figures* (1953). Oil on canvas. 152.5 × 116.5 cm.

Credit: Copyright The Estate of Francis Bacon. All rights reserved, DACS 2014. Photograph by Prudence Cuming Associates Ltd.

25 *Blue Velvet*: Dorothy framed by her furniture.

Credit: *Blue Velvet* (dir. David Lynch, 1986), © De Laurentiis Entertainment Group.

26 Francis Bacon, *Triptych—In Memory of George Dyer* (1971) (center panel). Oil on canvas. 198 × 147.5 cm.

Credit: Copyright The Estate of Francis Bacon. All rights reserved, DACS 2014. Photograph by Hugo Maertens.

27 *Twin Peaks: Fire Walk With Me*: Leland prepares to cross the landing.

Credit: *Twin Peaks: Fire Walk With Me* (dir. David Lynch, 1992), © Twin Peaks Productions, Inc.

28 *Twin Peaks*, episode two: Leland's blood coats the famous image of his daughter.

Credit: *Twin Peaks*, episode two (dir. David Lynch, 1990). © Lynch/Frost Productions, Propaganda Films, Spelling Entertainment Inc.

29 *Lost Highway*: the Madison house.

Credit: *Lost Highway* (dir. David Lynch, 1997), © Ciby 2000, Asymmetrical Productions.

30 The Schindler House in West Hollywood, designed by Rudolph M. Schindler in 1922.

Credit: Photograph by Yana Stoimenova.

31 *Lost Highway*: the Madisons' living room.
Credit: *Lost Highway* (dir. David Lynch, 1997), © Ciby 2000,
Asymmetrical Productions.

32 Diller + Scofidio, Slow House model (1989).
Credit: Photograph by Diller + Scofidio. Reproduced by
permission of Diller Scofidio + Renfro.

33 *Lost Highway*: The Mystery Man inside a desert shack.
Credit: *Lost Highway* (dir. David Lynch, 1997), © Ciby 2000,
Asymmetrical Productions.

34 The Park Plaza Hotel in Los Angeles.
Credit: Photograph by Yana Stoimenova.

35 *Wild at Heart*: Sailor, Lula and their Ford Thunderbird.
Credit: *Wild at Heart* (dir. David Lynch, 1990), © Polygram
Filmproduktion GmbH, Propaganda Films.

36 *Wild at Heart*: a classic couple on the run.
Credit: *Wild at Heart* (dir. David Lynch, 1990), © Polygram
Filmproduktion GmbH, Propaganda Films.

37 *Wild at Heart*: the epic traffic jam in El Paso.
Credit: *Wild at Heart* (dir. David Lynch, 1990), © Polygram
Filmproduktion GmbH, Propaganda Films.

38 *The Straight Story*: man and nature perfectly balanced.
Credit: *The Straight Story* (dir. David Lynch, 1999), © Walt Disney
Pictures, Picture Factory, Studio Canal, FilmFour.

39 *The Straight Story*: Lynch tracks a combine harvester.
Credit: *The Straight Story* (dir. David Lynch, 1999), © Walt Disney
Pictures, Picture Factory, Studio Canal, FilmFour.

40 *The Straight Story*: Alvin passes the Grotto of the Redemption.
Credit: *The Straight Story* (dir. David Lynch, 1999), © Walt Disney
Pictures, Picture Factory, Studio Canal, FilmFour.

41 Detail from Christian Tomaszewski, *On Chapels, Caves and Erotic
Misery* (2006). Mixed media installation.
Credit: Copyright Christian Tomaszewski. Photograph by Jason
Mandella, Georg Tassev, Laszlo Toth.

42 Details from Christian Tomaszewski, *On Chapels, Caves and Erotic Misery* (2006). Mixed media installation.

Credit: Copyright Christian Tomaszewski. Photograph by Jason Mandella, Georg Tassev, Laszlo Toth.

43 *Blue Velvet*: Dorothy on stage at the Slow Club.

Credit: *Blue Velvet* (dir. David Lynch, 1986), © De Laurentiis Entertainment Group.

44 *Twin Peaks*, episode fourteen: the giant on stage at the Roadhouse.

Credit: *Twin Peaks*, episode fourteen (dir. David Lynch, 1991), © Lynch/Frost Productions, Propaganda Films, Spelling Entertainment Inc.

45 *Mulholland Drive*: Rebekah del Rio collapses at Club Silencio.

Credit: *Mulholland Drive* (dir. David Lynch, 2001), © Studio Canal, Les Films Alain Sarde, Asymmetrical Productions.

46 *Mulholland Drive*: auditions at Paramount Studios.

Credit: *Mulholland Drive* (dir. David Lynch, 2001), © Studio Canal, Les Films Alain Sarde, Asymmetrical Productions.

47 *Twin Peaks*, episode two: the first appearance of the Red Room.

Credit: *Twin Peaks*, episode two (dir. David Lynch, 1990), © Lynch/Frost Productions, Propaganda Films, Spelling Entertainment Inc.

48 *Twin Peaks*, episode twenty-nine: the corridor of the Red Room.

Credit: *Twin Peaks*, episode twenty-nine (dir. David Lynch, 1991), © Lynch/Frost Productions, Propaganda Films, Spelling Entertainment Inc.

49 Workers' housing in the Księży Młyn district of Łódź.

Credit: Photograph by Richard Martin.

50 *Inland Empire*: Nikki's Hollywood mansion.

Credit: *Inland Empire* (dir. David Lynch, 2006), © Bobkind Inc—Studio Canal, Camerimage, Fundacja Kultury, Asymmetrical Productions.

51 *Inland Empire*: two men inside the Pałac Herbsta.

Credit: *Inland Empire* (dir. David Lynch, 2006), © Bobkind Inc—Studio Canal, Camerimage, Fundacja Kultury, Asymmetrical Productions.

52 The Pałac Herbsta in Łódź (right), with the refurbished Scheibler cotton mill behind it.

Credit: Photograph by Richard Martin.

53 *Inland Empire*: a prostitute on Hollywood Boulevard.

Credit: *Inland Empire* (dir. David Lynch, 2006), © Bobkind Inc—Studio Canal, Camerimage, Fundacja Kultury, Asymmetrical Productions.

54 *Inland Empire*: prostitutes by Plac Zwycięstwa.

Credit: *Inland Empire* (dir. David Lynch, 2006), © Bobkind Inc—Studio Canal, Camerimage, Fundacja Kultury, Asymmetrical Productions.

55 Plac Zwycięstwa in Łódź, with the Museum of Cinematography and former home of Karl Scheibler on the right.

Credit: Photograph by Richard Martin.

56 Roman Polanski's star on Ulica Piotrkowska.

Credit: Photograph by Richard Martin.

57 The Hollywood and Vine intersection in Los Angeles.

Credit: Photograph by Yana Stoimenova.

58 *Inland Empire*: Nikki enters the Orpheum Theater.

Credit: *Inland Empire* (dir. David Lynch, 2006), © Bobkind Inc—Studio Canal, Camerimage, Fundacja Kultury, Asymmetrical Productions.

59 The auditorium of the Orpheum Theater on Broadway.

Credit: Photograph by Yana Stoimenova.

60 Hotel Grand on Ulica Piotrkowska.

Credit: Photograph by Richard Martin.

61 *Inland Empire*: the alley behind the marketplace.

Credit: *Inland Empire* (dir. David Lynch, 2006), © Bobkind Inc—Studio Canal, Camerimage, Fundacja Kultury, Asymmetrical Productions.

62 The site of Lynch's proposed film studio in Łódź.

Credit: Photograph by Richard Martin.

Figures

Cover and inside cover: Senalda Road, Hollywood Hills.

1.1 *The Elephant Man*: Treves walks through Victorian London, p. 19.

Credit: *The Elephant Man* (dir. David Lynch, 1980), © Brooksfilms.

1.2 *The Elephant Man*: Merrick arrives at Liverpool Street station, p. 22.

Credit: *The Elephant Man* (dir. David Lynch, 1980), © Brooksfilms.

1.3 *Eraserhead*: negotiating the rubble of the post-war American city, p. 27.

Credit: *Eraserhead* (dir. David Lynch, 1977), © David Lynch and the American Film Institute for Advanced Studies.

1.4 "Eraserhood" exhibition poster by Karli Cox (2013), p. 29.

Credit: Copyright Eric Bresler. Poster design by Karli Cox.

1.5 *Eraserhead*: Henry begins his lonely urban walk, p. 30.

Credit: *Eraserhead* (dir. David Lynch, 1977), © David Lynch and the American Film Institute for Advanced Studies.

2.1 Lina Loos' bedroom in the Loos Apartment in Vienna (1903), p. 65.

Credit: Copyright Albertina, Vienna.

2.2 *The Elephant Man*: Merrick in his tiny attic room, p. 70.

Credit: *The Elephant Man* (dir. David Lynch, 1980), © Brooksfilms.

2.3 *Eraserhead:* Henry mulls things over, p. 72.

Credit: *Eraserhead* (dir. David Lynch, 1977), © David Lynch and the American Film Institute for Advanced Studies.

4.1 *The Elephant Man*: Merrick displayed in the lecture theater, p. 141.

Credit: *The Elephant Man* (dir. David Lynch, 1980), © Brooksfilms.

4.2 *Eraserhead:* the stage as catastrophe, p. 145.

Credit: *Eraserhead* (dir. David Lynch, 1977), © David Lynch and the American Film Institute for Advanced Studies.

4.3 Appartement de M. Charles de Beistegui in Paris, p. 154.

Credit: Copyright FLC/ADAGP, Paris and DACS, London 2014.

4.4 The Red Room set on the final day of filming for T*win Peaks* (1991), p. 156.

Credit: Copyright Richard Beymer. Photograph by Richard Beymer, with thanks to Rob Wilson.

4.5 *Orphée* (dir. Jean Cocteau, 1949): Orpheus enters "the zone," p. 159.

Credit: *Orphée* (dir. Jean Cocteau, 1949), © Andre Paulve Film, Films du Palais Royal.

BIBLIOGRAPHY

Albrecht, Donald, *Designing Dreams: Modern Architecture in the Movies* (London: Thames and Hudson, 1987)

Alexander, John, *The Films of David Lynch* (London: Letts, 1993)

Andersen, Thom, "Collateral Damage: Los Angeles Continues Playing Itself," *CinemaScope*, No. 20 (Autumn 2004)

Andrew, Geoff, *Stranger Than Paradise: Maverick Film-Makers in Recent American Cinema* (London: Prion, 1998)

Antonioni, Michelangelo, *The Architecture of Vision: Writings and Interviews on Cinema* (New York: Marsilio, 1996)

Appleyard, Donald, Kevin Lynch and John R. Myer, *The View from the Road* (Cambridge, MA: MIT Press, 1964)

Atkinson, Michael, *Blue Velvet* (London: BFI, 1997)

——, "*Inland Empire*," *Sight and Sound*, Vol. 17, No. 4 (April 2007)

Bachelard, Gaston, *The Poetics of Space*, trans. Maria Jolas (Boston: Beacon Press, 1994)

Ballard, J. G., *Crash* (London: Harper Perennial, 2008)

Banham, Reyner, *A Concrete Atlantis: U.S. Industrial Building and European Modern Architecture, 1900–1925* (Cambridge, MA: MIT Press, 1986)

——, *Los Angeles: The Architecture of the Four Ecologies* (Berkeley: University of California Press, 2001)

Barber, Stephen, *Abandoned Images: Film and Film's End* (London: Reaktion, 2010)

Barnett, Laura, "Portrait of the Artist: Nigel Coates, Architect," *The Guardian*, 12 October 2010

Barney, Richard A. (ed.), *David Lynch: Interviews* (Jackson: University Press of Mississippi, 2009)

Baudrillard, Jean, *America*, trans. Chris Turner (London: Verso, 1988)

Baudrillard, Jean, and Jean Nouvel, *The Singular Object of Architecture*, trans. Robert Bononno (Minneapolis: University of Minneapolis Press, 2002)

Beaumont, Matthew, and Gregory Dart (eds.), *Restless Cities* (London: Verso, 2010)

Beauregard, Robert A., *Voices of Decline: The Postwar Fate of US Cities* (Oxford: Blackwell, 1993)

de Beauvoir, Simone, *America Day by Day*, trans. Carol Cosman (London: Phoenix, 1999)

Beckman, Karen, *Crash: Cinema and the Politics of Speed and Stasis* (Durham, NC: Duke University Press, 2010)

Benjamin, Walter, *Reflections: Essays, Aphorisms, Autobiographical Writings*,
trans. Edmund Jephcott (New York: Schocken Books, 1986)
——, *Illuminations*, trans. Harry Zorn (London: Pimlico, 1999)
Bergfelder, Tim, Sue Harris, and Sarah Street, *Film Architecture and the
Transnational Imagination: Set Design in 1930s European Cinema*
(Amsterdam: Amsterdam University Press, 2007)
Berman, Marshall, *All That is Solid Melts into Air: The Experience of Modernity*
(London: Penguin, 1988)
Beuka, Robert, *SuburbiaNation: Reading Suburban Landscape in
Twentieth-Century American Film and Fiction* (New York: Palgrave
Macmillan, 2004)
Blake, Peter, *God's Own Junkyard: The Planned Deterioration of America's
Landscape* (New York: Holt, Rinehart and Winston, 1964)
Borden, Iain, *Drive: Journeys Through Film, Cities and Landscapes* (London:
Reaktion, 2013)
Borges, Jorge Luis, *The Aleph and Other Stories, 1933–1969*, trans. Thomas di
Giovanni (London: Jonathan Cape, 1971)
Breskin, David, *Inner Views: Filmmakers in Conversation* (Boston: Faber and
Faber, 1992)
Brodsly, David, *L.A. Freeway: An Appreciative Essay* (Berkeley: University of
California Press, 1981)
Bruno, Giuliana, *Atlas of Emotion: Journeys in Art, Architecture and Film*
(New York: Verso, 2002)
Bull, Synne, and Marit Paasche (eds.), *Urban Images: Unruly Desires in Film and
Architecture* (Berlin: Sternberg Press, 2011)
Burroughs, William, *Dead City Radio* (Import Music Services, 1995)
Carroll, David (ed.), *The States of "Theory": History, Art, and Critical Discourse*
(New York: Columbia University Press, 1990)
de Certeau, Michel, *The Practice of Everyday Life*, trans. Steven Rendall
(Berkeley: University of California Press, 1988)
Chion, Michel, *David Lynch*, trans. Robert Julian (London: BFI, 2006)
Chocano, Carina, "Inland Empire," *Los Angeles Times*, 15 December 2006
Christopher, Nicholas, *Somewhere in the Night: Film Noir and the American City*
(New York: Free Press, 1997)
Clarke, David B. (ed.), *The Cinematic City* (London: Routledge, 1997)
Cohan, Steven, and Ina Rae Hark (eds.), *The Road Movie Book* (London:
Routledge, 1997)
Colomina, Beatriz (ed.), *Sexuality and Space* (New York: Princeton Architectural
Press, 1992)
Colomina, Beatriz, *Privacy and Publicity: Modern Architecture as Mass Media*
(Cambridge, MA: MIT Press, 1994)
Conley, Tom, *Cartographic Cinema* (Minneapolis: University of Minnesota
Press, 2007)
Cook, Peter (ed.), *Archigram* (New York: Princeton Architectural Press, 1999)
Copjec, Joan, and Michael Sorkin (eds.), *Giving Ground: The Politics of
Propinquity* (London: Verso, 1999)

Corkin, Stanley, *Starring New York: Filming the Grime and the Glamour of the Long 1970s* (New York: Oxford University Press, 2011)

Cuff, Dana, "Enduring Proximity: The Figure of the Neighbor in Suburban America," *Postmodern Culture*, Vol. 15, No. 2 (January 2005)

David Lynch: The Air is on Fire (Paris: Fondation Cartier pour l'art Contemporain, 2007)

Davies, Norman, *God's Playground: A History of Poland, Volume II: 1795 to the Present* (Oxford: Clarendon Press, 1981)

Davis, Mike, *City of Quartz: Excavating the Future in Los Angeles* (London: Verso, 2006)

——, *Magical Urbanism: Latinos Reinvent the US City* (London: Verso, 2010)

Dear, Michael T., *The Postmodern Urban Condition* (Oxford: Blackwell, 2000)

Deleuze, Gilles, *Cinema I: The Movement-Image*, trans. Hugh Tomlinson and Barbara Habberjam (London: Continuum, 2005)

——, *Francis Bacon: The Logic of Sensation*, trans. David W. Smith (London: Continuum, 2008)

DeLillo, Don, *Americana* (London: Penguin, 2006)

Diani, Marco, and Catherine Ingraham (eds.), *Restructuring Architectural Theory* (Evanston, IL: Northwestern University Press, 1989)

Dimendberg, Edward, *Film Noir and the Spaces of Modernity* (Cambridge, MA: Harvard University Press, 2004)

Duany, Andres, Elizabeth Plater-Zyberk, and Jeff Speck, *Suburban Nation: The Rise of Sprawl and the Decline of the American Dream* (New York: North Point Press, 2001)

Edelstein, David, "They Cut Glass. And Hands," *New York Magazine*, 3 December 2006

Ehrenhalt, Alan, *The Great Inversion and the Future of the American City* (New York: Alfred A. Knopf, 2012)

Eisenstein, Sergei, "Montage and Architecture," trans. Michael Glenny, *Assemblage*, No. 10 (December 1989)

Fish, Robert (ed.), *Cinematic Countrysides* (Manchester: Manchester University Press, 2007)

Fitzgerald, F. Scott, *The Last Tycoon* (London: Penguin, 2001)

Ford, Henry, *Ford Ideals: Being a Selection from "Mr. Ford's Page" in the Dearborn Independent* (Dearborn, MI: Dearborn Publishing Company, 1922)

——, *My Life and Work* (Sydney: Cornstalk, 1924)

Foster, Hal, *The Art-Architecture Complex* (London: Verso, 2011)

Foucault, Michel, "Of Other Spaces," trans. Jay Miskowiec, *Diacritics*, Vol. 16, No. 1 (Spring 1986)

Frampton, Daniel, "Sublime Confusion," *The Philosophers' Magazine*, No. 47 (October 2009)

Freud, Sigmund, *Civilization and its Discontents*, trans. David McLintock (London: Penguin, 2002)

——, *The Uncanny*, trans. David McLintock (London: Penguin, 2003)

Gartman, David, *From Autos to Architecture: Fordism and Architectural Aesthetics in the Twentieth Century* (New York: Princeton Architectural Press, 2009)

Giedion, Sigfried, *Building in France, Building in Iron, Building in Ferroconcrete* (Santa Monica: The Getty Center for the History of Art and the Humanities, 1995)

Gifford, Barry, *Wild at Heart: The Story of Sailor and Lula* (London: Paladin, 1990)

Giles, Paul, *The Global Remapping of American Literature* (Princeton: Princeton University Press, 2011)

Gilmore, Mikal, "The Lost Boys," *Rolling Stone*, 6 March 1997

Gledhill, Christine (ed.), *Home is Where the Heart is: Studies in Melodrama and the Woman's Film* (London: BFI, 1987)

Gleyzon, François-Xavier (ed.), *David Lynch in Theory* (Prague: Litteraria Pragensia, 2010)

Godwin, K. George, "Lynchland: David Lynch and the Making of Eraserhead," *Ciné-Fantastique*, Vol. 4, Nos. 4–5 (September 1984)

Goldberg, Michael Alan, "There Goes the Eraserhood: Why Local Artists are Hoping to Preserve the Callowhill District's Gritty Past," *Philadelphia Weekly*, 11 July 2012

Hammond, Paul (ed.), *The Shadow and its Shadows: Surrealist Writings on Cinema* (San Francisco: City Lights Books, 2000)

Harrison, Martin, *In Camera: Francis Bacon: Photography, Film and the Practice of Painting* (London: Thames and Hudson, 2005)

Harvey, David, *The Condition of Postmodernity: An Enquiry into the Origins of Cultural Change* (Cambridge, MA: Blackwell, 2008)

Hatherley, Owen, *A Guide to the New Ruins of Great Britain* (London: Verso, 2010)

Hayden, Dolores, *Building Suburbia: Green Fields and Urban Growth, 1820–2000* (New York: Pantheon Books, 2003)

Heath, Stephen, *Questions of Cinema* (London: Macmillan, 1981)

Heidegger, Martin, *Poetry, Language, Thought*, trans. Albert Hofstadter (New York: Harper and Row, 1975)

Hines, Thomas S., *Richard Neutra and the Search for Modern Architecture* (New York: Rizzoli, 2005)

Hoberman, J., and Jonathan Rosenbaum, *Midnight Movies* (New York: Harper and Row, 1983)

Hodgson, Godfrey, *More Equal Than Others: America from Nixon to the New Century* (Princeton: Princeton University Press, 2004)

Hughes, David, *The Complete Lynch* (London: Virgin, 2003)

Huxtable, Ada Louise, *The Unreal America: Architecture and Illusion* (New York: New Press, 1997)

Imbert, Dorothée, *The Modernist Garden in France* (New Haven: Yale University Press, 1993)

Jackson, Kenneth T., *Crabgrass Frontier: The Suburbanization of the United States* (New York: Oxford University Press, 1985)

Jacobs, Jane, *The Death and Life of Great American Cities* (New York: Vintage, 1992)

Jacobs, Steven, *The Wrong House: The Architecture of Alfred Hitchcock* (Rotterdam: 010 Publishers, 2007)

James, Henry, *The American Scene* (London: Granville, 1987)

Jameson, Fredric, *Postmodernism, Or, The Cultural Logic of Late Capitalism* (London: Verso, 1993)

Jencks, Charles, *Heteropolis: Los Angeles, the Riots and the Strange Beauty of Hetero-Architecture* (London: Academy Editions, 1993)

Jenkins, Alan, "No Bed for Francis Bacon," *Times Literary Supplement*, 3 December 2008

Johnson, Jeff, *Pervert in the Pulpit: Morality in the Works of David Lynch* (Jefferson, NC: McFarland, 2004)

Kafka, Franz, *Metamorphosis and Other Stories*, trans. Willa and Edwin Muir (London: Vintage, 1999)

——, *The Diaries: 1910–1923*, trans. Joseph Kresh, Martin Greenberg and Hannah Arendt (New York: Schocken Books, 2000)

——, *Metamorphosis and Other Stories*, trans. Richard Stokes (London: Hesperus, 2002)

——, *Amerika*, trans. Willa and Edwin Muir (London: Vintage, 2005)

Kay, Jane Holtz, *Asphalt Nation: How the Automobile Took Over America, and How We Can Take It Back* (New York: Crown, 1997)

Khemsurov, Monica, "Eastern Promises," *New York Times*, 26 September 2010

Koolhaas, Rem, *Delirious New York: A Retroactive Manifesto for Manhattan* (New York: Monacelli Press, 1994)

Kreider, Tim, and Rob Content, "Reviews," *Film Quarterly*, Vol. 54, No. 1 (Autumn 2000)

Kubo, Michael, Irene Hwang, and Jaime Salazar (eds.), *Desert America: Territory of Paradox* (Barcelona: Actar, 2006)

Lamster, Mark (ed.), *Architecture and Film* (New York: Princeton Architectural Press, 2000)

Lavery, David (ed.), *Full of Secrets: Critical Approaches to Twin Peaks* (Detroit: Wayne State University Press, 1995)

Lavin, Sylvia, *Form Follows Libido: Architecture and Richard Neutra in a Psychoanalytic Culture* (Cambridge, MA: MIT Press, 2004)

Lawrence, D. H., *Studies in Classic American Literature* (London: Penguin, 1971)

Le Corbusier, *When the Cathedrals Were White: A Journey to the Country of Timid People*, trans. Francis E. Hyslop, Jr. (London: Routledge, 1948)

——, *Towards a New Architecture*, trans. Frederick Etchells (New York: Dover, 1986)

——, *The City of Tomorrow and its Planning*, trans. Frederick Etchells (New York: Dover, 1987)

Lefebvre, Henri, *The Urban Revolution*, trans. Robert Bononno (Minneapolis: University of Minneapolis Press, 2003)

Levy, Emanuel, *Small-Town America in Film* (New York: Continuum, 1991)

Lhamon, Jr., W. T., *Deliberate Speed: The Origins of a Cultural Style in the American 1950s* (Washington: Smithsonian Institutional Press, 1990)

Libeskind, Daniel, *Breaking Ground: Adventures in Life and Architecture* (London: John Murray, 2004)

Linstead, Stephen, and Alison Linstead (eds.), *Thinking Organization* (Oxford: Routledge, 2005)

Lippit, Akira Mizuta, "David Lynch's Secret Passages," *Flow*, Vol. 15, No. 6 (2012)

Loos, Adolf, *Spoken into the Void: Collected Essays 1897–1900* (Cambridge, MA: MIT Press, 1982)

Low, Setha, *Behind the Gates: Life, Security, and the Pursuit of Happiness in Fortress America* (New York: Routledge, 2003)

Luckhurst, Roger, *The Trauma Question* (London: Routledge, 2008)

Lynch, David, *Catching the Big Fish: Meditation, Consciousness, and Creativity* (London: Penguin, 2006)

Lynch, Kevin, *The Image of the City* (Cambridge, MA: MIT Press, 1960)

MacGillis, Alec, "Lost in Rural USA," *New Statesman*, 27 October 2008

MacKinnon, Kenneth, *Hollywood's Small Towns: An Introduction to the American Small-Town Movie* (Metuchen, NJ: Scarecrow Press, 1984)

McCarthy, Tom, "His Dark Materials," *New Statesman*, 11 January 2010

McCoy, Esther, *Vienna to Los Angeles: Two Journeys* (Santa Monica: Arts and Architecture Press, 1979)

McGowan, Todd, *The Impossible David Lynch* (New York: Columbia University Press, 2007)

Marx, Leo, *The Machine in the Garden: Technology and the Pastoral Ideal in America* (New York: Oxford University Press, 2000)

May, Elaine Tyler, *Homeward Bound: American Families in the Cold War Era* (New York: Basic Books, 1988)

Milun, Kathryn, *Pathologies of Modern Space: Empty Space, Urban Anxiety, and the Recovery of the Public Self* (New York: Routledge, 2007)

Morgan, Conway Lloyd, *Jean Nouvel: The Elements of Architecture* (London: Thames and Hudson, 1999)

Mulvey, Laura, *Visual and Other Pleasures* (Basingstoke: Macmillan, 1989)

——, *Fetishism and Curiosity* (Bloomington: Indiana University Press, 1996)

Mumford, Lewis, *The Highway and the City* (London: Secker and Warburg, 1964)

Nabokov, Vladimir, *Lolita* (New York: Vintage, 1997)

Neumann, Dietrich (ed.), *Film Architecture: Set Design from Metropolis to Blade Runner*, trans. Almuth Seebohm (Munich: Prestel, 1996)

Nieland, Justus, *David Lynch* (Urbana: University of Illinois Press, 2012)

Nochimson, Martha P., *The Passion of David Lynch: Wild at Heart in Hollywood* (Austin: University of Texas Press, 1997)

Odell, Colin, and Michelle Le Blanc, *David Lynch* (Harpenden: Kamera Books, 2007)

Olson, Greg, *David Lynch: Beautiful Dark* (Lanham, MD: Scarecrow Press, 2008)

O'Donoghue, Darragh, "Paradise Regained: *Queen Kelly* and the Lure of the 'Lost' Film," *Senses of Cinema*, Issue 27 (July 2003)

O'Neill, William L., *American High: The Years of Confidence, 1945–1960* (New York: Free Press, 1986)

Orr, John, *Contemporary Cinema* (Edinburgh: Edinburgh University Press, 1998)

——, *Hitchcock and Twentieth-Century Cinema* (London: Wallflower Press, 2005)

——, "A Cinema of Parallel Worlds: Lynch, Kieślowski and *Inland Empire*," *Film International*, Vol. 7, No. 1 (February 2009)

Pallasmaa, Juhani, *The Architecture of Image: Existential Space in Cinema*, trans. Michael Wynne-Ellis (Helskini: Rakennustieto, 2007)

Patterson, James T., *Restless Giant: The United States from Watergate to Bush v. Gore* (Oxford: Oxford University Press, 2005)

Pells, Richard, *Not Like Us: How Europeans Have Loved, Hated, and Transformed American Culture Since World War II* (New York: Basic Books, 1997)

Plath, Sylvia, *The Bell Jar* (London: Faber and Faber, 2005)

Powers, John, "Getting Lost is Beautiful: The Light and Dark World of David Lynch," *LA Weekly*, 19–25 October 2001

Pudovkin, V. I., *Film Technique and Film Acting: The Cinema Writings of V. I. Pudovkin*, trans. Ivor Montagu (London: Vision, 1954)

Raban, Jonathan, *Soft City* (London: Picador, 2008)

——, "Metronatural America," *New York Review of Books*, 26 March 2009

Rasmussen, Cecilia, " 'Wall Street of the West' Had Its Peaks, Crashes," *Los Angeles Times*, 11 June 2000

Reed, Christopher (ed.), *Not at Home: The Suppression of Domesticity in Modern Art and Architecture* (London: Thames and Hudson, 1996)

Reiss, Julie H., *From Margins to Center: The Spaces of Installation Art* (Cambridge, MA: MIT Press, 1999)

del Río, Elena, *Deleuze and the Cinemas of Performance* (Edinburgh: Edinburgh University Press, 2008)

Roach, John, and Mary Sweeney, *The Straight Story: A Screenplay* (New York: Hyperion, 1999)

Rodley, Chris (ed.), *Lynch on Lynch* (London: Faber and Faber, 2005)

Ross, Andrew, *The Celebration Chronicles: Life, Liberty, and the Pursuit of Property Values in Disney's New Town* (London: Verso, 2000)

Roth, Joseph, *Hotel Savoy*, trans. John Hoare (London: Granta, 2000)

Roth, Philip, *Shop Talk: A Writer and His Colleagues and Their Work* (London: Vintage, 2002)

Royle, Nicholas, *The Uncanny* (Manchester: Manchester University Press, 2003)

Rybczynski, Witold, *Home: A Short History of an Idea* (London: Heinemann, 1988)

Sargeant, Jack, and Stephanie Watson (eds.), *Lost Highways: An Illustrated Guide to the Road Movie* (London: Creation, 1999)

Sartre, Jean-Paul, *Literary and Philosophical Essays*, trans. Annette Michelson (London: Hutchinson, 1969)

Schaal, Hans Dieter, *Learning from Hollywood: Architecture and Film*, trans. Michael Robinson (Stuttgart: Axel Menges, 1996)

Schezen, Roberto, *Adolf Loos: Architecture 1903–1932* (New York: Monacelli Press, 1996)

Schneider, Cynthia, and Brian Wallis (eds.), *Global Television* (Cambridge, MA: MIT Press, 1988)

Sennett, Richard, *The Conscience of the Eye: The Design and Social Life of Cities* (New York: W. W. Norton, 1992)

Sheen, Erica, and Annette Davison (eds.), *The Cinema of David Lynch: American Dreams, Nightmare Visions* (London: Wallflower Press, 2004)

Shiel, Mark, *Hollywood Cinema and the Real Los Angeles* (London: Reaktion, 2012)

Shiel, Mark, and Tony Fitzmaurice (eds.), *Cinema and the City: Film and Urban Societies in a Global Context* (Oxford: Blackwell, 2001)

Shonfield, Katherine, *Walls Have Feelings: Architecture, Film and the City* (London: Routledge, 2000)

Silverman, Kaja, *The Acoustic Mirror: The Female Voice in Psychoanalysis and Cinema* (Bloomington: Indiana University Press, 1988)

Simmel, Georg, *Simmel on Culture: Selected Writings* (London: Sage, 2000)

Simon, Stephanie, "Words Don't Fail Iowans When Describing State," *Los Angeles Times*, 17 March 1999

Smith, Paul, "The Eisenman–Haneke Tapes," *Icon*, No. 55 (January 2008)

Soja, Edward W., *Postmodern Geographies: The Reassertion of Space in Critical Social Theory* (London: Verso, 1994)

——, *Thirdspace: Journeys to Los Angeles and Other Real-and-Imagined Places* (Cambridge, MA: Blackwell, 1996)

Speaks, Michael (ed.), *The Critical Landscape* (Rotterdam: 010 Publishers, 1996)

Sylvester, David, *Interviews with Francis Bacon* (London: Thames and Hudson, 2002)

Teaford, John C., *The Metropolitan Revolution: The Rise of Post-Urban America* (New York: Columbia University Press, 2006)

Thirlwell, Adam, "Czech Mates," *New Statesman*, 17 May 2010

Thomson, David, *The Whole Equation: A History of Hollywood* (New York: Alfred A. Knopf, 2005)

Till, Jeremy, *Architecture Depends* (Cambridge, MA: MIT Press, 2009)

Tirard, Laurent, *Moviemakers' Master Class: Private Lessons from the World's Foremost Directors* (New York: Faber and Faber, 2002)

Toles, George, "Auditioning Betty in *Mulholland Drive*," *Film Quarterly*, Vol. 58, No. 1 (Fall 2004)

Tournikiotis, Panayotis, *Adolf Loos* (New York: Princeton Architectural Press, 1996)

Updike, John, "Why Rabbit Had to Go," *New York Times*, 5 August 1990

——, *Rabbit, Run* (London: Penguin, 2006)

——, *Rabbit is Rich* (London: Penguin, 2006)

——, *Rabbit at Rest* (London: Penguin, 2006)

Valentine, Maggie, *The Show Starts on the Sidewalk: An Architectural History of the Movie Theatre, Starring S. Charles Lee* (New Haven: Yale University Press, 1994)

Vellay, Dominique, *La Maison de Verre: Pierre Chareau's Modernist Masterwork* (London: Thames and Hudson, 2007)

Venturi, Robert, Denise Scott Brown, and Steven Izenour, *Learning from Las Vegas: The Forgotten Symbolism of Architectural Form* (Cambridge, MA: MIT Press, 1977)

Vertov, Dziga, *Kino-Eye: The Writings of Dziga Vertov*, trans. Kevin O'Brien (London: Pluto Press, 1984)

Vidal, Ricarda, *Death and Desire in Car Crash Culture: A Century of Romantic Futurisms* (Oxford: Peter Lang, 2013)

Vidler, Anthony, *The Architectural Uncanny: Essays in the Modern Unhomely* (Cambridge, MA: MIT Press, 1992)

——, "The Explosion of Space: Architecture and the Filmic Imaginary," *Assemblage*, No. 21 (August 1993)

Vitruvius, *The Ten Books on Architecture*, trans. Morris Hicky Morgan (New York: Dover, 1960)

Walkowitz, Judith R., *City of Dreadful Delight: Narratives of Sexual Danger in Late-Victorian London* (London: Virago, 1992)

Wallace, David Foster, *A Supposedly Fun Thing I'll Never Do Again: Essays and Arguments* (New York: Back Bay, 1998)

Webber, Andrew, and Emma Wilson (eds.), *Cities in Transition: The Moving Image and the Modern Metropolis* (London: Wallflower Press, 2008)

Wenders, Wim, *On Film: Essays and Conversations* (London: Faber, 2001)

West, Nathanael, *Miss Lonelyhearts and The Day of the Locust* (New York: New Directions, 1969)

White, Morton, and Lucia White, *The Intellectual Versus the City: From Thomas Jefferson to Frank Lloyd Wright* (Cambridge, MA: Harvard University Press, 1962)

"(Why) is David Lynch Important? A *Parkett* Inquiry," *Parkett*, No. 28 (1991)

Wigley, Russell F. (ed.), *Philadelphia: A 300-Year History* (New York: W. W. Norton, 1982)

Wilentz, Sean, *The Age of Reagan: A History, 1974–2008* (New York: Harper, 2008)

Williams, Gregory Paul, *The Story of Hollywood: An Illustrated History* (Los Angeles: BL Press, 2005)

Wollen, Peter, *Paris Hollywood: Writings on Film* (London: Verso, 2002)

Woods, Paul A., *Weirdsville USA: The Obsessive Universe of David Lynch* (London: Plexus, 2000)

Wright, Frank Lloyd, *When Democracy Builds* (Chicago: University of Chicago Press, 1945)

——, *The Future of Architecture* (New York: Mentor, 1963)

Wright, Patrick, *Iron Curtain: From Stage to Cold War* (Oxford: Oxford University Press, 2007)

Yoshida, Nobuyuki, and Ai Kitazawa (eds.), *Jean Nouvel 1987–2006*. Special Issue of *Architecture and Urbanism* (April 2006)

Ziolkowski, Theodore, *Minos and the Moderns: Cretan Myth in Twentieth-Century Literature and Art* (Oxford: Oxford University Press, 2008)

Žižek, Slavoj, *The Art of the Ridiculous Sublime: On David Lynch's Lost Highway* (Seattle: Walter Chapin Simpson Center for the Humanities, 2002)

——, *The Parallax View* (Cambridge, MA: MIT Press, 2006)

——, *Violence: Six Sideways Reflections* (London: Profile, 2008)

Žižek, Slavoj, and Glyn Daly, *Conversations with Žižek* (Cambridge: Polity, 2004)

Žižek, Slavoj, Eric L. Santer, and Kenneth Reinhard, *The Neighbor: Three Inquiries in Political Theology* (Chicago: University of Chicago Press, 2005)

AUTHOR BIOGRAPHY

Richard Martin is a London-based writer and researcher specializing in modern American film, literature, art and architecture. He has taught at Birkbeck, Middlesex University and Tate Modern.

Index

Adams, Parveen 164
affect 6, 107, 134, 146–7, 149, 152, 158, 171, *see also* performance
Andersen, Thom 51–4
   Los Angeles Plays Itself 51
Antonioni, Michelangelo 7–8
apartments 1, 11, 22, 25–6, 35, 39–40, 48, 53–4, 61, 63, 65, 68–77, 79, 81, 83–6, 94, 99, 123, 127, 136, 152–4, *see also* interior design
Art Deco 25, 58, 69, 152

Bachelard, Gaston 2, 49, 63–4, 67, 69, 71–4, 77, 100, 131, 164
Bacon, Francis 67, 82–7, 97, 99, 102–3, 120–1, 133, 135–6, 143, 155, 174
Badalamenti, Angelo 118, 142
Ballard, J. G. 120, 122
   Crash 120
Banham, Reyner 10, 50, 56, 61, 96, 129
Barber, Stephen 59, 176
Baudrillard, Jean 105, 150, 169
Bauhaus 3
Beauvoir, Simone de 107–9
Beckett, Samuel
   Film 30–1
bedrooms 10, 65–6, 68–77, 85, 87–92, 97–9, 104, 158, 181, *see also* apartments; interior design
Benjamin, Walter 18, 21, 31, 91
Bergman, Ingmar 103, 126
   Wild Strawberries 126
Bertoia, Harry 97
Blue Velvet, *see* David Lynch
Brando, Marlon
   One-Eyed Jacks 149–50

Browning, Tod
   Freaks 139
Bruno, Giuliana 107

California 1, 6, 16, 44, 46, 49–62, 67, 78, 93–6, 104, 112, 114, 121, 150, 164, 166–72, 174–5, 178–9, 182, *see also* Los Angeles
Capra, Frank 55, 126
   It Happened One Night 126
car crashes 52, 120–3
Celebration (Florida) 33–4, 43, *see also* New Urbanism
Certeau, Michel de 18
Chamberlain, John 120
Chaplin, Charlie 30, 68
   Modern Times 30
Chareau, Pierre 3, 88
Chion, Michel 40, 115, 134–5
class 16, 35, 38, 41, 46, 58, 70, 73, 76, 78, 94–5, 98, 119, 122, 139–40, 172–3, *see also* social relations
Cocteau, Jean
   Orphée 116, 159–60
Cold War 36, 80, 86, 109, 143
Coen, Ethan and Joel
   Barton Fink 114
Colomina, Beatriz 66, 70, 88, 100, 102–3, 153
Conley, Tom 12, 111
corridors 2, 5–6, 9, 14, 46, 68–70, 76, 88, 99–101, 104, 136, 155–6, 158, 166–7, 180–1, 198n. 26
Cronenberg, David 7, 120
   Crash 120

curtains 2, 12, 34, 47, 59, 65, 67, 73, 81, 97, 133–5, 139–50, 152, 159, 176, *see also* interior design; movie theater; performance

Davis, Mike 61, 94–5, 100
Dear, Michael 166
Deleuze, Gilles 68, 84–5, 121, 135
DeLillo, Don
  Americana 126
del Rio, Rebekah 60, 146–7
DeMille, Cecil B.
  Samson and Delilah 148
Derrida, Jacques 50, 121
desert 104–5, 108, 114, 117–18, 121
digital cinema 173, 176–7
Diller and Scofidio 102
Dimendberg, Edward 28, 30, 59, 109
Disney Corporation 33–4, 43
Disney, Walt 36
Donen, Stanley
  Singin' in the Rain 60
doors 2, 8–9, 67, 69, 80, 91, 95–7, 150, 159, 164, 167, 169, 174–6, 181
downtown 2, 5–6, 23–5, 28, 31–2, 38, 56–62, 79, 113, 137, 146, 167, 170, 176, 181–2, *see also* movie theater; public space; urban decline
dreams 20, 25–7, 53–5, 60–3, 69, 71, 73–5, 77, 92, 100, 129, 152, 158, 160, 178, *see also* fantasy
Dune, see David Lynch

Eames, Charles and Ray 94, 97, 109
Eisenman, Peter 3, 7, 28, 49
Eisenstein, Sergei 7, 9, 82, 86, 125, 165
  Battleship Potemkin 86
  General Line, The 125
Elephant Man, The, see David Lynch
Elsaesser, Thomas 78, 89
Eraserhead, see David Lynch
European émigrés 53, 67, 78, 93–4, 170–1, 179, *see also* modernism

factories 1, 5–6, 17, 20–1, 25–7, 31, 35, 47, 56–7, 59, 69–70, 129, 169–73, 175–7, *see also* industry
fantasy, 4, 17–18, 26–7, 37, 39, 42, 48, 52, 54, 60, 74, 89, 100, 103–4, 108, 122–3, 134, 138, 141, 144–5, 149–50, 170, *see also* dreams
Fassbinder, Rainer Werner 80–1
  Berlin Alexanderplatz 80
  Fear Eats the Soul 80
Fellini, Federico 17, 127, 145
  La Strada 127
fences 33–7, 42, 80, 104–5, 113, 128, *see also* privacy; small towns; social relations
film noir 28, 54, 78–9, 81, 111, 157–8
film studios 8, 12, 52–4, 60, 147–51, 156, 165–6, 174–6, 181–2, 184
Fitzgerald, F. Scott
  Last Tycoon, The 157
Fleming, Victor
  Wizard of Oz, The 108, 115, 143
Ford, Henry 15, 20–1, 33, 42, 50, 93, 109, 116
Foster, Hal 185
Foucault, Michel 137–8, 150, 155, 159, 166–7
Freud, Sigmund 8, 38, 41, 64, 67, 99
Frost, Mark 36

Gehry, Frank viii–ix, 10, 58, 121, 168–9, 184–5
gender 89, 91–3, 142, 146–7, 178, 183
German Expressionism 87, 133
Giedion, Sigfried 99
Gifford, Barry 69, 113, 119, 124
Godard, Jean-Luc 10, 17, 57, 77, 82, 99, 102, 107, 117, 121–3, 145
  Breathless 123
  Contempt 57, 99, 102
  Histoire(s) du Cinema 77, 82
  Pierrot Le Fou 117, 121, 123
  Week End 107, 121–3
Googie architecture 55, 121
Greenaway, Peter
  Belly of an Architect, The 8

Groys, Boris 137, 140
Guston, Philip 110, 114, 119

Harvey, David 137
Hatherley, Owen 131
Heath, Stephen 164
Heidegger, Martin 133, 142
Hitchcock, Alfred 2, 46, 68, 77, 79, 81,
    85, 89, 91–3, 107–8, 128, 146,
    149, 152
    Lodger, The 89, 92
    Man Who Knew Too Much, The 146
    North by Northwest 128
    Notorious 89
    Rear Window 68, 72, 85, 149
    Rebecca 91
    Rope 68
    Shadow of a Doubt 46
    Spellbound 152
    Vertigo 92
Hollywood (California), ix–x, 21,
    32, 51–4, 96–9, 104, 149, 164–5,
    167–80, *see also* Los Angeles
Hollywood cinema 13, 20, 26, 40,
    52–62, 78, 80, 89, 93, 96, 108, 129,
    138, 142, 145–51, 164–5, 167–80,
    182–3
Hopper, Dennis
    Easy Rider 123
hotels 10, 16, 25, 35, 46, 58, 82, 104,
    114–15, 119, 146, 158, 174, 177

industry 15, 19–22, 24–32, 38, 47, 50,
    56, 111, 127, 129, 169–171, *see
    also* factories
Inland Empire, see David Lynch
interior design, viii–iv, 2, 4, 47, 54, 59,
    65–7, 73–4, 76–81, 84–6, 91–3,
    95–9, 101, 104, 114, 124, 127, 142,
    152–6, 158–60, 172–4, *see also*
    apartments; curtains
Izenour, Steven 109, 119, 121, 129

Jacobs, Jane 15, 21–3, 28, 31, 40, 42–3,
    48
James, Henry 24

Jameson, Fredric 11, 31
Jencks, Charles 50–1

Kafka, Franz 67–76, 84, 86, 99–100,
    103, 135, 143, 177, 179
    Amerika 135, 143
    'Burrow, The' 69, 74, 99–100
    'Metamorphosis' 69–76, 84, 103
    Trial, The 75
Keaton, Buster 30–1, 68, 163, 165–6,
    181
    Film 30–1
    High Sign, The 68
    Scarecrow, The 163, 165–6, 181
    Steamboat Bill Jr. 68
Kokoschka, Oskar 3
Koolhaas, Rem 1, 5, 7, 9, 56, 69, 121
Kubrick, Stanley
    2001: A Space Odyssey 158
    Shining, The 158–9
Kuleshov, Lev 165–6

labyrinths 151–2, 156–60
Lamour, Dorothy 174
Lang, Fritz 7, 8
    Secret Beyond the Door 8
Lavin, Sylvia 67, 78
Lawrence, D. H. 108, 126–7
Le Corbusier 1, 6, 18, 21, 30–1, 67,
    78, 98, 101–3, 116, 128–9, 133,
    153–5, 175
Lee, S. Charles 59, 153
Lefebvre, Henri 17
Lhamon Jr., W. T. 86
Libeskind, Daniel 121, 171–2, 175–6
Łódź viii, 5, 10, 14, 25, 166–80, 182,
    184
London 1, 6, 12, 15, 18–24, 26–9, 31,
    50, 57, 69–70, 73, 76, 113, 139,
    164, 198n. 26
Loos, Adolf 6, 64–8, 70, 81, 84, 87–8,
    97, 100, 102, 133, 142
Los Angeles ix–x, 4, 13, 16–17, 21,
    31–2, 36, 49–62, 67, 94–105, 114,
    146–50, 163–80, 184
Lost Highway, see David Lynch

Lynch, David
  art viii–ix, 4, 45–6, 92, 153, 169
  biographical information ix, 3–4,
    16, 24–5, 61, 75, 96–7, 124
  film and television works
  Alphabet, The 82
  Blue Velvet 11, 21, 28, 32–44, 46, 48,
    55, 64, 75, 78–86, 112–14, 136–7,
    142, 146, 181–2
  Dune 1, 2, 11, 19, 21, 107, 124, 140,
    182
  Elephant Man, The 18–23, 39, 47,
    69–76, 113, 120, 139–41, 143, 163,
    170–1, 180, 198n. 26
  Eraserhead 5, 9, 11, 18–19, 23–32,
    35, 50, 58, 68–77, 113, 124, 127,
    144–5, 152, 157, 165, 167, 170–1,
    182
  Grandmother, The 75, 88–9
  Industrial Soundscape 21
  Inland Empire viii, 5, 9, 14, 20–1, 40,
    51–2, 54, 59, 80, 82, 93, 119, 127,
    139, 147–51, 163–85
  Lost Highway ix, 10, 52, 64, 66, 69,
    94–105, 111, 113, 119–21, 131,
    141–2, 146, 163, 165, 178, 182–3
  Mulholland Drive 4, 11, 14, 21, 31,
    35, 51–62, 66, 81, 93, 96, 113, 138,
    146–50, 163, 165, 167, 175, 178,
    181
  *Premonitions Following an Evil
    Deed* 103
  Straight Story, The 19, 23, 37, 75,
    108, 110–12, 124–32, 164
  Twin Peaks 5, 11, 19–20, 35–7, 44–9,
    64, 69, 80–2, 85–93, 112–13, 118,
    124, 128, 136, 138–40, 143–4,
    150–61, 166, 182–3, 189n. 5
  Twin Peaks: Fire Walk With Me
    44–5, 49, 81–2, 85–93, 104, 113,
    119, 123, 132, 141–2, 151–61, 181,
    189n. 5
  Wild at Heart 21, 75, 82, 104, 108,
    110–28, 130–2, 141, 146, 149,
    164, 180
Lynch, Kevin 17–18, 45–6, 49, 111

McCarthy, Tom 57, 177
McGowan, Todd 4, 27, 39, 42, 113, 122,
  134–5, 177–8
McQueen, Steve 68
Majewski, Hilary 172, 177
Malick, Terrence
  Badlands 115
Meireles, Cildo 153
melodrama 42, 67, 77–8, 80, 87, 89, 96,
  111, 122, 166
Mendelsohn, Erich 129
Minnelli, Vincente 78, 89, 174
  Band Wagon, The 174
  Home from the Hill 89
modernism ix, 2, 5–6, 21, 52–3, 64–8, 84,
  94–105, 110, 129, 142–3, 154, 179
montage 5, 9–10, 51, 83, 94, 107, 111,
  117, 163–7, 173
movie theater viii, 6, 12, 14, 23, 58–62,
  68, 79–81, 107, 134–5, 137–8,
  141, 146–7, 153, 165, 170, 176–7,
  183, *see also* affect; curtains;
  performance; spectatorship
Mulholland Drive, see David Lynch
Mulvey, Laura 37, 42, 79, 80, 91–2,
  145–6
Mumford, Lewis 109, 111
Muñoz, Juan 153
music 39, 60–1, 115, 117–19, 134,
  140–7, 154–5, 161, 180
Muybridge, Eadweard 83, 86

Nabokov, Vladimir 86, 110, 117
  Lolita 110, 117
nature 15, 33, 39, 44–9, 52, 56, 71,
  124–32, *see also* woods
Neutra, Richard 3, 6, 53, 67–8, 78–9,
  88, 90, 93–4, 96, 98, 105, 142,
  170–1, 175, 179
New Orleans 114, 118–19
New Urbanism 16, 34–6, 43, 47
Nieland, Justus 4, 35, 97–8, 103, 136
Nolan, Christopher 114
  The Prestige 114
Nouvel, Jean viii–ix, 7, 10–14, 146,
  183, 185

Orr, John 107–8, 152, 160–1, 170

Pacific Northwest 1, 44–9, 163
Palin, Sarah 33–4, 36, 38, 42–3
Paramount Studios 27, 53–4, 61, 134,
        148–51, 165–6, 174–7, 181–2,
        see also film studios; Hollywood
        cinema; Los Angeles
Parreno, Philippe 136
Penn, Arthur
    Bonnie and Clyde 115, 123
performance 6, 14, 22–3, 59–60, 65–7,
        69, 72, 85, 93, 133–61, 166, 171,
        175, 183, *see also* affect; gender;
        spectatorship
Philadelphia 4, 15–16, 18–19, 23–33,
        42, 44, 46, 50, 56, 59, 62, 69, 76,
        94, 113, 145, 169, 182
photography 6, 54, 66–7, 73, 78, 83,
        92–3, 158, 169, 174
Plath, Sylvia
    Bell Jar, The 133, 138
Polański, Roman 170, 174
postmodernism 3, 4, 31, 34
Powell, Michael
    Peeping Tom 101
Preminger, Otto, 92–3, 179
    Laura 92–3
privacy 33, 45, 67, 72, 79, 83, 87–9,
        95–103, 135, 138, 144–5
psychoanalytic theory 4, 40–2, 64, 78, 99
public space 19, 22–3, 26, 79, 138,
        144, 156–7, 182, 184, *see also*
        downtown; urban decline

Raban, Jonathan 15, 17, 45, 47–8
radio 6, 38, 95, 101, 116–18, 177, 180
Ray, Nicholas 7, 79, 89, 96
    Bigger Than Life 89
    Rebel Without a Cause 96
Reagan, Ronald 32–4, 36–8, 40–3, 47
Reichardt, Kelly 45
Renoir, Jean 150
roads and highways 1, 5–6, 16, 36, 45,
        51–2, 96, 105, 107–33, 164, *see
        also* car crashes

Roth, Joseph
    Hotel Savoy 170–1
Roth, Philip 110, 115, 119
Rubinstein, Arthur 177
'Rust Belt' 16, 18, 25, 31, 169

St. Paul 32, 38–9
Sartre, Jean-Paul 51
Scheibler, Karl 172, 174
Schindler, Rudolph Michael 3, 6, 53,
        94, 96–7, 175
Schneider, Alan
    Film 30–1
Scorsese, Martin
    Taxi Driver 31, 58
Scott, Ridley
    Thelma and Louise 115
Scott Brown, Denise 34, 109–10, 119,
        121, 129
Sennett, Richard 42, 56–7
sexuality 25, 42, 65–6, 75–6, 80, 82–4, 97,
        104, 115, 124, 135, 142, 146, 183
Shiel, Mark 50, 59, 62
Silverman, Kaja 146
simultaneity 151–2, 163–7, 175, 177,
        179–80, 182, 184
Sirk, Douglas 42, 78, 80–1, 89, 179
    All That Heaven Allows 80
    Written on the Wind 89
skyscrapers 21, 31, 56
small towns 15–16, 32–49, 51, 78–80,
        87, 90, 128
social relations 6, 17, 21, 23–4, 28,
        31–44, 46–9, 55, 59–61, 73–6,
        87, 90, 94–7, 117–18, 122, 127–8,
        139–40, 167–8, *see also* class
Soja, Edward 17, 50–1, 58, 151, 160,
        163–4
sound 2, 60, 65–6, 71, 91, 141–2,
        145–7, 152–5
spectatorship 12, 22–3, 40, 64–8,
        72, 78–81, 83–5, 101, 107, 111,
        122, 131, 134–5, 139–40, 145–7,
        149, 153–4, 164, 175, *see also*
        movie theater; performance;
        surveillance

staircases 2, 5–6, 68, 78–9, 86–91, 93, 97, 118, 157, 169
Stone, Oliver
    Natural Born Killers 126
    Nixon 114
Straight Story, The, see David Lynch
subjectivity 7, 12, 21, 38, 40, 42, 46, 66, 74, 76, 100–3, 117–18, 135, 140, 144, 146–7, 157, 177–9, 185
suburbs 12, 15–16, 24, 31, 34–6, 43–4, 50, 58, 64, 78, 80–1, 94, 103, 109, 143, 166, 169, 175, 178
"Sun Belt" 16, 18, 31
Surrealism 152, 154–5, 160
surveillance x, 22–3, 40, 64–8, 72, 79, 82–5, 87, 95–6, 99–103, 139, 143, *see also* spectatorship
Swanson, Gloria 178

Tarkovsky, Andrei
    Stalker 133
Taut, Bruno 7
television 57–8, 64, 78–82, 86, 97, 104, 143, 160, 177, 182
Thirlwell, Adam 179
Thomson, David 52
Tomaszewski, Christian 136
traffic jams 107, 112, 114, 120–4, 131
Twin Peaks, see David Lynch
Twin Peaks: Fire Walk With Me, see David Lynch

uncanny, the 28, 37, 52, 58, 60, 64, 88, 92, 147, 151, 171, 175, 184, *see also* corridors; psychoanalytic theory; staircases
Updike, John 24–6, 31
    'Rabbit' novels 24–6
urban decline 5–6, 16, 18–19, 23–32, 58–9, 62, 79, 144, 157, 169–72, 175–6, 182, *see also* downtown; movie theater; 'Rust Belt'
urban grid 24, 26, 51, 56–8, 108, 183, *see also* downtown

urban regeneration viii, 28, 30, 32, 168–9, 184

van der Rohe, Mies 3, 142, 179
Van Sant, Gus 45
Venturi, Robert 34, 109–10, 119, 121, 129
Vertov, Dziga 9–10, 103, 166, 172
    Man With a Movie Camera 103
Vidler, Anthony 64, 88, 99
Vidor, Charles
    Gilda 54, 145
Vidor, King
    Fountainhead, The 8
vinyl records 12, 21, 57, 173
Virilio, Paul 101, 111, 127
Vitruvius 6–7, 175
von Stroheim, Erich 178
    Queen Kelly 178

Wajda, Andrzej 171, 173–4
    Promised Land, The 171, 173–4
Wenders, Wim 7, 10, 17
West, Nathanael 94, 173
    Day of the Locust, The 94
Wild at Heart, see David Lynch
Wilder, Billy 54, 68, 148–9, 178–9
    Apartment, The 68
    Sunset Boulevard 54, 148–9, 178
Wilmington (North Carolina) 38, 114
Winding Refn, Nicolas
    Drive 114
windows ix, 66, 69, 71–3, 96–7, 101–2, 123, 158, 181, *see also* apartments; spectatorship; surveillance
woods 1–2, 44–9, 108, 119, 128, 132, 155, 157
Wright, Frank Lloyd, Jr. ix, 3
Wright, Frank Lloyd, Sr. 3, 7, 15, 47, 59, 67, 80, 89, 93–4, 98, 105, 124, 126, 129, 133
Wright, Patrick 143

Žižek, Slavoj 4, 32, 40–1, 44, 100, 134, 169